Endorsed by
University of Cambridge
International Examinations

Heinemann
IGCSE

D1579674

Business Studies

Rob Jones

www.pearsonis.com

Free online support
Useful weblinks
24 hour online ordering

Heinemann

Part of Pearson

79 537 175 4

Contents

Section 4: People in business

Section 5: Regulating and controlling business activity

Introduction

This book has many features that will help you during the course. These features are described below.

Getting started

The material at the start of each chapter, on a purple background, provides an introduction to the topic covered in the chapter.

DID YOU KNOW?

In the US about 10 million manual jobs have been lost during the past 10 years. Machines and automated systems have replaced humans. During this time, businesses have invested more than $100 billion in robotics and supporting systems.

Did you know?

The 'Did you know' boxes are not specifically required by the syllabus, but are designed to widen your knowledge and deepen your understanding.

Questions

There are questions throughout the book to check your understanding of each unit or topic.

QUESTION 1

Mirza and Associates is a small firm of solicitors based in Lahore, Pakistan. There are four partners in the business and each one specialises in a specific area of law:
- Salim Hussain is an expert in property law and deals with property ownership disputes.
- Tariq Zaman deals with tax and corporate matters for business clients.
- Nasir Ahmed is a legal advisor for colleges and universities.
- Tariq Mirza is responsible for administration and also deals with criminal cases.

(a) Use this case as an example to explain what is meant by a partnership.

(b) How does this case illustrate one of the main advantages of partnerships?

Key terms

Key terms help you identify important information.

Key terms

De-industrialisation – the decline in manufacturing.
Primary sector – production involving the extraction of raw materials from the earth.
Secondary sector – production involving the conversion of raw materials into finished and semi-finished goods.
Tertiary sector – the provision of services in the economy.

What is business activity?

Getting started...

Some people try to make money by setting up a business. They might do this because they want to work for themselves. Or they think they can make more money than if they work for someone else. Or perhaps they have been made redundant and cannot find another job. Running a business is hard work, but the rewards can be worth it. Look at the example below.

Okkas Taverna

In 2008 Marios and Alexia Okkas opened Okkas Taverna, a restaurant catering for tourists in Cyprus (see Figure 1.1). The couple no longer wanted to work for another employer. Both had previous experience in catering. Alexia had worked as a waitress in Limassol, while Marios was employed as a chef in Paxos. The couple used €15,000 of their own money to set up the business. Before trading began they had to:

▲ **Figure 1.1** A Greek restaurant

- obtain a €10,000 bank loan;
- find suitable premises and decorate the restaurant area;
- obtain a fire certificate to meet health and safety regulations;
- buy furniture and kitchen equipment;
- employ two part-time staff to help out when busy;
- advertise the restaurant in the local area.

Marios ran the kitchen. He was responsible for menu design, dealing with suppliers and preparing the food. Alexia ran the restaurant area. She waited on tables, settled bills and looked after the customers. Marios and Alexia worked long hours, but it was worth it because in 2009 Okkas Taverna made a profit of €34,600.

(a) Why do you think Marios and Alexia opened a restaurant?

(b) State three resources used by Marios and Alexia when setting up their business.

(c) Why do you think businesses exist?

Business activity

A **business** is an organisation that provides **goods** or **services**. The example above illustrates many features of business activity.

- Business activity produces an output – a good or service. A restaurant service is being provided by Marios and Alexia.

- Goods and services are consumed. Tourists consume the service provided by Marios and Alexia.

- Resources are used up. Food and drinks, furniture, people, gas and electricity are examples of the resources used by Okkas Taverna. Money, such as the €10,000 bank loan is also a resource. The resources used by businesses are often called the *four factors of production*. These are explained briefly in Figure 1.2.

- A number of business functions may be carried out. Production, marketing, administration (the paper work), managing staff and financial control are examples. Production in the above case involved the provision of meals in a restaurant. Marketing involved advertising in the local area.

- Businesses can be affected by external factors. This means they are affected by things that they cannot control such as government laws, changes in consumer tastes and competitors. Marios and Alexia had to obtain a fire certificate because of health and safety regulations.

- Businesses aim to make a profit. Most businesses are set up by people to make money. In this case Okkas Taverna made a profit of €34,600 for Marios and Alexia in 2009.

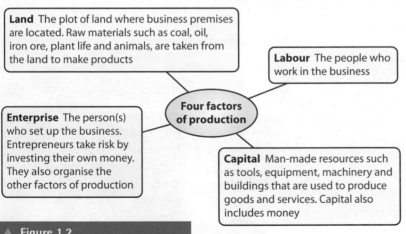

Land The plot of land where business premises are located. Raw materials such as coal, oil, iron ore, plant life and animals, are taken from the land to make products

Labour The people who work in the business

Four factors of production

Enterprise The person(s) who set up the business. Entrepreneurs take risk by investing their own money. They also organise the other factors of production

Capital Man-made resources such as tools, equipment, machinery and buildings that are used to produce goods and services. Capital also includes money

▲ **Figure 1.2**
The four factors of production

Raw materials	Processes	Product
Wood	Joining	
Glass	Glazing	
Paint	Painting	Conservatory
Floor tiles	Tiling	
Window fittings		
Other raw materials		
$11,500		**$29,000**
	Value added =	**$17,500**

▲ **Figure 1.3**
Adding value when constructing a conservatory

Goods and services

Businesses provide a wide range of goods and services. Some produce products for consumers – ordinary people. These are called **consumer goods**. Products sold by one business to another are called **producer goods**. Some businesses serve both consumers and producers. For example, the Taj Mahal hotel in Mumbai caters for both tourists and business people.

Adding value

Business activity involves adding value to resources. **Added value** is the difference between the cost of raw materials and the price charged:

Value added = selling price − cost of raw materials

In Figure 1.3 a builder uses raw materials such as wood, glass, floor tiles, window fittings and paint to build a conservatory. The builder uses processes such as joining, glazing, painting and tiling to construct the conservatory. The value added in this case is $17,500 ($29,000 − $11,500). It is the difference between the cost of the raw materials and the price of the conservatory. However, $17,500 is *not* the profit made by the builder. Part of the $17,500 will be used to meet other costs such as motor expenses, administration, insurance and wages.

QUESTION 1

Imad Arshad is a jeweller. He owns a small shop in Dehli and makes items of jewellery in a workshop at the back. One of his customers paid 4,500 rupees (Rs) for a brooch. He made it from silver and jade and designed it himself. The cost of the silver was Rs 1,000 and the cost of the jade Rs 900. He also used other materials costing Rs 200.

(a) Calculate the value added in this example.

(b) Explain the difference between value added and profit.

Satisfying needs and wants

Businesses have to satisfy people's **needs** and **wants**. Needs are the requirements for human survival. Some are physical such as water, food, warmth, shelter and clothing. If these needs cannot be met, humans will die.

Humans also have other desires. These are called wants and include holidays abroad, a better house, a bigger car, more status, more love, a better education and a cleaner environment. These wants are *infinite*. Most people want more than they already have. It is human nature. Unfortunately, the resources used by businesses are *finite*. This means there is a limited amount. Economists say that resources are **scarce**.

To survive, businesses must produce goods and services that satisfy people's needs and wants. They also need to understand that these may change over time. Also, other businesses will be attempting to do the same. This shows that businesses operate in a *changing and competitive environment* (see Chapter 9).

The purpose of business activity

Businesses exist to provide goods and services. However, different types of organisation provide goods and services for different reasons. They have a different purpose.

- **Private enterprise** Most businesses are owned privately by individuals or groups of individuals. They are *private sector* (see Chapter 10) businesses. In the UK there are over four million privately owned businesses. Most of these are small or medium-sized. The aim or goal of a private enterprise is to make money – a *profit* for the owners. The aims and objectives of private sector businesses are discussed in Chapter 5.

Key terms

Added value – the difference between the cost of raw materials and the selling price.

Business – an organisation that produces goods and services.

Consumer goods – goods and services sold to ordinary people (consumers) rather than businesses.

Goods – physical products such as a mobile phone, packet of crisps or a pair of shoes.

Needs – basic requirements for human survival.

Producer goods – goods and services produced by one business for another.

Scarce resources – the amount of resources available is limited.

Services – non-physical products such as banking, car cleaning and waste disposal.

Wants – people's desires for goods and services.

- **Non-profit making organisations** Some organisations in the private sector are non-profit making. Organisations such as charities, pressure groups, clubs and societies exist for other reasons. For example, charities such as Oxfam exist to raise money for 'good' causes. Pressure groups, such as Greenpeace, exist to influence decision makers in politics and business. Clubs and societies, such as the scouting association and sports clubs, provide opportunities and facilities for people with common interests.

Non-profit making organisations aim to meet the needs and wants of their members, or those that they aim to support.

- **Public enterprise** Some goods and services are provided by organisations owned by central or local government. These are *public sector* organisations (see Chapter 10) and examples in the UK include the National Health Service (NHS), the Post Office, the Bank of England and public libraries. The main purpose of public enterprise is to provide goods and services that private enterprise fails to provide adequately. Most goods and services provided in the public sector are free. They are paid for from taxes. Public sector organisations do not normally aim to make a profit. They try to provide good quality services.

QUESTION 2

The Li Ka Shing Foundation is a charity founded in 1980 by Hong Kong business man Li Ka Shing. Its mission is to develop 'a culture of giving' in Chinese society. The money raised by the Li Ka Shing Foundation is used for education and healthcare projects. For example, in 2005, the foundation gave HK$1 billion to the University of Hong Kong. To date the Li Ka Shing Foundation, and other charities established by Mr. Li, have donated HK$10.7 billion (see Figure 1.4).

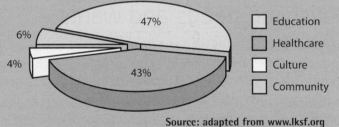

Source: adapted from www.lksf.org

▲ Figure 1.4
Donations made by Li Ka Shing Foundation as of 15 April 2009 – by type

(a) Using this case as an example, explain what is meant by a non-profit making organisation.

(b) What is the purpose of the Li Ka Shing Foundation?

Chapter review – SurgiCo

SurgiCo is a private sector business that designs and manufactures surgical instruments. The company aims to be the world's leading supplier of high-quality and cost-effective instruments. In 2008, the business made a profit of $780,000 on sales of $4.3 million. This was an increase on the previous year when the profit was $685,000. In 2008, the business moved to new premises. This helped SurgiCo to improve its manufacturing processes. For example, since the move the business has bought some specialist machinery which has helped to improve quality.

(a) SurgiCo makes producer goods. Explain what this means. (2 marks)

(b) What examples of capital are used by SurgiCo? (2 marks)

(c) Explain how SurgiCo meets needs. (4 marks)

(d) How does SurgiCo add value? (4 marks)

(e) Explain how the aims or goals of SurgiCo might differ from those of the hospitals which it supplies. (8 marks)

Chapter 2

Business classification

Getting started...

Businesses operate in different sectors. In developed countries, such as the US and the UK, most businesses provide services. They may be fitness centres, insurance brokers or retailers, or provide services for businesses such as market research or IT support. In some countries, such as China, there are large numbers of manufacturers. Finally, in less developed countries most businesses will concentrate on producing agricultural goods. Look at the businesses below.

◀ **Figure 2.1**
Examples of business activity in different sectors

(a) Which of the businesses above are concerned with (i) agriculture; (ii) manufacturing; (iii) services?

(b) Which of the above businesses are most likely to be common in (i) Africa; (ii) Western Europe?

Primary sector

Business activity is classified into three sectors. In the **primary sector** business activity involves extracting raw materials from the earth. Examples include:

- **Mining and quarrying** where raw materials such as coal, iron ore, copper, tin, salt and limestone are dug out of the ground. This sector also includes the extraction of oil and gas. Saudi Aramco, the largest oil producer in the world, is an example of a business that extracts oil.

- **Fishing**, which involves netting, trapping, angling and trawling fish. It also includes catching or gathering other types of sea food such as mussels, prawns, lobsters, crabs, scallops and oysters. China is the world's largest fish producer.

- **Forestry**, which involves managing forests to provide timber for wood products. It also involves protecting the natural environment, providing access and facilities to the public and managing wildlife habitats.

- **Agriculture**, which involves a range of farming activities. This is probably the most important primary sector activity for most countries. Most agriculture is concerned with food production, but other examples include ornamental or exotic products such as cut flowers, nursery plants and tropical fish.

Secondary sector

In the **secondary sector** business activity involves converting raw materials into finished or semi-finished goods. Examples include metal working, car production, textile production, chemical and engineering industries, aerospace manufacturing, energy utilities, engineering, food processing, construction and shipbuilding. In many countries this sector has declined in recent years.

Tertiary sector

The **tertiary sector** involves the provision of services. There is a wide variety of services and some examples are given below:

- **Professional services** such as accountancy, legal advice and medical care.

- **Transport** such as train, taxi, bus and air services.

- **Household services** such as plumbing, decorating, gardening and house maintenance.

- **Leisure services** such as television, tourism, swimming pools and libraries.

- **Financial services** such as banking, insurance, and pensions.

- **Commercial services** such as freight delivery, debt collection, printing and employment agencies.

Key terms

De-industrialisation – the decline in manufacturing.
Primary sector – production involving the extraction of raw materials from the earth.
Secondary sector – production involving the conversion of raw materials into finished and semi-finished goods.
Tertiary sector – the provision of services in the economy.

QUESTION 1

Jill and Ronnie Sanchez have owned a farm for 40 years. They grow a range of root vegetables such as carrots, swedes, turnips and parsnips. They have a contract to supply two local supermarkets and also sell to other shops in the area. In the 1970s, Jill and Ronnie employed up to 12 workers; however, because of mechanisation they now just employ three.

(a) Using examples from this case, explain the difference between the primary and the tertiary sectors.

(b) Look at Figure 2.2. What has happened to the number of people employed in agriculture in the UK since 1960?

(c) Explain one possible reason for the pattern described in (b).

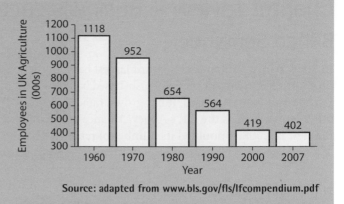

Source: adapted from www.bls.gov/fls/lfcompendium.pdf

▲ **Figure 2.2** Employment in agriculture, UK 1960-2007

Changes in sectors

The number of people employed in each sector does not stay the same. Different sectors grow and decline over time. In the UK, before the Industrial Revolution began in the late 18th century, most production was in the primary sector. During the 19th century secondary production expanded rapidly as manufacturing grew as a result of the Industrial Revolution. However, in the last 60 years the tertiary sector has started to expand at the expense of manufacturing. The decline in manufacturing is called **de-industrialisation**. Figure 2.3 shows the pattern of employment in manufacturing and services in the UK between 1960 and 2007. Similar patterns can be identified in other developed nations. Why has manufacturing declined in developed countries while services have grown?

- People may prefer to spend more of their income on services than manufactured goods. There has also been a decline in demand for the goods produced by some of the traditional industries in manufacturing, such as shipbuilding and textiles.

- Recently there has been fierce competition in the production of manufactured goods from developing countries such as India, China and Brazil.

- As countries develop the public sector grows. Since the public sector mainly provides services, this adds to the growth of the tertiary sector.

- Advances in technology means employment in manufacturing falls because machines replace people.

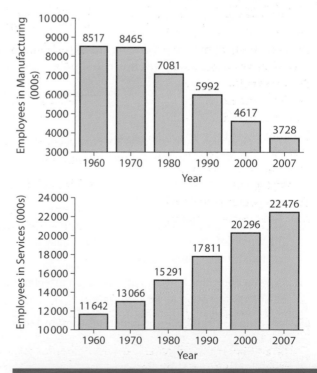

▲ **Figure 2.3**
The numbers of people employed in manufacturing and services in the UK 1960–2007

Chapter review – Business sectors

Banco Santander

In 2008, Banco Santander, the third largest bank in the world, made a profit of €8,876 billion. The Spanish-based bank also has operations in Europe and Latin America. It has grown rapidly recently since buying other banks such as the UK's Abbey, Alliance & Leicester and Bradford & Bingley. In 2008, it doubled its number of retail outlets.

Source: adapted from www.santander.com

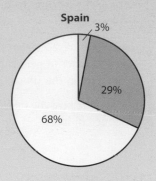

Spain
3%
29%
68%

VT Garments

Thailand is one of the world's largest textile manufacturers and VT Garments is one of the largest producers in the country. It produces a range of clothes such as ski jackets and pants, shorts, jogging suits and T-shirts. Its customers include The North Face, Nike, Patagonia and Nautica. The business has grown rapidly in the last 20 years. In 1981 it employed 120 people. By 2007 this had increased to 3,500.

Source: adapted from www.vtgarment.com

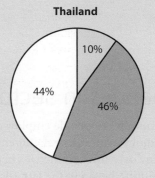

Thailand
10%
44%
46%

Wagagai Ltd

Wagagai Ltd is a flower farm in Uganda. The company began in 1998 exporting roses to the Netherlands. Soon after the farm diversified into chrysanthemum cuttings. Today, about 260 million chrysanthemum cuttings are produced in more than 22 acres of greenhouses. In 2005 the owners stopped producing roses and approached German company Selecta First Class about producing cuttings. This was a success and Selecta and Wagagai formed a joint venture to supply international markets.

Source: adapted from www.greenhousegrower.com

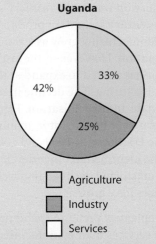

Uganda
33%
42%
25%

☐ Agriculture
■ Industry
☐ Services

Source: adapted from World Development Report, World Development Indicators, World Bank

(a) Using examples from the case above explain what is meant by
   (i) secondary production; (ii) tertiary production.   **(4 marks)**

(b) Look at Figure 2.4. Which nation relies most on the secondary sector for its output? Explain your answer.   **(2 marks)**

(c) (i) What is meant by de-industrialisation?   **(2 marks)**
    (ii) Which of the countries in Figure 2.4 have been subject most to de-industrialisation?   **(2 marks)**

(d) How do you think VT Garments has been affected by de-industrialisation in western countries?   **(2 marks)**

(e) What do you think are the main causes of de-industrialisation? **(8 marks)**

▲ **Figure 2.4**
Sector output in Uganda, Thailand and Spain (GDP %). GDP (Gross Domestic Product) is the total output in the economy

Chapter 3

Business size and growth

Getting started...

Most businesses are small in size. They may be owned by one person and employ no other people. They are likely to supply a local market and make just enough profit to keep the owner happy. On the other hand, some businesses are very large. They may be owned jointly by many shareholders. They may employ thousands of people and make billions of dollars profit. Look at the two examples below.

Sandeep Stores

Sandeep Stores is a corner shop located in Delhi. It sells spices and dried fruits and has been run by the Sandeep family for over 70 years. Over 95% of the Indian retail market is made up of small, family run businesses like this one. Dilip Sandeep understands local tastes and makes sure that he can meet the needs of the local market. In 2008 the shop made a profit of $12,000.

Tata Group

Tata Group is the largest business in India. It is involved in the production of steel, motor cars, chemicals, electricity and watches. It also provides a range of services such as telecommunications, IT consultancy, hotels and hospitality. The company employs more than 350,000 people and has operations in over 80 different countries. In 2008, Tata had a turnover of $62.5 billion and made a profit of $5.4 billion (see Figure 3.2).

▲ **Figure 3.1**
Spices for sale in a shop in India

(a) What evidence is there to suggest that Tata group is a large business?

(b) What evidence is there to suggest that Sandeep Stores is a small business?

(c) To what extent has Tata Group grown since 1992?

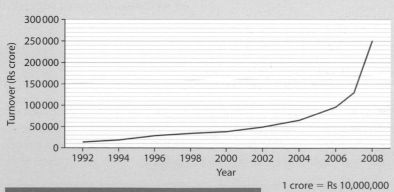

1 crore = Rs 10,000,000

▲ **Figure 3.2** Tata Group turnover 1992–2008

DID YOU KNOW?

In 2008 Ergon Energy, the Australian energy company, had capital employed of AUS$2,523.8 million. In contrast, Kresta Holdings, the Australian window and soft furnishings company, had capital employed of AUS$20.48 million. Clearly, Ergon is the largest business.

Methods of measuring business size

What is the difference between a large business and a small business? When does a small business become large? How might size be measured?

Turnover The sales revenue or turnover of a business could be used to measure size. For example, BP, the UK oil company, is a very large business. Its turnover in 2008 was $361 billion.

The number of employees A business with thousands of employees may be considered large. For example, Ford the US car giant, employed over 280,000 people in 2008.

The amount of capital employed Capital employed is the amount of money invested in a business. The more money invested, the larger the business.

Market share It could be argued that a business with a 43% market share, is larger than one that has a 9% market share in the same industry. Coca-Cola, for example sells over 50% of all cola drinks worldwide.

	Small	Medium-sized	Large
Turnover	< €10m	€10m to €50m	> €50m
No. of employees	< 50	50 to 249	> 249
Capital employed	< €10m	€10m to €43m	> €43m

▲ **Figure 3.3** The size of firms as defined by the EU

EU definitions of size

The EU classifies the size of firms according to turnover, the number of employees and the capital employed. The definitions are summarised in Figure 3.3.

Problems with measuring size

In practice, measuring the size of a business may not be easy.

- A highly automated chemical plant may only employ 45 people, but have a turnover of €50 million. According to the number of employees, the European Union (EU) would class it as a small business. However, according to the level of turnover it could be classed as a large business.

- A business with a turnover of €56 million may have capital employed of just €32 million. Therefore, according to turnover it is large, but the size of its capital employed suggests that it is medium-sized!

QUESTION 1

Casio Computer Co. Ltd is based in Japan and makes electronic goods. It is best known for its calculators, audio equipment, cameras, musical instruments, and watches. In 1957 Casio released the world's first electric calculator. The company employs over 13,000 people and had a turnover of ¥623 billion (€4.8 billion) in 2008. Casio also made a profit of ¥3.946 billion (€30.64 million) in the same year.

(a) Using evidence from the case determine whether Casio is a small, medium or large business.

Methods of growth

Once a firm is established in a market it is common for owners to grow the business. How might a company grow?

Internal growth is when a firm expands without involving other businesses. **Organic growth** means that the firm expands by selling more of its existing products. This could be done by selling to a wider market. Internal growth is often a slow process.

External growth is a faster method of growth. This can be by **acquisition** or **takeover** of other businesses or by **merging** with them. A takeover is when one company buys control of another. A merger usually means that two companies have agreed to join together and create a new company.

Reasons why businesses grow

- **Survival** In some industries firms may not survive if they remain small. Staying small might mean that costs are too high. They may not be able to compete with larger rivals. Also, small firms may be taken over by a larger firm.
- **Gain economies of scale** As firms grow in size they will enjoy economies of scale. This means that unit costs will fall and profits will improve. This is explained in Chapter 36.
- **Increase future profits** By growing and selling larger volumes, a firm will hope to raise profits in the future.
- **Increase market share** Larger firms may be able to dominate the market. For example, they might be able to raise prices or control part of the market. Some staff may enjoy the status and power associated with a high market share. For example, it could be argued that Richard Branson enjoys the publicity that goes with leading a large company such as Virgin.
- **Reduce risk** Risk can be reduced through *diversification*. Branching into new markets and new products means that if one product fails, success in others can keep the company going. For example, Stagecoach, the UK coach business, branched out into the provision of rail services when British Rail was privatised.

QUESTION 2

In June 2009, Xstrata approached fellow mining group Anglo American to discuss a possible £41 billion merger. In a statement confirming the approach, Xstrata described a deal between the two companies as 'highly compelling'. The Anglo-Swiss company said it had already identified 'substantial' savings from combining the businesses. Analysts believe that combining the two businesses would save £400 million. The merged company would also have a wider product range and access to more international markets.

Source: adapted from www.guardian.co.uk

(a) Using this case as an example, explain what is meant by external growth.

(b) Explain two reasons why growth in this case is likely to benefit the companies.

Problems connected with growth

- **Diseconomies of scale** If a business grows too big, unit costs may start to rise. This may be caused by *diseconomies of scale* (see Chapter 36). For example, there may be communication problems as the organisation grows. To overcome this problem a business should plan carefully before growing rapidly.

- **Resistance from shareholders** Businesses owned by shareholders may be forced to use profits to increase dividend payments rather than fund growth. To avoid such resistance the backing of shareholders is needed, by promising higher dividends in the future when the company has grown, for example.

- **Lack of expertise** Businesses that diversify into new areas may lack expertise. For example, a Chinese computer manufacturer may not have the skills required to manufacture cars. To overcome this problem, a business could recruit people who have expertise in the new areas. Alternatively, it could retain key staff when taking over a company in a new line of business.

- **Lack of funds** A business needs funds to grow. For example, a business will need money to pay for an acquisition. If funds cannot be raised, growth may be prevented.

Key terms

Internal growth – expansion that doesn't involve other businesses.
Merger – the joining together of two businesses, usually to create a third new company.
Organic growth – growth in current activities without joining or buying another business.
Takeover or **acquisition –** the purchase of one business by another.

Chapter review – Sainsbury

Sainsbury began as a small dairy shop in London in 1869. Today it is one of the UK's largest supermarket chains with a turnover of £20,383 million in 2009 (see Figure 3.4). The company, owned by shareholders, now employs over 150,000 people, serves over 18 million customers a week and has a market share of around 16%. Its large stores offer 30,000 products including a range of non-food products and services. Sainsbury also has an internet-based home delivery shopping service that is available to 88% of UK households.

(a) What evidence is there to suggest that Sainsbury is a large business? (2 marks)

(b) Calculate the percentage growth in Sainsbury's turnover between 2005 and 2009. (2 marks)

(c) Much of Sainsbury's growth has been organic. What does this mean? (2 marks)

(d) Outline two possible reasons why Sainsbury has grown. (4 marks)

(e) Discuss two problems that Sainsbury might encounter when growing and how it might overcome them. (10 marks)

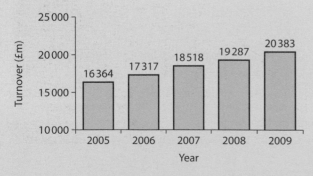

Figure 3.4
Sainsbury's turnover 2005–2009

Chapter 4

Key features of an economy

Getting started...

Different countries have different types of economy. For example, in poor parts of the world, where natural resources are limited, economies may be very basic. People may provide for their own needs by hunting and gathering. In many western countries, where economies are well developed, most of the nation's resources are used to produce services. Finally, newly developing countries may be producing a lot of manufactured goods. Look at the examples below.

Saudi Arabia

Saudi Arabia's national income in 2009 was $468 billion. Saudi Arabia has an oil-based economy with strong government controls over major economic activities. The government owns most of the key industries such as oil, telecommunications and mining. Saudi has more than 20% of the world's petroleum reserves and is the world's largest exporter of petroleum.

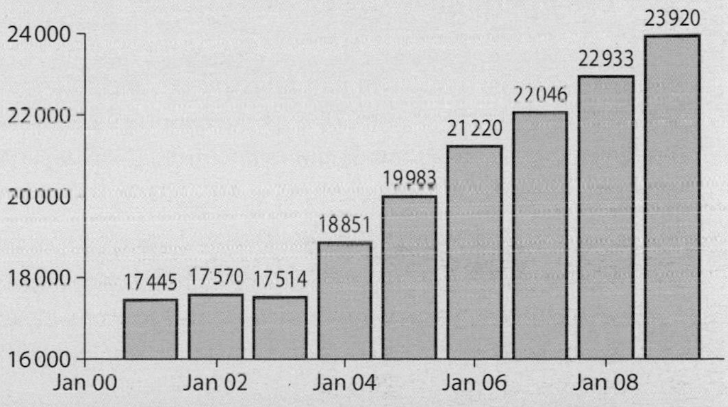

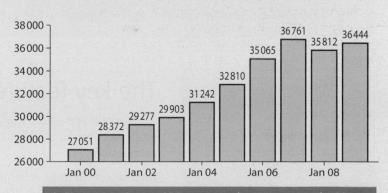

▲ **Figure 4.1** Saudi Arabia GDP per capita (income per head) US$

Canada

Canada's national income was $1,400 billion in 2009. The Canadian economy is diversified and highly developed. The Canadian economy relies heavily on foreign trade and the US is its largest trade partner. Canada is one of the few developed nations that is a net exporter of energy. Canada also exports motor vehicles and parts, machinery, aircraft, telecommunications equipment and electronics.

(a) What do Figures 4.1 and 4.2 show about the wealth of Canada and Saudi Arabia?

(b) Which country has the most balanced economy? Explain your answer.

(c) In which economy does the government play a significant role?

▲ **Figure 4.2** Canada GDP per capita (income per head) US$

Subsistence economies

An economy is a system that aims to solve the economic problem. The main function of an economy is to allocate a nation's resources between different uses. This is explained in Chapter 10.

Some poor countries have very basic economies where people provide for their own needs. These are called **subsistence economies**. People grow food and fish and hunt to satisfy hunger. They build their own houses from natural materials. They produce only what they need. However, people may swap goods with each other if they have surpluses. This is called **bartering**.

Subsistence economies have no businesses or infrastructure. Some communities travel from place to place looking for a location that provides food. They may settle for a period of time before moving on. Subsistence economies can be found in Africa and parts of South America, Asia and the Arctic.

QUESTION 1

Papua New Guinea is rich in natural resources, including minerals, timber and fish, and produces a variety of agricultural products. About 75% of the country's population relies on the subsistence economy. The minerals, timber and fish sectors are dominated by foreign businesses. Manufacturing is limited and agriculture supports more than 85% of the population.

Papua New Guinea is highly dependent on imports for manufactured goods. Industry accounts for only 9% of GDP and contributes little to exports. Small-scale industries produce goods such as beer, soap, concrete products, clothing, ice cream, canned meat, furniture, plywood, and paint. The small domestic market, high wages and high transport costs limit business development.

Source: adapted from www.geographyiq.com

(a)   To what extent is Papua New Guinea a subsistence economy?

(b)   Outline three features of a subsistence economy.

(c)   What is limiting business development in Papua New Guinea?

KEY FACT

Goods such as food, clothes, leisure and entertainment are usually produced by private businesses.

The key features that shape economies

Most economies in the world are either developed or developing. In these economies businesses play a huge role. What influences the shape of economies?

Businesses In most economies businesses produce products that aim to meet customer needs. They also provide employment. Through employment people earn money to buy goods and services. Businesses are owned either by private individuals or the state. The market system (see Chapter 10) ensures that businesses supply products that people want. Other goods, such as education, street lighting, roads and protection, are provided by the state.

Government The role played by the government can vary. Its main role is to provide a legal framework within which businesses can operate.

In some countries the government provides a lot of public services, such as education, healthcare, housing, public transport, social services and community services.

Monetary system A developed economy could not function without a monetary system. Subsistence economies do not use money because people provide goods for themselves, they do not buy anything. However, in modern economies money is needed as a medium of exchange. People work for money and then spend it on goods and services.

Infrastructure Businesses would struggle to operate without an efficient infrastructure. Businesses need good transport and communication links such as motorways, airports, ports, telecommunication links and rail networks. They also require power supplies, schools and hospitals. Economies will struggle to develop without an infrastructure.

International trade All developed economies are open. This means that businesses are free to trade goods and services overseas. International trade gives businesses larger markets to target. It also provides consumers with more choice and cheaper goods.

Specialisation One feature of a modern economy is **specialisation**. This is where an individual, business, region or country produces a limited range of goods. Individuals specialise at work by doing one task or job. Businesses also specialise. For example, Ford makes cars, Sony makes electronic products and BP is an oil company. Different countries specialise as well. For example, Saudi Arabia specialises in oil production. The pattern of specialisation in a country is likely to influence the shape of the economy.

KEY FACT

The government is likely to:
- pass laws to protect the rights of people and punish offenders;
- issue money and control the monetary system;
- provide essential services such as policing, defence and the judiciary;
- prevent businesses from exploiting employees and consumers.

Business sectors

Chapter 2 showed that business activity is classified according to the type of production that takes place. Primary production involves agriculture, mining and fishing, secondary production involves manufacturing, construction and processing, and tertiary production involves the provision of services.

The shape of an economy is influenced by how much is produced in each sector. For example, most developed countries have very large tertiary sectors. In contrast, poor countries tend to have large primary sectors because they rely heavily on agriculture or mining. Some of the newly developed nations such as China, Brazil and India have large manufacturing sectors. Over a period of time, as economies become more developed, the tertiary sector grows at the expense of the primary and secondary sectors.

QUESTION 2

Bangladesh

The Bangladeshi economy has grown 5-6% per year since 1996. However, the country is poor, overpopulated and poorly governed. More than half of national income is generated through the service sector. However, nearly two-thirds of Bangladeshis are employed in the agriculture sector – rice is the single most important product. Garment exports and money from Bangladeshis working overseas help the economy to grow.

Brazil

Brazil is one of the fastest growing economies in the world. It has large and growing agricultural, mining, manufacturing and service sectors. The Brazilian economy is the biggest in South America. Its main exports are transport equipment, iron ore, soya beans, footwear, coffee, autos and machinery. Brazil accounts for 25% of global exports of raw cane and refined sugar. It is also the world leader in soya bean exports and is responsible for 80% of the planet's orange juice.

Source: adapted from www.cia.gov

(a) Look at Figure 4.3. Describe the key differences between the Bangladeshi and Brazilian economies.

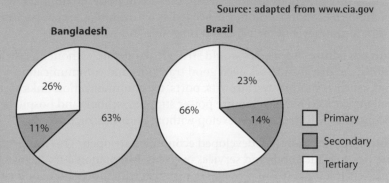

Figure 4.3 ▶
Employment by sector – Bangladesh and Brazil

 DID YOU KNOW?

Around half of the forests that once covered the planet are now gone. Forests are important for the survival of the planet. At least 120 out of 620 living primate species will be extinct in the next 10 to 20 years at current rates of habitat loss. Many other species are under threat, such as tigers, mountain gorillas and pandas.

Impact of business on the environment

Evidence suggests that as countries develop environmental damage increases. For example, governments are becoming concerned about global warming, which may be changing weather patterns and climates. Some of the greenhouse gases that contribute to global warming come from businesses such as power generators. As business activity increases there is more pollution. Also, economic development means that car ownership and air travel increases. The emissions from cars and aircraft also add to global warming.

Some business development destroys wildlife habitats and spoils the natural environment.

Resource depletion

In addition to the loss of forests many other resources are at risk. Here are some examples:

• Non-renewable resources, such as oil, coal, gas and minerals, cannot be replaced. Therefore, as business development gathers pace the amount of these resources is reduced. Once they have run out, future generations will have to do without.

• Fish stocks are falling. The world's marine catch increased from 18.5 million tons in 1950 to 82.5 million tons in 1992. This staggering growth is threatening millions of people who depend on fishing for their livelihoods.

• Fertile soil, which is needed to grow food, is being lost. About 40% of the world's agricultural land is badly affected. This is due to deforestation, poor farming practices, overgrazing, urban sprawl and land pollution.

Sustainable development

Many governments are talking about **sustainable development**. This means that people should satisfy their needs and enjoy better living standards without reducing the quality of life of future generations. Business development that denies resources to future generations is not sustainable. This means that resources used by businesses and consumers need to be reduced. For example, businesses could:

- design packaging that can be reused or recycled;
- reduce or stop using hazardous chemicals and processes that produce harmful by-products;
- use more energy-efficient equipment or renewable energy sources;
- explore ways of selling waste to other businesses as a by-product;
- stop unnecessary activities – for example, replace business travel with conference calls.

Key terms

Bartering – a system of exchange involving the swapping of goods.
Specialisation – in business, the production of a narrow range of products.
Subsistence economies – where people provide for their own needs, by hunting and gathering, for example.
Sustainable development – the idea that people should satisfy their basic needs and enjoy improved living standards without compromising the quality of life of future generations.

Chapter review – China

China is now the second largest economy in the world. Exports have boosted economic growth and account for 39.7% of its national income (see Figure 4.4). China's main exports are office machines, computers, telecommunications equipment, electrical machinery and clothing. China's growth has been so fast that large quantities of the world's resources have been used up. For example, in 2003 China consumed:

- half of the world's output of cement,
- a third of the world's output of steel,
- a fifth of the world's output of aluminium,
- nearly a quarter of the world's output of copper.

This raised world commodity prices. For example, the price of crude oil rose above $100 a barrel in 2007. Also, coal prices have risen and the prices of some steel products have almost doubled. China's hunger for resources has also caused a world shipping shortage.

Another problem caused by China's rapid growth is pollution. There have been thousands of incidents of water, air and land pollution. For example, Jilin Petro Chemical was fined $125,000 for its pollution of the Songhua River.

Source: adapted from www.democraticunderground.com

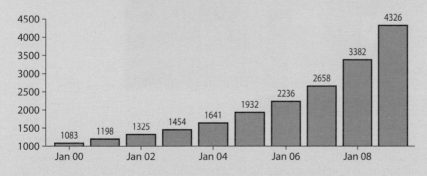

Figure 4.4
China's national income (GDP) – US$ billions

(a) Look at Figure 4.4. What evidence is there in the case to suggest that China's economy is in good shape? **(4 marks)**

(b) Which business sector do you think is most important to China? **(2 marks)**

(c) Using examples from the case, discuss the impact that rapid economic development in China has had on:
(i) the environment; (ii) resource usage. **(6 marks)**

(d) What is meant by sustainable development? **(2 marks)**

(e) What measures might Chinese businesses take to adopt a more sustainable approach to development? **(6 marks)**

Chapter 5

Business objectives

Getting started...

Businesses exist to produce goods and services for consumers and other businesses. However, the owners of businesses will want to achieve certain goals. Most business owners want to make a profit. They risk their own money when setting up a business and aim to make a financial return. There are other aims and objectives that businesses might try to achieve. Look at the two examples below.

The Bahrain Central

The Bahrain Central is a three-star hotel located in Manama, the capital of Bahrain. The owners of the hotel have recently met with the manager and agreed a two-year plan to increase profitability. The owners want to raise profit from 120,000 to 200,000 Bahraini Dinars. The manager hopes to cut costs and increase room occupancy by advertising more to business customers.

▲ **Figure 5.1** A hotel in the Middle East

British Airways

British Airways (BA) lost a record £401 million in 2008 and is struggling to survive. BA said it would ground aircraft, slash seat numbers and postpone the purchase of 12 A380 superjumbos as it faces a fall in passengers. BA has also said that it would cut its summer capacity by 3.5% instead of the original 2.5%.

In addition, BA staff voted for a pay cut to save jobs. However, senior managers turned them down. Unite, the union that represents 28,000 of BA's 40,000 workforce, put forward the pay plan to help BA save more than £200 million. This was after managers wrote to all staff asking them to volunteer to work for nothing.

Source: adapted from abcnews.go.com

(a) What is (i) The Bahrain Central; and (ii) BA trying to achieve?

(b) Describe briefly the measures being taken by (i) The Bahrain Central; and (ii) BA to achieve their aims.

The need for and importance of objectives

Businesses are more likely to be successful if they set goals or objectives. Businesses need to have goals for the following reasons:

- Employees need something to work towards. Goals help to motivate people. For example, sales staff might get bonuses if they reach certain sales targets.

- Without goals owners might not have the 'spark' needed to keep the business going. Owners might lose grip and allow their business to 'drift'. This might result in business failure.

- Goals help to decide where to take a business and what steps are necessary to get there. For example, if a business aims to grow by 10%, it might decide that launching products overseas might be the best way to achieve this.

- It is easier to assess the performance of a business if objectives are set. If objectives are achieved it could be argued that the business has performed well.

Aims and objectives

The **aims** of a business are what the business wants to achieve in the long term. Aims tend to be general and examples are: to be the 'best' in the market; to be the 'market leader'. The **objectives** of a business are the goals or targets that need to be met in order to achieve an aim. For example, a business might set annual sales targets to help grow the business.

Private sector objectives

In the *private sector* (see Chapter 10), where businesses are owned by individuals or groups of individuals, the objectives below are common.

Survival All businesses will consider survival as important. However, from time to time survival may be *the* most important objective. For example, when a business first starts trading it may be vulnerable. The owners may lack experience and there may be a shortage of resources. Therefore, a target for a new business may be to survive in the first 12 months. The survival of a business might also be threatened when trading conditions become difficult. In the example above, British Airways took a number of measures to ensure that the large airline survived the recession in 2009–2010.

Profit Most businesses aim to make a profit because their owners want a financial return. Some businesses try to **maximise profit**. This means they make as much profit as they possibly can. For example, companies, which are owned by shareholders, may try to maximise profits. This is because shareholders often put pressure on companies to pay out large *dividends*.

 DID YOU KNOW?

Owners of many small businesses are happy to make a satisfactory level of profit – just enough to fund a comfortable lifestyle, perhaps.

Growth Some owners want to grow their business. This is because larger businesses enjoy a number of benefits. For example, they:

- may enjoy lower costs;
- have a larger market share;
- enjoy a higher public profile;
- make more profit in the future.

The growth of a business might also benefit a wider range of *stakeholders* (see Chapter 6). For example, employees are likely to benefit from the growth of a business because their jobs will be more secure.

Increase market share Businesses often want to build a larger market share. They may be able to do this if they can win customers from competitors. Businesses with a large market share may be able to dominate the market. They may be able to charge higher prices, for example.

Image, reputation and social responsibility In recent years many businesses have tried to improve their image and develop a good reputation. One way of doing this is to take into account the needs of others such as customers, the local community and employees. If a business has a bad image or a poor reputation it may lose customers.

QUESTION 1

Thomas Cook Group plc is one of the world's leading leisure travel groups. It had sales of £8.8 billion, 22.3 million customers and 31,000 employees in 2008. It has 93 aircraft, 3,400 travel stores and interests in 86 hotels and holiday resorts. Thomas Cook is number one or number two in its core markets and has a clear strategy for the future. Thomas Cook aims to:

Improve performance in mainstream tour operating, make significant advances in independent travel, travel-related financial services and emerging markets, and grow overall revenue and profit.

Source: www.thomascookgroup.com/media/tcg_strategy_day.pdf

(a) Describe the main objective(s) of Thomas Cook.

(b) Do you think Thomas Cook will be concerned about its image and reputation as an objective? Explain your answer.

SMART objectives

The setting of business objectives may achieve more if they are SMART. This means that they should be:

- **S**pecific – stating clearly what is trying to be achieved.
- **M**easurable – capable of numeric measurement.
- **A**greed – have the approval of everyone involved.
- **R**ealistic – able to be achieved given the resources available.
- **T**ime specific – state a time by which they should be achieved.

An example of a SMART objective might be for a business to increase turnover by 8% in the next 12 months.

Mission statements

Some businesses write a **mission statement** when setting aims and objectives. This describes the purpose of a business. Mission statements are often directed at stakeholders such as customers, employees and shareholders. They:

- help a business to focus;
- provide a plan for the future;
- make clear to all stakeholders what the business is trying to achieve.

Figure 5.2 shows the mission statement for Unilever, the 'soups to soaps' company.

Our mission

Unilever's mission is to add vitality to life. We meet everyday needs for nutrition, hygiene and personal care with brands that help people feel good, look good and get more out of life.

▲ **Figure 5.2**
Unilever mission statement

Public sector aims and objectives

The aims and objectives of *public sector* organisations (see Chapter 10) are likely to be different from those in the private sector. For example, schools, hospitals, government departments and council run services are not likely to make a profit. Generally, public sector objectives are linked to quality of service and reducing costs. Examples of public sector objectives may include:

- Increasing special needs provision in schools.
- Increasing response time by the emergency services.
- Reducing specific crime rates.
- Reducing waste sent to landfill.
- Increasing the number of students entering higher education.

QUESTION 2

The UK National Health Service (NHS) has hit its target to treat patients within a maximum of 18 weeks from referral by their doctor. It said the average wait for treatment for admitted patients is now 8.6 weeks. For example:

- Cataract removal waiting times have halved – from 20 weeks in March 2007 to 10 weeks in January 2009.
- Waiting times for a heart bypass have halved from 14 to seven weeks.
- Audiology referral to treatment time now stands at around five weeks.

UK Health Secretary Alan Johnson said:

> *Achieving the shortest waits since NHS records began is a tremendous achievement for staff and I congratulate them for all their hard work. Meeting the standard nationally five months before it came into effect shows the commitment of the whole health service to improving patients' experiences.*

Source: adapted from www.hsj.co.uk

(a) Using examples from the case, explain what sort of objectives are set by public sector organisations.

(b) Why doesn't the NHS aim to make a profit like a private sector health service?

Key terms

Aims – what a business tries to achieve in the long term.

Mission statement – a brief summary of a firm's aims and objectives.

Objectives – the goals or targets set by a business to help achieve its long-term purpose.

Profit maximisation – making as much profit as possible in a given time period.

What determines business objectives?

The objectives set by a business are determined by a range of factors. For example, the size of firms may be important. Small businesses tend to aim to make enough profit to satisfy the owners. In contrast, large companies may try to maximise profit or grow rapidly. Stakeholders can also influence the objectives of a business. This is discussed in Chapter 6.

Finally, a business may have more than one objective. For example, a business may try to grow and become a market leader. Also, long-term objectives may differ from short-term objectives. For example, in the early stages of business start-up survival may be the main objective. But in the long term profit will become more important.

Chapter review – Boston Pizza International

Boston Pizza International (BPI) operates a pizza franchise in Canada. It has over 300 restaurants and operates three of these as corporate restaurants. These serve as franchisee training centres and allow BPI to test new menu items and other policies. The following information about the company is given:

- BPI had sales of over $830 million in 2008.
- Sales growth has averaged 5.7% for the last 10 years.
- Menus include health check options.
- The Boston Pizza Foundation has raised over $9 million for charities since 1990.
- It was named Franchisor of the Year by the Quebec Franchise Council in 2007.
- It was named No. 3 in Canada's 10 Most Admired Corporate Cultures.

(a) Use an example from this case to explain what is meant by a business objective. **(2 marks)**

(b) (i) Using this case as an example, explain what is meant by a mission statement. **(2 marks)**
(ii) What is the purpose of a mission statement? **(2 marks)**

(c) What evidence is there in the case to suggest that Boston Pizza International is concerned about its image and reputation? **(4 marks)**

(d) Explain why it is important to a company like Boston Pizza International to have aims and objectives. **(10 marks)**

our corporate mission statement

To be a world class franchisor through selecting and training people to profitably manage an outstanding foodservice business. To achieve this goal we are innovative and responsible in our approach to business. We work as a team providing attention to detail but never losing sight of the larger picture. We recognize the need to provide leadership in all areas of operations, marketing and restaurant development.

Figure 5.3
Boston Pizza mission statement

Source: adapted from www.bostonpizza.com

Chapter 6

Stakeholders and their objectives

Getting started...

Business activity can have an affect on different groups in society. For example, if a business launches a new product, who will be affected? The customers may benefit if the new product meets their needs more effectively. The owners might also benefit if the product is successful and more profit is made by the business. Look at the example below.

The Sultan Center (TSC)

The Sultan Center operates 11 retail outlets and owns a growing number of convenience stores in Kuwait. Its operations also include restaurants, catering, trading, fashion, telecommunications, security, and investments. TSC has expanded successfully throughout the Middle East with interests in Oman and Jordan. TSC has a 15% share of the retail market in Kuwait and employs about 3,500 staff. The company is owned by shareholders.

Source: adapted from www.sultan-center.com

(a) Identify three groups of people who have an interest in TSC.

(b) If TSC decided to extend its opening hours how might the groups identified in (a) be affected?

Figure 6.1 ▶
The Sultan Center in Kuwait

Business stakeholders

Any individual or group that has an interest in the operation of a business is called a **stakeholder**. Owners have a financial 'stake' in the business because they have invested some of their own money. Some stakeholders rely on the success of a business for their livelihoods. Figure 6.1 shows the different business stakeholders.

Figure 6.2 ▶
Business stakeholders

Owners

A business belongs to its owners. However, not all owners are the same. Many small businesses are owned by individuals, families or small groups of people. These people are often called **entrepreneurs**. They are responsible for setting up and running the business. They make all the key decisions and their main aim is to make a profit. Entrepreneurs usually depend on the business for their livelihood.

Larger businesses, such as companies (see Chapter 14), are owned jointly by **shareholders**. Shareholders invest money in a business and get a share of the profit called a **dividend**. Although individuals are free to buy shares in *public limited companies* (see Chapter 14), most shareholders are financial institutions such as pension funds, investment banks and insurance companies. They want high dividends and growth.

Customers

Customers buy the goods and services that businesses sell. Most customers are *consumers* who use or 'consume' products. However, some may be other businesses.

Customers want good quality products at a fair price. If they do not get this they will spend their money elsewhere. Customers have a powerful influence on businesses. If a business cannot produce goods that satisfy customers, they are not likely to survive. Customers are more aware today about the range of products available and about their rights as consumers.

Employees

Employees work for businesses. They may be employed to carry out a wide variety of tasks depending on the type of business. Employees depend on businesses for their livelihood. Most employees have no other sources of income and rely on wages to live on. However, they have other needs. They will need to be trained so that they can do their jobs properly. They want good working conditions, fair pay and benefits, job security and opportunities for promotion. Safety at work is also important as are issues to do with equal opportunities.

Managers

Managers help to run businesses. In small businesses the owner will carry out managerial tasks. Management involves:

- **Organising and decision making** Managers are often employed to run the different departments in businesses such as marketing, production, finance and human resources. They are responsible for the work carried out in their departments and for the people employed to do the work. Managers have to show leadership, solve problems, make decisions, settle disputes and motivate workers.

- **Planning and control** Managers are likely to help plan the direction of the business with owners. They also have to control resources such as finance, equipment, time and people.

- **Accountability** Managers are accountable to the owners. This means they have to 'shoulder the blame' if things go wrong.

KEY FACT

Employees are often represented at work by *trade unions*. When they are, they also become stakeholders. The needs of employees are often in conflict with those of other stakeholders such as owners and managers.

 ### DID YOU KNOW?

Managers may have needs in addition to those of general employees. For example, they may expect bonus payments if they perform well and expense allowances when travelling on company business. They may also want extra benefits such as a company car, free health insurance and more flexibility.

QUESTION 1

Boart Longyear, one of the world's largest drilling contractors and manufacturers, operates in 40 countries. Examples of its products include diamond and hard rock drills, exploration equipment and environmental tools. In 2009, the Australian-based company scrapped its dividend after cutting 2,000 jobs because of a downturn in the mining sector. The number of people employed in the Asia-Pacific region is currently about 2,600, down from 3,200 in September. Boart said the job cuts would save about $AUS123 million. The company has also imposed a wages freeze and reduced managerial salaries.

Source: adapted from http://business.theage.com.au

(a) Which stakeholder will be affected by Boart's decision to scrap the dividend?

(b) How will employees and managers be affected by Boart's recent actions as a result of the downturn in the mining sector?

(c) How might customer objectives be affected by Boart's actions?

Financiers

Financiers lend money to a business. They may be banks but could be individuals such as family members or private investors such as *venture capitalists* (see Chapter 22). Clearly these stakeholders have a financial interest in a business and will be keen for it to do well. Financiers will expect their interest payments to be met and their money returned at the end of the loan period. They will also want clear communication links with the business.

Suppliers

Businesses that provide raw materials, components, commercial services and utilities to other businesses are called **suppliers**. Relations between businesses and their suppliers must be good because they rely on each other. Businesses want good-quality resources at reasonable prices. They also want prompt delivery, *trade credit* (buy now, pay later) and flexibility. In return suppliers will require prompt payment and regular orders. Businesses that fail to pay promptly can cause cash flow problems for suppliers.

The local community

Most businesses are likely to have an impact on the local community.

• **Positive impact** A business may employ a lot of people that live in the local community. If the business does well, the local community may prosper. There may be more jobs, more overtime and possibly higher pay. This will have a knock-on effect in the community. For example, shops, restaurants and cinemas may benefit from extra spending.

• **Negative impact** A business may be criticised by the local community. For example, if a noisy factory decides to work night shifts, there may

Key terms

Dividends – the proportion of profit given to shareholders in return for their investment.
Entrepreneurs – people who set up and run businesses.
Managers – individuals who are accountable for more work than they could undertake alone.
Shareholders – individuals or financial institutions that own shares in companies.
Stakeholders – an individual or group with an interest in the operation of a business.
Suppliers – businesses that provide resources to other businesses.

be complaints from local residents. Also, if a business closes down, the impact on a local community can be devastating. In the 1980s when lots of coal mines were closed in the UK, many mining communities suffered badly as a result of very high unemployment.

The government

The government has an interest in all businesses. Generally the government will want businesses to be successful. They provide employment, generate wealth and pay taxes. Taxes from businesses and their employees are used to fund government expenditure. It helps to pay for benefits, hospitals, schools and other services. If businesses fail, the government loses tax revenue and has to pay benefits to the unemployed.

QUESTION 2

In January 2009, Woolworths, one of the most famous retailers in the UK, closed down. As a result, 27,000 people lost their jobs. The firm's 807 British outlets have been closing in stages since the end of December 2008 following clearance sales.

Woolworths went into administration in November 2008 with debts of £385 million. Unfortunately the company could not be saved. The administrators are now trying to sell off individual sites, with stores in popular high street locations expected to be reopened by other businesses.

Source: adapted from bbc.co.uk/news

(a) How might
   (i)   financiers;
   (ii) suppliers;
   (iii) the government be affected by the closure of Woolworths?

Objectives and conflict

Conflict can arise in a business because *stakeholder objectives* are different. For example, the owners may come into conflict with employees. The owners want to make profit and will try to keep costs down. But employees may want more pay to meet rising living costs. Employees' objectives will cost the business more money so the owners may not agree. This type of conflict can cause problems. Employees may go on strike for example.

Chapter review – Ohms Electricals

Ohms Electricals sells household appliances such as kettles, irons, toasters, food blenders, televisions and digital radios. It is based in Durban, South Africa and has recently started Internet selling. This resulted in the closure of some stores in rural areas because of dwindling trade. In 2008, 12 stores were closed and 150 people were laid off. Although new jobs have been created in online selling, further job losses are expected. A spokesperson for Ohms Electricals said: 'We understand the difficulties some employees will face when moving into online selling. But the company will save over R120 million. This will help the long term survival of the business.'

In an effort to improve cash flow managers have forced suppliers of electrical goods to extend the credit period from 60 days to 120 days. This has resulted in some friction. One supplier said: 'We just can't do this, Ohms is a good customer but we cannot wait any longer for payment. We have bills of our own to pay.'

(a) Use an example from the case to explain what is meant by a stakeholder. (2 marks)

(b) How are customers likely to benefit from online selling at Ohms Electricals? (2 marks)

(c) How are (i) owners; (ii) employees likely to be affected by the changes being made at Ohms Electricals? (4 marks)

(d) Outline the objectives (needs) of suppliers. (4 marks)

(e) Describe the conflict between stakeholders in the case and discuss the possible consequences. (8 marks)

▲ **Figure 6.3**
Examples of the products made by Ohms Electricals

Chapter 7

Government economic policy and business

Getting started...

Businesses are likely to do well if the economy is stable. This means that prices should not be rising too fast, unemployment should be low and the economy should be growing steadily. The government uses economic policy to help keep the economy stable. However, economic policies can affect businesses directly at a local, national and international level. Look at the example below.

2008–2009 Recession

In 2008, many countries were hit by a recession. It was caused by a financial crisis that started in America. The main problem was that banks cut back on their lending. This caused problems for businesses because they need to borrow money to fund their activities. Also, consumers borrow money to buy certain goods and services. As a result many governments took measures to encourage lending, ease the recession and help businesses. Some examples used by the UK government are outlined below.

- VAT (tax on spending) was reduced from 17.5% to 15%.
- Interest rates were slashed from 4.5 % to 0.5%.
- A 'scrap and save' car scheme was introduced (£2,000 off the price of a new car if the old one is scrapped – provided it is over 10 years old).
- Banks such as LloydsTSB, HBOS, Northern Rock and RBS were taken into public ownership to prevent them from collapsing.

(a) How might a restaurant benefit from the reduction in VAT?

(b) How might a house builder be affected by the cut in interest rates?

(c) What affect might the 'scrap and save' scheme have on the Nissan car factory in Sunderland?

The role of the government in the economy

It is the job of the government to manage the economy. As a result most governments have economic objectives. These are outlined below.

Promote economic growth An increase in output in the economy is called **economic growth**. It is good for the economy to grow because living standards rise.

Maintain price stability The government will want to keep **inflation** low. Inflation means that prices are rising and this can harm the economy. For example, it means that business costs will rise and people will have to pay more for their shopping.

Reduce unemployment When people cannot find a job **unemployment** occurs. Unemployment is bad for the economy because it is a waste of resources. Also, the government has to pay benefits to the unemployed, which come from taxes.

Control the balance of payments Some governments get concerned if *imports* are much higher than *exports* (see Chapter 11). It might mean that a country is relying too heavily on foreign goods and services. Also, a country has to pay its way. It cannot import more than it exports indefinitely.

The need for government intervention

Boom and recession Over time economies will grow. For example, most western economies grow at around 2% a year. However, the pattern of growth is often uneven (see Chapter 62).

- When an economy grows very quickly a *boom* is said to exist. This means that spending, incomes and business output will be high. Unemployment will be low and businesses will generally do well. However, if growth is too fast prices might rise too quickly.

- On the other hand, it is possible for economic growth to be flat. Or worse still it could be negative. This means that output falls. If this happens a *recession* is said to exist. As a result businesses suffer and unemployment rises.

This uneven pattern of growth means that governments have to intervene in the economy.

Control the impact of businesses Governments often have to intervene to protect people and the environment from businesses.

- Employees may need protection to ensure they are provided with a safe working environment and not exploited. In many countries, government legislation exists to provide such protection (see Chapter 58).

- Consumers may need protection from businesses. Sometimes businesses can become very powerful. They may develop a **monopoly**. This means they will have very little competition. Intervention may be needed to stop monopolists exploiting consumers. Consumer protection is discussed in Chapter 59.

- Some business activity may damage the environment. For example, a business might lower its costs by dumping waste into a river. This could kill plant and animal life. Many governments use legislation to help protect the environment from businesses. This is discussed in more detail in Chapter 60.

Support businesses Some government intervention aims to help and support businesses.

- **Local support** Local business support usually comes from local government. For example, local governments often provide free advisory services to new and small businesses. This helps local businesses to survive and flourish.

> **KEY FACT**
>
> During a recession the government may try to 'kick-start' the economy. The government will want to stop unemployment from rising and help businesses to recover. On the other hand, during a boom the government might intervene to reduce inflation.

- **National support** Central government often gives support to businesses. For example, it might reduce the amount of 'red tape' in business. This might reduce costs and improve efficiency. During a recession the government might reduce income tax. This would boost demand for all businesses.

- **International support** The government might help firms that export. For example, it could provide exporters with protection from bad debts. This means that if an overseas customer fails to pay for goods, the government pays.

Impact of intervention

Government intervention will affect business decision making. Generally, intervention raises costs and restricts business activity. Some examples are shown in Figure 7.1.

One of the most important ways in which the government influences business decision making is through *interest rates* and *taxation*. This is discussed below.

Subsidies may be given to businesses that make 'green products' such as solar heating systems. This would encourage businesses to produce 'green products'.

Employment subsidies may be given to firms that create jobs in a depressed area. This would influence business decisions relating to recruitment.

Free government advice and training may be given to businesses that launch products overseas. This might affect the decision whether to risk exporting or not.

A council may offer firms rent free units if they are located on a local industrial estate. This would affect business location decisions.

New legislation may force construction companies to increase the energy efficiency of buildings. This would influence the decision on which materials to use in production.

▲ **Figure 7.1**
Examples of the impact of government intervention on business decision making

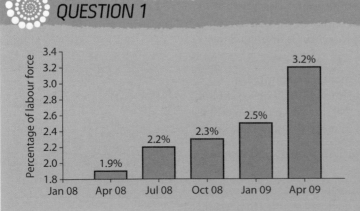

QUESTION 1

(a) What evidence is there in Figure 7.2 to suggest that Singapore went into recession in 2008–2009?

(b) How might a Singapore holiday company selling luxury cruises react to the pattern shown in Figure 7.2.

◄ **Figure 7.2**
Unemployment in Singapore

Taxation

Governments can affect business decision making using **fiscal policy**. This involves changing taxation and government spending to influence the economy. Taxes are paid by businesses and individuals. Different countries have different taxes. The main taxes used in the UK are shown in Figure 7.3.

Direct taxes (taxes on income)

Income tax	*Paid on all personal income and that from self-employment*
National Insurance contributions	*Paid by businesses and individuals on employees' earnings*
Corporation tax	*Paid by companies based on how much profit they make*
Capital gains tax	*Paid on the capital gain (profit) made when selling an asset*
Inheritance tax	*Paid on money transferred to another individual*

Indirect taxes (taxes on spending)

Value Added Tax (VAT)	*Paid mainly when buying goods and services (except food)*
Excise duties	*Paid when buying certain goods such as petrol and tobacco*
Customs duties	*Paid when buying certain goods from abroad*
Council tax	*Paid by residents to the local council to help fund local services*
Business rates	*Paid by businesses to the council to help fund local services*

▲ **Figure 7.3**
The main taxes used in the UK

Examples of the impact changes in taxation might have on businesses are:

- If income tax is lowered, there would be more spending in the economy. Businesses may respond by increasing production or raising prices.

- Businesses may respond to higher corporation tax by cutting investment or reducing dividends.

- An increase in VAT would raise prices so demand might fall. However, businesses may decide to cut profit margins to keep prices the same.

Generally, lower taxes are better for businesses than higher taxes. This is because high taxes will reduce demand and discourage work and enterprise.

QUESTION 2

In 2009, the New Zealand government announced some tax changes to help businesses. They were expected to save small and medium-sized businesses $480 million over four years. The changes were also designed to help businesses manage their cash flows. This is because businesses could delay paying their tax. The measures included:

- Reducing the amount of tax that businesses pay in advance.

- Reducing interest rates on underpaid and overpaid tax. From 1 March 2010 the rate for underpayments has been cut from 14.24% to 9.73% and the rate for over-payments from 6.66% to 4.23%.

- Lifting the GST (sales tax) registration threshold from $40,000 to $60,000. This means that small businesses do not have to charge GST until their turnover is $60,000.

Source: adapted from www.nzherald.co.nz

(a) How will the tax measures introduced in New Zealand support businesses?

(b) Why do businesses prefer lower taxes?

Key terms

Economic growth – an increase in income, output and expenditure over a period of time.

Fiscal policy – using changes in taxation and government expenditure to manage the economy.

Inflation – a rise in the general price level.

Interest – the price of borrowed money.

Monetary policy – using changes in interest rates and the money supply to manage the economy.

Monopoly – where a market is dominated by one supplier.

Unemployment – when people are out of work and cannot find a job.

Interest rates

Interest is paid to lenders when money is borrowed. Businesses and consumers have to pay interest if they take out loans and overdrafts or use credit cards. Over time interest rates can change. This is because they are used to help manage the economy. In many countries, the central bank sets the rate of interest. The use of interest rates to help control the economy is part of the government's **monetary policy**.

Changes in the interest rate can have a big impact on businesses. Generally, high interest rates are bad for businesses for the following reasons:

- Costs rise when interest charges increase. This will reduce profit.

- The purchase of capital goods funded by borrowing is discouraged because it is more expensive.

- People's mortgage payments rise so they have less to spend.

- Demand for goods bought with borrowed money will fall because it is dearer.

Changes in the interest rate will have a bigger impact on those businesses which have lots of debt, and those which produce goods bought with borrowed money such as cars, houses and consumer durables.

Chapter review – Government measures to support businesses

Most governments set a *budget* each year that outlines their spending plans for the future. The budget also states how revenue is to be raised from taxes. In 2009, a government budget contained some measures to help businesses. Some examples are outlined below.

- Tax allowances on investment were increased (this makes investment cheaper).

- Loss relief was extended. This means that a business loss can be offset against profits in a certain time period. This reduces the tax paid by businesses.

- Money was provided to firms investing in renewable energy, such as wind farms and solar power.

- Dividends paid by multinational businesses to foreign investors will be exempt from tax.

(a) A manufacturer is considering the construction of a new warehouse. How might the decision be affected by the 2009 budget measures? **(2 marks)**

(b) How might the budget measures influence businesses with foreign investors? **(2 marks)**

(c) Outline the role of the government when managing the economy. **(4 marks)**

(d) Explain why businesses prefer lower interest rates. **(4 marks)**

(e) Do you think there is a need for government intervention in the economy? **(8 marks)**

Chapter 8

Impact of technology on business

Getting started...

The development of new technology continues to have a huge impact on businesses. New technology results in new products that provide new market opportunities for businesses. It also helps to improve efficiency and makes work a lot easier for many people. Look at the example below.

Electric cars

Most car manufacturers are trying to develop alternatives to petrol-fuelled vehicles. This is because of the high oil price and the damage done by cars to the environment. Most big car makers plan to launch an electric car by 2012. General Motors has developed the Chevrolet Volt, which should be ready in 2010. BMW is launching a test fleet of electric Minis. Daimler is working on an electric Smart city car. In addition, Honda and Toyota already have their hybrid cars that run on a combination of petrol and electricity.

Nissan has recently launched an electric vehicle (EV) prototype. The car will use a battery that will recharge in four hours when plugged into the mains. The car is expected to cost about 4 cents a mile to run. Nissan also said that several hundred new jobs would be created in Sunderland (UK) where it plans to make the batteries for the car.

▲ Figure 8.1 An EV

Source: adapted from www.wired.com/autopia/2009/04/we-drive-nissan/

(a) What has prompted the development of electric cars?

(b) Outline briefly two advantages to consumers of EVs.

(c) How might Nissan's workers be affected by the development of EVs?

The impact of technology on costs

New technology in business lowers costs. Also, technology usually means that people are replaced by machines and production becomes more efficient. Some examples are given below.

• In the primary sector the use of tractors, mechanical harvesters, grain-drying machines and automatic feeding systems have helped to lower costs in agriculture. Chemicals and pesticides have also helped to increase the amount of crops produced.

• In the secondary sector the introduction of robots on production lines has reduced costs. They are cheaper to employ than people because they can work 24/7. Computer aided design (CAD) is used to design products such as cars, aircraft, plastic containers, gardens, furniture and clothing. This improves accuracy and speeds up the whole design process. As a result design costs are lower.

DID YOU KNOW?

In some factories production is entirely automated. Computers are used to design products and the information is then fed into computer numerically controlled machines (CNCs) that can carry out tasks such as cutting, milling, sewing, moulding and welding.

- The use of technology in service industries has reduced costs. In the leisure industry bookings for hotels and transport can be made online, which reduces administration costs. In banking costs have been reduced through the use of ATMs for dispensing cash. Internet banking has also helped to reduce costs because customers can manager their accounts online.

- The use of information and communications technologies (ICT) has helped to reduce administration and communication costs in business. For example, many routine tasks can be carried out quickly by computer. These may include customer invoicing or billing. Huge amounts of data can be gathered, processed, manipulated, stored and retrieved using computer databases. A wide range of different information can be sent electronically anywhere in the world instantly.

DID YOU KNOW?

In the US about 10 million manual jobs have been lost during the past 10 years. Machines and automated systems have replaced humans. During this time, businesses have invested more than $100 billion in robotics and supporting systems.

The impact of technology on labour requirements

Unfortunately, the introduction of new technology often results in job losses. However, although technology results in job losses, new jobs are also created. For example, new technology has to be researched, designed, manufactured, installed, operated and maintained. However, these jobs tend to be skilled and different from those that the technologies replace. This means that businesses need people with new skills. It also means that the development of technology provides opportunities for people to learn new skills.

QUESTION 1

Vidéotron provides cable television, Internet access and wireless telephone services in Quebec, Canada. Recently, the company introduced an automated system to deal with administration when handling service calls. This involved giving field technicians BlackBerry smartphones with a special application. The system had the following benefits:

Savings of $1.6 million over three years The new system was about 40% less expensive than giving each technician a laptop. When combined with staff reduction costs and improved efficiency, Vidéotron believes it will save approximately $1.6 million over three years.

Reduces the need for dispatchers Switching from a paper- and phone-based system to the BlackBerry application has reduced staff costs by 40% and phone calls by 35%.

More effective and happier technicians The BlackBerry solution helps technicians to work faster and reduces customer waiting time.

Source: adapted from http://na.blackberry.com

(a) What impact did the automated administration system have on Vidéotron's costs?

(b) How might Vidéotron's labour requirement have been affected by the new system?

The impact of technology on production methods

Production has become more **capital intensive** in many industries. This means that more machinery is used in production instead of other resources such as labour. Some examples are as follows:

- Automation is common in the food industry. The processing, canning, bottling and packaging of food and drinks is carried out on production lines using *continuous production* (see Chapter 35). Production lines are controlled by computers and can run non-stop for long periods.
- Car manufacturing makes increasing use of robots, automatic presses and CAD. Even windscreens can be fitted by a robot.
- Sheet glass production may be entirely automated. Raw materials are fed into a mile-long plant at the start. Then, after going through a number of processes (mixing, melting, cooling, cutting and stacking) sheets of glass are loaded automatically on to lorries and driven straight to customers.

The impact of technology on marketing

Some examples of the impact of technology on marketing are outlined below:

- IT has made market research easier. The gathering, processing and presentation of market research data is cheaper using IT. Also, large amounts of data can be handled. Data can also be gathered online. This is more convenient for consumers and therefore more data is likely to be gathered. It is also cost effective.
- In advertising, TV adverts use the latest film technology and special effects to make adverts more sensational and entertaining.
- There is a growing selection of advertising media (see Chapter 32).
- The Internet is used to promote products. Many businesses have their own websites where information about products is updated regularly.
- Prices may be lower if goods and services can be traded online.
- Businesses can market their goods more widely using the Internet. The Internet also allows businesses to advertise internationally at a low cost.

DID YOU KNOW?

Advertisers use electronic messaging on the 'touchlines' at sports events and in city centres on the side of buildings. Information about products can also be sent direct to mobile phones.

QUESTION 2

Quividi, a French software company, has developed a device that analyses the faces of passers-by who look at outdoor advertising. The software measures the attention different consumers (men and women, older and younger people) are paying to outdoor media. The hidden camera:
- counts the number of viewers;
- provides information on viewership such as dwell time (the amount of time the viewer spends looking at the advert) and attention time;
- shows the age and gender of viewers;
- provides information about the links between viewership and content. For example, it can tell what sort of people look at an image showing an attractive landscape.

Source: adapted from www.technologyinmarketing.com/2009_02_01_archive.html

(a) Explain how businesses might benefit from the technology illustrated in this case.

(b) Outline briefly two advantages of gathering market research data online.

What is e-commerce?

E-commerce involves the use of electronic systems to buy and sell products. Most e-commerce takes place online. There are two main types.

Business to consumers (B2C) This is the selling of goods and services by businesses to consumers. Some e-commerce is done entirely electronically. For example, an individual can make a payment, download some music and listen to it on their laptop, iPod or iPhone. However, a great deal of e-commerce still involves trading in physical goods such as clothes and consumer durables. This is called **e-tailing** and involves ordering goods online and taking delivery at home. Most large retailers now have online services. Some other examples of B2C e-commerce include:

- tickets for air, rail and coach travel;
- tickets for sports fixtures, cinema, theatre and attractions such as theme parks;
- holidays, weekend breaks and hotel rooms;
- music for MP3 players;
- a wide range of goods on ebay, the auction site.

Business to business (B2B) This involves businesses selling to other businesses online. In some cases the services sold to consumers are also available to businesses. Examples include travel tickets, accommodation, financial services and physical goods such as furniture. Businesses can also use specialist software to purchase resources. The software helps to find the cheapest supplier and carries out all the paperwork.

Benefits to consumers of e-commerce

Some consumers really like e-commerce. For example, those who:
- live in rural and isolated locations;
- do not have the time to go shopping;
- dislike going to shops;
- have mobility problems.

Online shopping can be cheaper because business costs are lower. It can be done 24 hours a day, seven days a week (24/7) and there is generally a huge amount of choice. People can also shop from different locations such as at work, at home or travelling on a train. All they need is access to the Internet – via a laptop or a mobile phone.

Benefits of e-commerce to businesses

- Businesses involved in e-tailing do not have to meet the costs of operating stores (although some do both). With lower costs they can reduce prices and attract more customers.
- Costs of processing transactions is reduced (mainly because they are paperless).
- Documents such as purchase orders and invoices can be exchanged online.

Key terms

Capital intensive – methods of production that use greater quantities of capital (machinery and plant) than other resources such as labour.
E-commerce – the trading of goods and services electronically.
E-tailing – the sale of physical goods online.

- Payments can be made and received online.

- B2C businesses can offer goods to a much wider market. Many now offer their products internationally.

- Businesses can serve their customers 24/7. Online trading can be done when the shops are closed.

- Businesses have more choice when locating their operations. This is because they do not have to be close to their customers. This means they can be based in cheaper locations.

Threats of e-commerce

Many businesses and consumers are happy to trade electronically. However, there are some threats, which are summarised in Figure 8.2.

Threats to businesses

Competition is now more fierce – from overseas sellers for example.

Lack of human contact – this might not suit some customers.

Reliance on delivery services – e-tailers often lack control on the quality of delivery.

Break in service – websites may crash and Internet connections can get lost.

Security risk – computer hackers might gain access to sensitive information.

Threats to consumers

Cannot physically see goods – might not suit some customers.

Poor after sales service – for example, customers may find it difficult to return goods.

Some customers excluded – for example, those without Internet access and credit/debit cards.

Security risk – computer hackers might gain access to personal information.

Bogus traders – there is more potential for 'scams' online, which can result in lost money.

Receiving goods – people at work may have problems with delivery times.

Time consuming – for example, with so much choice making comparisons may be difficult.

▲ Figure 8.2
Threats of e-commerce to businesses and consumers

Chapter review – Aston Villa FC

Aston Villa FC is an English Premier League soccer club. In the 2008–2009 season it had 26,000 season ticket holders and an average attendance at matches at its ground, Villa Park, of over 40,000. Like most football clubs it has a website. Fans and visitors to the site can:

- buy match tickets and Aston Villa merchandise from the official online store;
- get up-to-date news about the club;
- obtain information about the club, its activities and football in general;
- watch match highlights and interviews with the manager and players;
- organise transport to away matches;
- subscribe to AVTV (Aston Villa's TV channel) and live match commentaries.

Aston Villa's commercial arm also provides services to businesses. For example, it has conferencing facilities where businesses can hold meetings and put on exhibitions. The club also provides hospitality packages for businesses on match days. Details of these are available on the website and facilities can be booked online.

(a) State two groups of consumers who may prefer online shopping. (2 marks)

(b) Use this case as an example to explain the difference between B2C and B2B e-commerce. (4 marks)

(c) Outline two benefits to Aston Villa of using e-commerce. (4 marks)

(d) Do you think Aston Villa's customers benefit from e-commerce? (10 marks)

Chapter 9

Business reaction to market changes

Getting started...

Businesses operate in dynamic markets. This means that markets change over time resulting in new spending patterns. A wide range of factors can affect what consumers buy. Markets have also become more competitive, which makes it more difficult for businesses to be successful. Look at the information below.

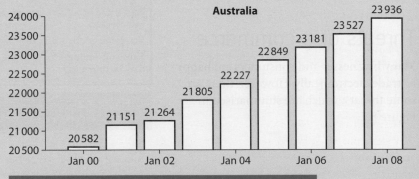

▲ **Figure 9.1** GDP per capita (income per head) – Australia

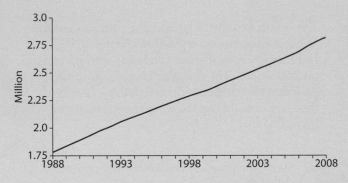

In the 12 months to 30 June 2008, the number of people aged 65 years and over in Australia increased by 67,600 people - a 2.4% increase. The proportion of the population aged 65 years and over increased from 10.8% to 13.3% between 1988 and 2008.

◀ **Figure 9.2**
Australian population over the age of 65

(a) How might (i) a business selling luxury holidays abroad; (ii) a domestic budget hotel chain in Australia react to the pattern shown in Figure 9.1?

(b) How might (i) a toy manufacturer; (ii) a private hospital in Australia react to the pattern shown in Figure 9.2.

What is a market?

Goods and services are sold by businesses in markets. A market exists when buyers and sellers communicate and exchange goods for money. Some examples of markets are:

• **Consumer goods markets**: where products like food, cosmetics and magazines are sold.

- **Markets for services**: these are varied and could include services for individuals, such as banking, or business services, such as cleaning.
- **The housing market**: where people buy and sell properties.
- **Commodity markets**: where raw materials such as oil, copper, wheat and coffee are traded.

Changes in consumer spending patterns and business reactions

Over time market conditions are likely to change. For example, a market might become less attractive to a business because prices are falling. This means it is harder to make a profit. Spending patterns may change over time for a number of reasons. Some examples are summarised in Figure 9.3.

Economic conditions During a boom spending levels will be high and businesses will benefit from rising demand. They may react by increasing production or raising prices. In contrast, during a recession spending falls. Businesses may react by cutting production, laying off staff and cutting other costs.

Consumer tastes Consumers tastes change over time. For example, in recent years there has been an increase in spending on organic foods. Changes in consumer tastes may arise from changes in *society*. For example, social websites such as Facebook and Bebo have grown out of the rising trend in electronic communication. Businesses have to react quickly to such changes. They need to supply products that meet consumer needs and wants. They can follow changes in consumer tastes by carrying out *market research*.

Population – size, age and structure

- In most countries populations are growing. As a result there will be more demand.

- Populations are also aging. This means higher demand for products bought by the elderly. Examples might include healthcare, retirement homes and specialist holidays for the elderly.

- In some countries changes in the structure of the population can affect spending patterns. For example, in Australia ethnic groups such as South East Asians and Indians have grown. This means that spending on ethnic foodstuffs may rise.

Income Increased incomes means consumers can buy more products. In countries such as China, India and Brazil incomes have increased sharply in the last 10–15 years. As a result, spending on leisure goods in particular has risen fast. Businesses must react by supplying more.

Technology Changes in technology is one of the main reasons for changes in consumer spending patterns. New products resulting from research and development (R&D) create new markets. Examples include satellite navigation systems, digital radio, electric vehicles and new computer games. Businesses operating in markets where technology changes quickly need to invest in R&D in order to compete. However, some firms survive by copying new products developed by others.

DID YOU KNOW?

Historically, markets were *places* where buyers and sellers would meet to exchange goods. Today it is possible to trade goods without buyers and sellers meeting up. For example, trading can be done over the telephone, using newspapers, through mail order or on the Internet.

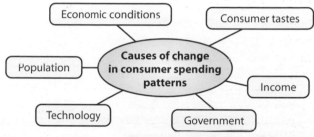

▲ Figure 9.3
Changes in consumer spending patterns – causes

KEY FACT

Some governments have introduced 'scrap and save' schemes to encourage consumers to scrap their old cars and buy a new one. This helps to take older 'polluting' cars off the road and supports the car industry during the recession.

Government The government can affect consumer spending patterns in two ways:

- It can boost or dampen consumer spending using fiscal policy or monetary policy. For example, if income tax is increased consumers will have less disposable income and spending will fall. On the other hand, if interest rates are cut consumer spending will rise as people borrow more to spend (see Chapter 7).

- Some government legislation may affect spending patterns. New environmental legislation will encourage consumers to buy 'green' products, for example.

Businesses have to be aware that changes in markets will occur over time. Those that anticipate changes and react quickly are more likely to succeed. Businesses will need to be flexible and creative to survive.

 ## QUESTION 1

India has always been a tea drinking nation. However, coffee has become more popular, especially among the young. Also, Indian middle-class consumers want to be a part of global lifestyle and culture. Leading coffee retailers such as Café Coffee Day, Barista and Costa Coffee have all been trying to take advantage of this trend. Although tea costs a few rupees and coffee up to Rs100, rising incomes in the country also means that an increasing number of consumers can afford to visit coffee shops.

India has now becoming one of the fastest growing coffee markets in the world. As a result, Starbucks, the largest coffee shop chain in the world, is planning to enter the market. According to researchers, the coffee retail business in India is worth over Rs8 billion ($17 million), and there is the potential for up to 3,000 coffee retail outlets.

Source: adapted from http://trak.in

(a) What is expected to happen to consumer spending on coffee in India in the future?

(b) State two possible reasons for the growing popularity of coffee in India.

(c) How has Starbucks responded to the trend in India?

Why have markets become more competitive?

Competition often causes changes in market conditions. Competition is the rivalry that exists between businesses when selling goods in a particular market.

Many markets have become more competitive. There are a number of reasons for this:

- **Globalisation:** Competition has increased because markets have become *global*. This means that many businesses sell into international markets. Some are multinationals and supply markets in many different countries resulting in more competition.

- **Legislation:** Governments must ensure that markets are competitive. This is because without competition consumers may be exploited.

- **More information**: Markets are more competitive if consumers have more information about products. The Internet provides a huge amount of information about businesses and their products. With more information consumers can make better judgments about products when shopping.

- **New enterprise culture**: In some countries more people have been encouraged to set up businesses. Governments have been trying to develop an enterprise culture by giving help to new entrepreneurs. In many Eastern European countries, people have been allowed to set up businesses for the first time. More businesses means more competition.

 DID YOU KNOW?

On the internet there are price comparison sites such as *comparethemarket.com*. These search for the cheapest suppliers.

The impact of competition on consumers

Most consumers would say that competition is desirable for the following reasons:

- **Lower prices**: In a competitive market firms cannot overcharge consumers. If one firm tries to raise its price, it may lose business. This is because in a competitive market consumers can switch from one supplier to another.

- **More choice**: Competition means there are lots of alternative suppliers to choose from. Suppliers may try to *differentiate* their products from those of rivals. This helps to widen choice even more for consumers.

- **Better quality**: Firms that offer poor quality goods in a competitive market will lose business. Consumers are rational and will look for value for money. Therefore, businesses are under pressure to provide quality products and good customer service.

 DID YOU KNOW?

In the highly competitive soft drinks market the choice of products is huge. Firms are constantly bringing out new flavours and changing their packaging.

 ## QUESTION 2

The UK market for clothes is competitive. Clothes are sold from a variety of different outlets.

- **Independent shops and boutiques** are usually small clothes retailers that operate from just one location. They may have an individual range, specialise in a certain style or serve a market *niche*.

- **Multiples** such as Next, Wallis, Jaeger and Monsoon have stores all over the country. Each chain has a standard product line, standard store front, standard prices and a standard layout.

- **Variety chains** such as Marks & Spencer, Primark, BHS and Debenhams, sell a wide range of different products but clothes feature very highly.

- **Supermarkets** are diversifying and many of them now sell clothes.

- **Online sales** of everything are currently growing rapidly. This includes clothes.

In March 2009, Debenhams announced that it was cutting prices by up to 50%. When the department store slashed prices before Christmas, rivals such as Marks & Spencer followed suit. The latest price cuts may force competitors to do the same. **Source: adapted from www.mirror.co.uk**

(a) Using this case as an example, explain what is meant by competition in a market.

(b) How will the Internet make the clothing market more competitive?

(c) Outline two impacts on consumers resulting from competition in the UK clothes market.

Key terms

Competition – the rivalry that exists between firms when trying to sell goods to the same group of customers.
Innovation – the commercial exploitation of a new invention.
Market – a set of arrangements that allows buyers and sellers to communicate and exchange goods and services.

The impact of competition on businesses

Generally, businesses do not welcome competition. Most firms would prefer to dominate the market and operate without rivals. If there is no competition, a business can charge a higher price. The main disadvantage to a business operating in a competitive market is that sales and profit will be limited.

In competitive markets firms have to give consumers value for money. This involves:

- being efficient to keep costs down;
- providing good-quality products with high levels of customer service;
- charging prices that are acceptable to customers;
- **innovating** by constantly reviewing and improving the product.

Chapter review – EMI and the music market

In 2007, sales of CDs fell 13% in the US. In contrast, sales of downloaded songs rose 34%. Consumers often prefer digital music because they can download individual songs from an album. This means they do not have to buy the whole album. They also like the idea of downloading immediately to listen to their purchases. However, there is evidence that music listening is increasing. For example, the number of consumers listening to music on social networks sites climbed from 15% in 2007 to 19% in 2008.

EMI, the oldest record company in the world, has been affected by these changes. EMI reacted by generating more revenue from the activities in which its artists are involved. For example, in 2002, EMI agreed an £80m deal with pop singer Robbie Williams. The deal meant that EMI got a share of the revenue from all the artist's activities. This included recorded music, publishing, concerts and merchandising.

Source: adapted from www.zdnet.com/news

(a) State two reasons why markets in general have become more competitive in recent years. **(2 marks)**

(b) Without competition consumers may be exploited. What does this mean? **(2 marks)**

(c) How might spending patterns in the music market be affected by **(i)** recession; **(ii)** an aging population. **(4 marks)**

(d) Explain how EMI is reacting to changes in the music market. **(4 marks)**

(e) Analyse the impact of competition on consumers in the music market. **(8 marks)**

Chapter 10

Mixed and market economies

Getting started...

Goods and services are produced by organisations to meet the needs and wants of consumers. However, the way in which different countries organise the choice, production and distribution of goods will vary. Look at the two sets of images in Figure 10.1 below.

SET 1

SET 2

 Figure 10.1 Services and goods

(a) Who provides the goods and services shown in the two sets of photographs in Figure 10.1?

(b) Why do you think there are two sets of providers? Explain your answer.

The economic problem

All countries have to deal with what economists call the **basic economic problem**. The problem, which is summarised in Figure 10.2, arises because the world's resources are scarce or *finite* and people's wants are *infinite*. More resources are needed than are available. Therefore decisions have to be made about how to allocate a nation's resources between different uses.

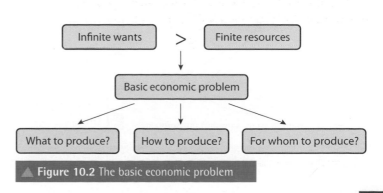

Figure 10.2 The basic economic problem

Overcoming the basic economic problem involves making some important decisions:

- **What to produce?** It is impossible to produce all the goods that people want. Therefore a country must decide which goods will be produced. For example, should resources be used to provide more libraries, expand the armed forces, make more cars, make more toys or train more doctors?

- **How to produce?** Goods can be produced using different production methods. The four factors of production can be organised in different ways to produce the same goods. For example, in China a lot of clothes manufacturers use large quantities of labour in production. However, in many western countries the same goods are produced using hi-tech machinery.

- **For whom to produce?** Once goods have been produced they have to be distributed. This means goods have to be shared out in some way. For example, should everyone get exactly the same or should some receive more than others?

There are different solutions to the basic economic problem. This is because different courses of action can be taken when making the decisions above. The way in which they are made depends on what sort of *economic system* a country has.

The public and private sectors

An **economy** is a system which attempts to solve the basic economic problem. In any economy goods and services may be provided by the **public sector** or the **private sector**. In the private sector, individuals are free to set up businesses and supply products to anyone who wants to buy them. In the public sector, government organisations provide services such as healthcare, education, refuse collection, social care and street lighting. Most public sector services are provided free and paid for by taxes.

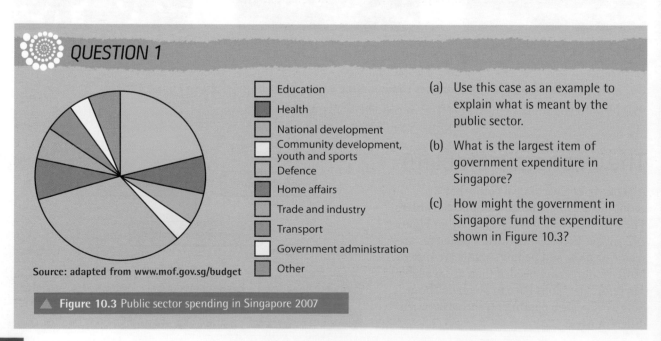

QUESTION 1

Education
Health
National development
Community development, youth and sports
Defence
Home affairs
Trade and industry
Transport
Government administration
Other

Source: adapted from www.mof.gov.sg/budget

(a) Use this case as an example to explain what is meant by the public sector.

(b) What is the largest item of government expenditure in Singapore?

(c) How might the government in Singapore fund the expenditure shown in Figure 10.3?

Figure 10.3 Public sector spending in Singapore 2007

Types of economy

Different countries have different economic systems. This is because political systems and styles of government vary in different countries. For example, before the break-up of the Soviet Union in 1991, production in most Eastern European countries was organised by the government. On the other hand, some governments believe that goods and services should be produced by private sector businesses.

There are three types of economy:

- In a **market** or **free enterprise economy** most goods and services are provided by private businesses. The role of the public sector is very limited. The allocation of resources is largely determined by *market forces*.

- In a *command or planned economy* the state chooses, produces and distributes goods. All resources belong to the state and the government plans and organises production. Goods are distributed from state outlets where they are sold to consumers at fixed prices.

- A **mixed economy** relies on *both* the public sector and the private sector to provide goods and services.

The market economy

In a market economy goods and services are produced by businesses in the private sector.

The role of the public sector is limited to:

- passing laws to protect the rights of people and punish offenders;

- issuing money and controlling the monetary system;

- providing essential services such as policing, defence and the judiciary;

- preventing businesses from exploiting employees and consumers.

What to produce? This is decided by consumers. Businesses produce goods and services that are designed to meet the needs and wants of consumers. Businesses that produce unwanted products will fail. Resources will be attracted into markets where businesses are thriving. Resources will be released from *declining industries*.

How to produce? In market economies businesses make this decision. Businesses aim to make a profit. Therefore they will choose production methods that minimise costs. Competition in market economies forces firms to keep costs down and prices low.

For whom to produce? Businesses produce goods and services that consumers buy with money. The amount of money consumers have depends on their wealth and income. In market economies individuals own the factors of production. For example, workers can earn money by selling their labour and business owners receive profit. Those individuals with the most money can by the most goods and services.

 DID YOU KNOW?

Tourism is growing all over the world. This means that the number of businesses in the tourist industry will increase. There will be more hotels, travel agents, restaurants and airlines. As a result more resources will be used by those businesses.

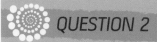

QUESTION 2

There are no examples of pure market economies. However, Brazil is a country where more than 80% of goods and services are produced in the private sector. Brazil is one of the fastest growing emerging economies in the world. Figure 10.4 shows that national income has nearly trebled since 2004.

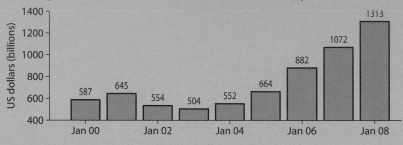

Figure 10.4
Brazil Gross Domestic Product (GDP)

(a)   Who decides what goods should be produced in Brazil?

(b)   How are goods and services distributed between people in Brazil?

(c)   What is the main role of the government in Brazil?

Key terms

Basic economic problem – allocation of a nation's scarce resources between competing uses that represent infinite wants.

Economy – a system that attempts to solve the basic economic problem.

Market or free enterprise economy – an economy where goods and services are provided by businesses in the private sector.

Mixed economy – an economy where goods and services are provided by both the private and the public sectors.

Private sector – the provision of goods and services by businesses that are owned by individuals or groups of individuals.

Public sector – government organisations that provide goods and services in the economy.

The mixed economy

In reality, no economy is an entirely planned or free market. Most countries in the world have mixed economies. Production decisions are made jointly between the private and public sectors. This is because market economies and planned economies have problems.

What to produce? A mixed economy recognises that some goods are best provided by the private sector. Consumer goods such as food, clothes, leisure and entertainment are best chosen by consumers. The market system ensures that businesses produce the goods that people want. Other goods, such as education, street lighting, roads and protection, are better provided by the state. The public sector tends to provide services that the private sector might overlook.

How to produce? In the private sector goods are provided by businesses with the aim of making a profit. Competition exists between these firms and this provides choice and variety for consumers. Businesses will use production methods that maximise quality and minimise costs.

Public sector services are provided by government organisations. They will attempt to supply them efficiently. However, some public sector goods are produced by the private sector. For example, the government is responsible for the provision of roads and motorways in many countries. However, the government often pays private sector construction companies to carry out such work.

For whom to produce? Goods produced in the private sector are sold to anyone who can afford them. In contrast, most public sector goods are provided free to everyone and paid for from taxes. In a mixed economy the state helps people who cannot work – because of illness or disability, for example. A system of financial benefits exists to make sure that people do not starve.

What are the main differences between mixed economies and market economies?

Generally, the public sector plays a greater role in the provision of goods and services in mixed economies. However, there are some specific differences:

- Certain important goods and services such as education, roads and rail links, health and social care are 'underprovided' in market economies. For example, only the wealthy could afford to send their children to the privately run schools.

- Market economies do not provide benefit systems for the disadvantaged such as the disabled and the unemployed.

- Taxes in market economies will be much lower than in mixed economies. This is because they do not have to pay for public services.

- Prices will be lower in market economies because taxes on sales and profits will be lower. However, some services like education may be free in mixed economies.

- There may be more choice in market economies. This is because in mixed economies competition may not exist in some markets. For example, transport in some mixed economies is provided only by the public sector.

KEY FACT

Different governments will determine the 'degree of mixing' in this type of economy. Some countries, such as Sweden, allow the government to play a greater role in the economy. For example, government expenditure in Sweden is around 60% of its national income. In such countries social provision is greater but taxes will be higher.

Chapter review – Mixed and market economies

Figure 10.5 shows the government expenditure as a percentage of national income for a selection of countries.

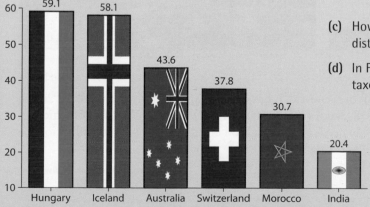

Source: adapted from anepigone.blogspot.com

▲ **Figure 10.5** Government expenditure as a percentage of national income for a selection of countries 2007

(a) What is meant by a mixed economy? **(2 marks)**

(b) In Figure 10.5, in which country does the public sector play the greatest role? Explain your answer. **(2 marks)**

(c) How would you expect goods and services to be distributed in India? **(2 marks)**

(d) In Figure 10.5, in which country would you expect taxes to be highest? Explain your answer. **(2 marks)**

(e) How might private sector businesses benefit from public sector spending? **(2 marks)**

(f) What are the main differences between mixed and market economies? **(10 marks)**

Chapter 11

International trade

Getting started...

Trade between nations has grown a lot in recent years. One reason for this is that many countries have become more open. International trade takes place for a number of reasons. Look at the examples below.

The UK

Historically, the UK bought raw materials from abroad and sold manufactured goods. However, the UK now sells a lot of services abroad such as media, banking, insurance and business services. On the other hand the UK buys machines, manufactured goods, food, beverages and tobacco from overseas. For example, it buys fresh produce such as pineapples, citrus fruits, salad stuff and vegetables.

Maldives

The Maldives is a group of small islands in the Indian Ocean. They are beautiful and tourism is the Maldives' largest industry. It accounts for 28% of GDP and more than 60% of the Maldives' imports. Over 90% of government tax revenue comes from import duties and other tourist taxes. Fishing is the second largest sector, but with so few natural resources the country is poor by international standards.

Figure 11.1 An island in the Maldives ▶

Saudi Arabia

Saudi Arabia is one of the biggest producers of oil in the world. It has considerable reserves, estimated at 266.8 billion bbl/day in 2007 (bbl is the volume). In 2008, Saudi's oil production was 9.2 million bbl/day, of which around 8 million bbl/day were sold overseas. It only needs about 1 million bbl/day for its own consumption. Saudi Arabia's main trading partners are America and Japan.

Source: adapted from www.cia.gov

(a) Why do you think Saudi Arabia sells so much oil abroad?

(b) Why does the UK buy fresh foods from overseas?

(c) In which two industries are businesses in the Maldives most likely to operate?

International trade

International trade benefits the world. It creates opportunities for business growth, increases competition and provides more consumer choice. However, there are some specific reasons why countries trade with each other:

- **Obtain goods that cannot be produced domestically**: Many countries are unable to produce certain goods. This is because they lack the natural resources needed for such production. In the example, the UK cannot produce foods like tropical fruits because it does not have the right climate.

- **Obtain goods that can be bought more cheaply from overseas**: Some countries can produce goods more efficiently than others. This may be because they have cheaper resources. For example, China can produce cheap manufactured goods because it has a cheap labour.

- **Improve consumer choice**: International trade provides more consumer choice. One reason is because countries both buy and sell the same products. For example, Toyota (Japan) and Ford (US) both manufacture cars. They also sell their vehicles in both countries and consumers welcome the choice this provides.

- **Sell off unwanted commodities**: Some countries have so much of a resource they could never use it all themselves. In the example above Saudi Arabia has huge reserves of oil. It produces far more than it can use. Saudi businesses can generate revenue from selling unwanted oil overseas.

QUESTION 1

Poland became an open economy after the break up of the Soviet Union in 1991. In the last decade Poland's foreign trade increased almost ten-fold. Poland exports processed fruit and vegetables, meat, dairy products, vehicles, aircraft and vessels. Most of Poland's imports are capital goods and inputs for manufacturing. Examples include machinery, chemicals, minerals, fuels and lubricants.

(a) (i) Describe the pattern of international trade in Poland over the time period shown in Figure 11.2.

(ii) What might account for the pattern identified in (i)?

(b) Why do you think Poland imports:
(i) capital goods;
(ii) inputs such as minerals and fuels?

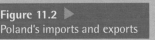
Figure 11.2 ▶
Poland's imports and exports

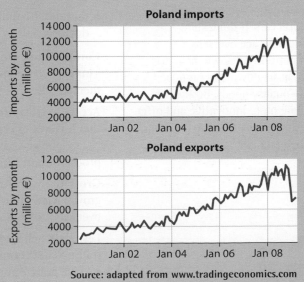

Source: adapted from www.tradingeconomics.com

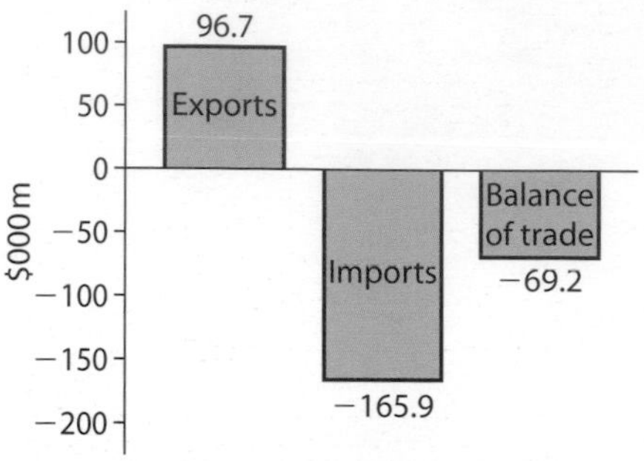

Visible and invisible trade

Goods and services sold overseas are called **exports**. Those bought from other countries are called **imports**. Economists distinguish between **visible trade** and **invisible trade**.

- Visible trade is to do with buying and selling physical goods. For example, India sells textiles, leather goods, gems and jewellery overseas. These are all visible exports for India. On the other hand, India buys oil, fertiliser and chemicals from overseas. These are examples of visible imports for India. The difference between total visible exports and imports is called the **visible balance** or the **balance of trade**. Figure 11.3 shows India's visible trade in 2008–2009. The balance of trade is −$69,181 million ($96,732 − $165,913). It has imported more goods than it has exported.

- Invisible trade involves buying and selling services. For example, the money India gets from tourists is recorded as an invisible export. On the other hand, India pays foreign carriers to transport goods to other countries. Payments for this service are recorded as invisible imports.

Source: adapted from www.indiaonestop.com

▲ **Figure 11.3**
India's visible balance (April to September 2008–2009)

KEY FACT

Germany both imports and exports cars. If domestic producers face overseas competition, they will have to keep costs down and produce high-quality goods. Businesses may be more innovative and offer consumers better value for money if they face foreign competition.

Benefits and opportunities resulting from international trade

More and more countries encourage **free trade**. This is where a country allows foreign businesses access to its markets. The government does not restrict imports. At the same time domestic businesses are encouraged to sell goods and services abroad. This creates benefits and opportunities.

Consumer choice One of the main benefits of free trade is that consumers get more choice. For example, consumers in Norway will be able to buy goods:

- that are impossible to produce in their climate, such as tropical fruits and wine;
- made from materials that are not available in Norway, such as gold and diamonds;
- that other countries produce more cheaply, such as cars and consumer durables.

Competition Free trade often provides competition for businesses. This is because most countries import goods that they can also produce themselves.

Access to cheap resources Some countries have lots of cheap resources that businesses can use to keep their costs down. For example, China has cheap labour, so it is common for western manufacturers to outsource production to Chinese businesses.

Growth International trade provides opportunities for businesses to grow. Firms often find that domestic markets become saturated. By selling overseas, businesses can generate more sales and more profit.

Less risk Selling into different international markets reduces risk when trading conditions become poor. For example, a multinational may survive poor trading conditions in European markets if it has stable or growing markets in the Far East.

QUESTION 2

Samsung is one of the world's largest multinationals. Based in South Korea it has numerous international businesses including:

- Samsung Electronics, the world's largest electronics company;
- Samsung Heavy Industries, one of the world's largest shipbuilders;
- Samsung Engineering & Construction, a major global construction company.

Samsung accounts for more than 20% of South Korea's total exports. IT is the leader in many domestic industries, such as the financial, chemical and retail industries. Samsung is also the sponsor of the English Premier League football club, Chelsea.

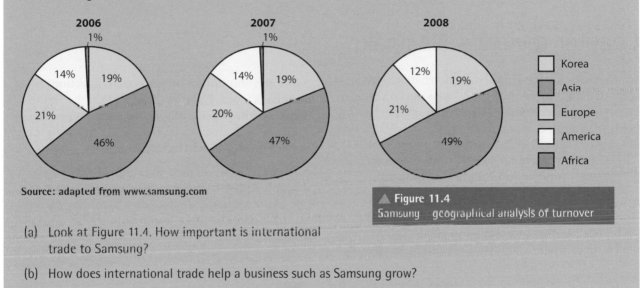

Source: adapted from www.samsung.com

▲ Figure 11.4
Samsung – geographical analysis of turnover

(a) Look at Figure 11.4. How important is international trade to Samsung?

(b) How does international trade help a business such as Samsung grow?

Problems and threats resulting from international trade

Unfortunately there may be some drawbacks to free trade.

Overspecialisation A country may become too dependent on a narrow range of goods. For example, some developing nations may rely too much on primary goods. If demand or prices fall for these goods, nations will suffer a loss of trade and income. This could result in unemployment and hardship.

Competition Competition benefits consumers, but businesses can struggle. For example, in the US shrimpers have been hit very hard from overseas competitors. Bayou La Batre, the seafood capital of Alabama, has lost 200 of the 300 shrimping vessels it had in 2005. The competition from Thailand, Vietnam, Indonesia and China is very fierce. Also, western manufacturers are finding it hard to compete with those in the Far East.

Environmental damage Because free trade helps global economic growth, it is likely to result in more environmental damage. For example, as nations become wealthier, their demand for cars and air travel will

Key terms

Balance of trade or visible balance – the difference between visible exports and visible imports.
Exports – goods and services sold overseas.
Free trade – trade between nations that is completely without government restrictions.
Imports – goods and services bought from overseas.
Invisible trade – trade in services.
Visible trade – trade in physical goods.

rise. This will increase carbon emissions and global warming. Also, more resources will be used up. For example, South America rainforests are being destroyed to make way for biofuel production.

Other threats Free trade may increase the development gap. This is where wealthy nations get richer faster than developing countries. There may also be a loss of culture if foreign ideas and products are allowed to dominate. For example, some countries may become too 'Americanised'. Countries may also lose control over matters that affect them. For example, in the UK many laws are now determined by the EU.

Chapter review – Nampak

South Africa has benefited from international trade since its economy became more open in 1994. It has lots of mineral resources and is a major exporter of gold, platinum, coal and diamonds. South Africa also has a growing tourist industry. In contrast, South Africa imports machinery, foodstuffs, chemicals, petroleum products and scientific instruments.

Nampak is an emerging multinational based in Sandton, South Africa. It manufactures packaging such as drinks cans, aerosol cans, bottles, labels, tissue paper, tubes, crates and drums. It also makes plastic,

paper and aluminium products for confectionery and snack foods. Nampak is selling into the rest of Africa and has operations in 10 countries (see Figure 11.5). In 2009, this will be expanded to 11 with the development of a new factory in Angola.

Nampak also has markets in Europe. For example, it supplies plastic bottles to the dairy industries. It is one of the leading manufacturers of folding cartons for the food industry in Europe and makes cartons, leaflets and labels for the healthcare market.

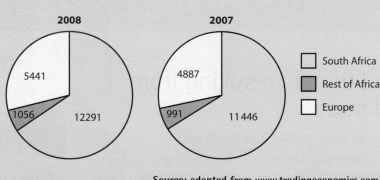

Source: adapted from www.tradingeconomics.com

▲ **Figure 11.5**
Nampak turnover 2007–2008 (R million)

(a) Using examples from this case, explain two reasons why nations trade. **(2 marks)**

(b) Using an example from this case explain what is meant by an invisible export. **(2 marks)**

(c) How much does Nampak rely on international trade for its revenue? **(2 marks)**

(d) Outline two benefits to South African consumers of international trade. **(4 marks)**

(e) What are the opportunities and threats to Nampak of international trade? **(10 marks)**

Chapter 12

Problems of entering new markets abroad

Getting started...

Many businesses are keen to sell in markets abroad. This is because they can increase their sales, make more profit and spread their risk. However, when entering markets abroad they might hit problems. Look at the example below.

Boots entry into the Japanese market

A few years ago Boots, the UK pharmacy, health and beauty retailer, tried to enter the Japanese market. To improve the chances of success Boots joined together with the Japanese company Mitsubishi Corporation. However, the venture failed and about two years later Boots closed its four Japanese stores. It lost £3 million last year on sales of £10.5 million and £12 million in the previous year. Boots has lost around £128 million in international markets in the last four years.

Boots was wise to get the support of Mitsubishi. However, it did not realise how complex the market was. The Japanese retail market is demanding and over-crowded. Many companies, including retail giants Wal-Mart, have failed in Japan. Recession, falling prices, competition and overcautious consumers all help to make the Japanese retail market challenging. One reason for failure is because foreign retailers have tried to compete with local stores selling the same merchandise.

▲ **Figure 12.1** A Boots store

Source: adapted from www.independent.co.uk

(a) How did Boots reduce its risk when entering the Japanese market?

(b) How much did Boots lose in the Japanese market?

(c) Why did Boots fail with its Japanese venture?

Why do businesses enter markets abroad?

As a result of *globalisation* many businesses need protection from foreign competition. One approach is to enter markets abroad and compete on an international scale. For many businesses this approach is necessary for survival. There are some specific reasons for entering markets abroad:

- **Profit**: Selling abroad can increase sales and raise profits. Also, some markets abroad may be more profitable than those at home. For example, manufacturing and distribution costs may be lower.

DID YOU KNOW?

The Nigerian Export–Import Bank provides help for Nigerian exporters. It provides insurance, credit in local currency, bank loans and a trade information system designed to help businesses entering markets abroad.

KEY FACT

In some countries, certain products cannot be sold because of cultural differences. For example, a Scottish whisky producer cannot sell into markets populated by Muslims. This is because alcohol is against their religion.

- **Less risk**: By selling into different international markets it is easier to deal with a downturn in any single market. Relying on the home market for all sales is risky.

- **Lack of domestic demand**: Some businesses sell abroad because the home market is *saturated*. Selling in markets abroad allows a business to continue growing.

- **Government help**: Businesses entering markets abroad may get help from the government.

Problems when entering markets abroad

Businesses are likely to encounter difficulties when entering markets abroad. Problems often arise because of a *lack of local knowledge* and a *lack of contacts*. For example, a German car manufacturer is not likely to have much knowledge about motoring in countries such as Libya, Kenya, Indonesia and Iran. A number of differences may exist between domestic markets and those abroad.

Cultural differences Most countries have different cultures, which may cause problems. For example, there are likely to be language differences. A business will need to translate product labels, information and instructions. This will help overseas consumers to understand what the product is about.

Legal differences Different countries often have different legal systems. Therefore businesses may have to change production, packaging and marketing methods:

- Some countries have strict consumer protection legislation. Products may have to be modified to gain entry into markets abroad.

- The information required on product labels will vary across nations. For example, more information is needed on American food labels than anywhere else in the world.

- In some countries it is illegal to advertise certain goods on the television. For example, in the EU, cigarettes cannot be advertised on the TV.

- Many countries place environmental restrictions on products. For example, there are restrictions on emissions from motor cars in some countries.

Political differences Some countries are politically unstable. These may be avoided by businesses searching for new markets. This is because investment in politically unstable countries could be lost. Businesses should also be aware that a change in government can bring about new opportunities. For example, since the break-up of the Soviet Union in 1991, business development from foreigners is now welcome in Eastern Europe.

Economic and social differences Businesses must recognise that economic conditions vary around the world. For example, incomes, taxes, import restrictions, interest rates and unemployment levels might be different. There are also likely to be social differences. For example, the role of females, literacy levels, fashions and trends, and the habits and attitudes of social groups should be taken into account.

Differences in business practice and conduct The way business is conducted may differ between nations. For example, in Japan it is common to exchange gifts with new business partners. Trading hours can be very different. There may also be financial differences such as different currencies and in some countries there may be lots of paperwork.

Barriers to trade

When entering markets abroad one problem is overcoming trade barriers. These may be put in place by governments to protect domestic industries.

- Many governments put taxes on imports. These are called **tariffs** or **customs duties**. These reduce demand for imports and raise revenue for the government.

- A **quota** limits the amount a business can sell in a country. By restricting the quantity of imports, domestic producers are protected from foreign competition.

- Another approach to protectionism is to give a **subsidy** to domestic producers. This involves giving financial support, such as grants or tax breaks, to exporters. Subsidies may also be given to domestic producers to help compete with imports. Subsidies lower the prices of domestic goods.

- Some countries reduce imports by insisting that foreign goods meet strict regulations and specifications. These are known as *administrative barriers*. For example, toys from the Far East might be returned if they fail to meet health and safety regulations.

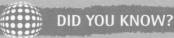

DID YOU KNOW?

In Spain most business stops for a 'siesta' in the middle of the day. This allows people to rest for a few hours.

 ## QUESTION 1

The following advice is offered to foreign businesses entering Egyptian markets for the first time:

- Understand the importance of religious issues in the decision making process.
- Who you know and who you are is very important.
- To help develop the initial contacts it is often necessary to appoint a go-between. This person will arrange meetings and act as a bridge into the culture.
- Time is very flexible and meetings may start very late and last for many hours. It is difficult to schedule a series of meetings on the same day.
- Meetings may start with coffee and a great deal of small talk. Do not try to rush this process.
- It is important to offer lavish compliments to your host – and be prepared to receive them in return.
- People may stand much closer to you than you are comfortable with. Try not to back away as this can seem stand-offish.

Source: adapted from www.worldbusinessculture.com/Egyptian-Business-Negotiation.html

(a) Using examples from the case, explain how differences in business conduct might be a problem for a western company entering the Egyptian market.

(b) In 2007, tariffs on goods coming into Egypt were reduced on most goods except cars, to less than 10%. How might this benefit a business entering the Egyptian market?

Dealing with problems when entering markets abroad

Generally, when entering new markets abroad preparation is vital. This may involve doing market research. Identifying legal, cultural, bureaucratic, economic and social differences will also be important. To help overcome problems businesses can use a number of approaches when entering foreign markets.

Franchising This involves allowing another person or business to trade under your name (see Chapter 13). The franchisee will pay an initial fee plus a share of sales or profits in the future. The advantage of this is that someone local will take the risk in the foreign market. However, profits are shared with the franchisee.

Exporting This is where goods are manufactured in the home country and then sold into overseas markets. This is probably the most common approach. It reduces the risk of entering new markets because production is not transferred overseas. Exporters often use agents to sell their goods. This is because they are familiar with the foreign market.

Licensing This involves giving an overseas manufacturer a licence to make and sell a product. This eliminates transport costs. Another advantage of this approach is that the licensee takes all the risk. However, profit is shared with the licensee.

Direct investment This approach is the most risky. It involves setting up production in an overseas market. This is expensive but could give the largest return because:

* profit is not shared;
* resources such as labour may be cheaper;
* distribution costs are lower;
* government help might be available because jobs are created;
* trade barriers are avoided.

Joint venture This involves sharing the costs and responsibilities of entering a foreign market with another business – ideally, one that is based in that market. The main advantage of this approach is that the risk is shared. Also, each business can draw on its own strengths in the venture.

Mergers and takeovers Some companies prefer to buy a business that is already established in a market abroad. This makes it a lot easier but may be an expensive approach. It has similar advantages to that of direct investment.

Key terms

Quota – a physical limit on the quantity of imports allowed into a country.
Subsidy – financial support given to a domestic producer to help compete with overseas firms.
Tariffs or customs duties – a tax on imports to make them more expensive.
Trade barriers – measures designed to restrict trade.

QUESTION 2

Toyota, the giant Japanese corporation, has invested £1.85 billion in manufacturing plants in the UK. Toyota employs around 4,000 people in the UK and has an assembly plant in Derbyshire. It also has an engine manufacturing plant in North Wales. Toyota located in the UK because of its tradition of vehicle manufacturing. The UK also has a large domestic car market. In addition, the UK offered transport links to Toyota's European customers and its 230 British and European suppliers. Another reason was the excellent workforce and favourable working practices.

Source: adapted from www.toyotauk.com

(a) What approach did Toyota use to enter the UK and European markets?

(b) Outline the possible advantages of this approach to entering a foreign market.

Chapter review – CFWshops

Children and Family Wellness Shops, known as CFWshops, is a network of 65 health clinics in Kenya. They operate as franchises and serve 450,000 people located in rural areas. Each outlet is run by an experienced nurse or health worker.

Franchisees pay a deposit of $300 for a franchise. They also borrow $1,700 to help with start-up costs. Franchisees receive training in CFWshops' standards and procedures. Medicines are purchased in bulk at head office and are then distributed to all franchisees. Savings from bulk-buying are passed on to patients. For example, the average cost of treatment is less than $1.00.

Source: adapted from www.changemakers.com/en-us/node/1199

(a) Describe the approach used by the HealthStore Foundation (the US owner of CFWshops) to enter the Kenyan market. **(4 marks)**

(b) Outline two problems that the Healthstore Foundation might have encountered when developing the CFWshops in Kenya. **(4 marks)**

(c) Do you think trade barriers will slow down the development of CFWshops? **(4 marks)**

(d) To what extent has the Healthstore Foundation overcome the problems associated with entering markets abroad? **(8 marks)**

Sole traders, partnerships and franchises

Getting started...

There are several different types of business organisation. They vary according to size, type of ownership and legal status. Look at the examples below.

Luke's Kaffeestrube

Luke Burger is the owner of Luke's Kaffeestrube, a bakery and cafe located in Swakopmund, Namibia. He set up the business in 2001 when he bought a small disused bakery for N$20,000. Two years later he decided to open a cafe by extending the premises. He thought the cafe would provide another outlet for some of the cakes and pastries produced in the bakery. The cafe serves shoppers, workers and tourists. It is busy and Luke employs two other staff. He recently invested N$50,000 of his own money to refurbish the cafe.

R & H Photography Services

Andrea Rolton and Gillian Hammond are business partners. They provide photography services in Darwin, Australia. Andrea has a degree in photographic art and is responsible for the production work. Gillian spends most of her time promoting the business. She develops contacts and handles the administration. Andrea and Gillian set up the business in 2005 by investing AUS$20,000 each. They used the money to buy photography equipment and a studio in central Darwin.

▲ Figure 13.1
A photographer at work

(a) Who owns the businesses in the above examples?

(b) State one advantage and one disadvantage of owning a business with a partner.

(c) Business owners have to take risks. What risks are taken in the above examples?

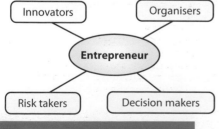

▲ Figure 13.2
The roles of the entrepreneur

Entrepreneurs

People who set up businesses are called entrepreneurs. They are the owners and without them businesses would not exist in the private sector. The roles played by entrepreneurs in business are summarised in Figure 13.2.

- Entrepreneurs are *innovators* because they try to make money out of a business idea. Such ideas might come from spotting a gap in the market, a new invention or market research. However, many people set up a business by copying or adapting what another business does.

- Entrepreneurs are responsible for *organising* other factors of production. They buy or hire resources such as materials, labour and equipment. These resources are used to make products. Organising involves giving instructions, making arrangements and setting up systems.
- Since entrepreneurs are the owners they have make all the key *decision*s. They may make decisions on how to raise finance, product design, choice of production method, prices, recruitment and wages.
- Entrepreneurs are *risk takers*. This is because they risk losing any money they put into the business if it fails. However, if the business is successful they will be rewarded with profit.

Unincorporated and incorporated businesses

Businesses vary according to the legal form they take:

- In **unincorporated businesses** there is no legal difference between the owner and the business. Everything is carried out in the name of the owner. These businesses tend to be small and owned by one person, or a small group of people.
- An **incorporated business** is one that has a separate legal identity from that of its owners. In other words, the business can sue, be sued, taken over or *liquidated*. Incorporated businesses are often called *limited companies* and the owners are shareholders. This is discussed in the next chapter.

Features of a sole trader

A **sole trader** or **sole proprietor** is the simplest form of business organisation. It has one owner but can employ any number of people. Sole traders may be involved in a wide range of business activity. In the primary sector they may be farmers or fishermen. In the secondary sector they may be small builders or manufacturers. However, it is in the tertiary sector where most sole traders will be found. Many are retailers running small shops. Others may offer services such as web design, tutoring, hairdressing, taxi driving and garden maintenance.

Setting up as a sole trader is simple because there are no legal requirements. However, all sole traders have **unlimited liability**. This means that if the business fails, a sole trader can lose more money than was originally invested. This is because a sole trader can be forced to use personal wealth to pay off business debts. The advantages and disadvantages of operating as a sole trader are summarised in Figure 13.3.

Advantages

All the profit is kept by the owner
Independence – the owner has complete control
It is simple to set up with no legal requirements
Flexibility – e.g. can adapt to change quickly
Can offer a personal service because they are small
May qualify for government help

Disadvantages

Have unlimited liability
May struggle to raise finance – too risky for lenders
Independence may be a burden
Long hours and very hard work
Usually too small too exploit economies of scale
No continuity – the business dies with the owner

▲ Figure 13.3
Advantages and disadvantages of a sole trader

Features of a partnership

A *partnership* exists when between 2 and 20 people jointly own a business. The owners will share responsibility for running the business. They also share the profits. Partnerships are often found in professions such as accountants, doctors, estate agents and solicitors.

There are no legal formalities to complete when a partnership is formed. However, partners may draw up a **deed of partnership**. This is a legal document that states partners' rights in the event of a dispute. It states:

- how much capital each partner will contribute;
- how profits (and losses) will be shared among the partners;
- the procedure for ending the partnership;
- how much control each partner has;
- rules for taking on new partners.

The advantages and disadvantages of partnerships are summarised in Figure 13.4.

Advantages

Easy to set up and run – no legal formalities
Partners can specialise in their area of expertise
The burden of running a business is shared
More capital can be raised with more owners
Financial information is not published

Disadvantages

Partners have unlimited liability
Profit has to be shared
Partners may disagree and fall out
Any partners' decision is legally binding on all
Partnerships still tend to be small

▲ Figure 13.4
Advantages and disadvantages of partnerships

Mirza and Associates is a small firm of solicitors based in Lahore, Pakistan. There are four partners in the business and each one specialises in a specific area of law:
- Salim Hussain is an expert in property law and deals with property ownership disputes.
- Tariq Zaman deals with tax and corporate matters for business clients.
- Nasir Ahmed is a legal advisor for colleges and universities.
- Tariq Mirza is responsible for administration and also deals with criminal cases.

(a) Use this case as an example to explain what is meant by a partnership.

(b) How does this case illustrate one of the main advantages of partnerships?

Key terms

Deed of partnership – a binding legal document that states the formal rights of partners.

Franchise – where a business (the franchisor) allows another operator (the franchisee) to trade under their name.

Incorporated business – where the business has a separate legal identity from that of its owners.

Partnership – a business owned by between two and 20 people.

Sole trader or sole proprietor – a business owned by a single person.

Unincorporated business – where there is no legal difference between the owner and the business.

Unlimited liability – where the owner of a business is personally liable for all business debts.

Features of franchises

One approach to running a business is to buy a **franchise**. This may suit someone who wants to run a business but does not have their own business idea. Owners of franchises are called *franchisors*. They have developed a successful business and are prepared to allow others, the *franchisees*, to trade under their name. Franchisees pay fees to the franchisor. Examples of some international franchises are McDonald's, Subway and Avis.

What does the franchisor offer the franchisee?
- a licence to trade under the recognised *brandname* of the franchisor;
- a start-up package including help, advice and essential equipment;
- training in how to run the business and operate the systems used by the franchise;
- materials, equipment and support services that are needed to run the business;
- marketing support that is organised on behalf of all franchisees;
- an exclusive geographical area in which to operate.

In return for these services the franchisee has to pay certain fees:
- a start-up fee – a lump sum;
- an ongoing fee (usually based on sales).

QUESTION 2

Mr & Mrs Idly is an Indian franchise selling snacks from kiosks. It aims to provide customers with healthy and wholesome snacks at affordable prices. Mr & Mrs Idly is the only fast food franchise selling idly and dosai (Indian food) from a kiosk. Franchisees are provided with:

- a market and feasibility study;
- an established brandname and logo;
- technical support and exclusive knowhow;
- operating manuals;
- access to cheap materials;
- help with negotiations and site selection;
- assistance with hiring and training employees.

Under the franchise agreement the kiosk space is to be owned or leased by the franchisee. Franchisees may only sell approved Mr & Mrs Idly products. Also, the kiosk and equipment are purchased by the franchisee. Franchisees are expected to maintain high standards of hygiene and look after the counters.

Source: adapted from mrandmrsidly.com/franchise.html

(a) Use this case as an example to explain how franchisors make money.

(b) Outline one advantage to a franchisee of taking out a franchise in Mr & Mrs Idly.

Chapter review – Marek Jonata

The fishing industry in Indonesia is very important. Marek Jonata is a fisherman and owns a sail boat that cost about $1,000. For five years, Marek worked most days of the week fishing for groupers, rabbitfish and slipmouth. He saved most of his profits because he wanted to buy a powered boat. This would have greater capacity and he could make more money.

In 2009, Marek decided that he would never be able to save for a powered boat. He also found that banks would not lend him $4,000 to match his own savings to buy the new boat. Marek had his eye on a Searay 270 Sundancer with a 2003 quickload trailer, a 7.4 litre engine and all fishing equipment. The only way he could afford the boat would be to take on a partner. One of his fishing colleagues, Endang Witarsa, said he would join Marek as a business partner. However, Marek was not sure that going into business with someone else was the right thing to do.

(a) Marek is an entrepreneur. What does this mean? (2 marks)

(b) State the four roles of an entrepreneur. (2 marks)

(c) Sole traders are unincorporated businesses. What does this mean? (2 marks)

(d) Operating as a sole trader, Marek has unlimited liability. Explain what this means. (4 marks)

(e) Discuss the advantages and disadvantages of operating as a partnership and suggest whether Marek should take on a partner. (10 marks)

Chapter 14

Limited companies and joint ventures

Getting started...

Limited companies have different features from sole traders and partnerships. They have different types of owners and raise capital in different ways. They are also set up and run differently. Look at the examples below.

Airport to Hotel

Airport to Hotel is a limited company. It was set up by Paul Stanyer when he lost his job at travel agent Thomas Cook. It provides travel agents with transfer services between airports and hotels. Airport to Hotel operates in 70 countries and has links with easyJet and other airlines. It is also launching a ski shuttle service to winter holiday destinations. Sales grew 84% a year from £1.4m in 2004 to £8.6m in 2007. Half of the shares in Airport to Hotel are owned by Hong Kong-based Unifol International, a group of investors.

Source: adapted from www.fasttrack.co.uk

▲ **Figure 14.1** People being transferred from an airport

Bank of East Asia (BEA)

BEA is run by the Chairman, Sir David Li, and 17 directors. The company is quoted on the Hong Kong stock exchange and owned by shareholders. BEA is the largest independent local bank in Hong Kong and has branches in the US, Canada, the UK, the British Virgin Islands, and South-east Asia. Worldwide BEA has 240 outlets and employs over 10,000 people. The bank's turnover was HK$6,793 million in 2008.

Source: adapted from www.hkbea.com/hk/index.htm

(a) Use examples from the above cases to explain who (i) owns limited companies; (ii) runs limited companies?

(b) Comment on the size of limited companies such as those above compared to sole traders and partnerships.

Limited companies

Limited companies are incorporated. This means that they have a separate legal identity from their owners. They can own assets, form contracts, employ people, sue and be sued. What are the main features of limited companies?

- The owners have *limited liability*. If a limited company has debts, the owners can only lose the money they originally invested. They cannot be forced to use their own money to pay debts run up by the business.

- Capital is raised by selling shares. Each shareholder owns a number of these shares. They are the joint owners of the company. They are entitled to vote on important matters such as who should run the company. They also get dividends paid from profits. Those with more shares will have more control and get more dividends.

- They are run by directors elected by the shareholders. The board of directors, headed by a chairperson, is accountable to shareholders. He/she should run the company as the shareholders wish. If the company performs badly, directors can be 'voted out' at an *Annual General Meeting (AGM)*.

- Whereas sole traders and partnerships pay income tax on profits, companies pay corporation tax.

- To form a limited company it is necessary to follow a legal procedure. This is outlined below.

Forming a limited company

Some important documents must be sent to the *Registrar of Companies* before a limited company can be formed. The two most important ones are shown in arc shown in Figure 14.2.

If these documents are acceptable the company will get a *Certificate of Incorporation*. This allows it to trade as a limited company. The shareholders have a legal right to attend the AGM and should be told of the date and venue in writing.

Memorandum of Association
This sets out the constitution and gives details about the company. The following details must be included:
- name of the company;
- name and address of the company's registered office;
- objectives of the company and the nature of its activities;
- amount of capital to be raised and the number of shares to be issued.

Articles of Association
This document deals with the internal running of the company. The Articles include details such as:
- rights of shareholders depending on the type of share they hold;
- procedures for appointing directors;
- length of time directors should serve before re-election;
- timing and frequency of company meetings;
- arrangements for auditing company accounts.

▲ **Figure 14.2**
Memorandum of Association and Articles of Association

Private limited companies

Most *private limited companies* tend to be small or medium-sized. Some features of private limited companies are as follows:

- Their business name ends in *Limited* or *Ltd*.

- Shares can only be transferred 'privately' (from one individual to another). All shareholders must agree on the transfer and they cannot be advertised for sale.

- They are often family businesses owned by family members or close friends.

- The directors of these firms tend to be shareholders and are involved in the running of the business.

- Figure 14.3 lists the advantages and disadvantages of private limited companies.

Advantages
Shareholders have limited liability
More capital can be raised
Control cannot be lost to outsiders
Business continues if a shareholder dies
Has more status – e.g. than a sole trader

Disadvantages
Financial information has to be made public
Costs money and takes time to set up
Profits are shared between more members
Takes time to transfer shares to new owners
Cannot raise **very** large amounts of money

▲ **Figure 14.3**
Advantages and disadvantages of private limited companies

Sir Anwar Pervez founded Bestway as a single grocery store in 1963. Since then Bestway has grown to become one of the largest cash-and-carry operators. The group's other interests include food processing, cement factories in Pakistan and a 31% stake in a Pakistani bank.

Bestway is an example of a large private limited company. It employs over 5,000 staff and sales reached £1,895 million in 2008. Sir Anwar Pervez and his family own 66% of the company. The rest is owned by managers.

Source: adapted from www.fasttrack.co.uk

(a)   Who controls the Bestway Group?

(b)   Analyse two advantages to Bestway of operating as private limited company.

KEY FACT

When 'going public' a company is likely to publish a *prospectus*. This advertises the company to potential investors. It also invites them to buy shares before a *flotation*.

Advantages

Huge amounts of capital can be raised
Shareholders have limited liability
They can exploit economies of scale
May be able to dominate the market
Shares can be bought and sold very easily
May have a very high profile in the media

Disadvantages

Setting up costs can be very expensive
Outsiders can take control by buying shares
More financial information has to be made
   public
May be more remote from customers
More regulatory control due to Company
   Acts
Managers may take control rather than
   owners

▲ **Figure 14.4**
Advantages and disadvantages of public limited companies

Public limited companies

Public limited companies (plcs) tend to be larger than private limited companies. Their shares can be bought and sold by the public on the stock exchange. Any person or organisation can buy shares in plcs.

'Going public' can be expensive because:

- the company needs lawyers to ensure that the prospectus is 'legally' correct;
- the prospectus has to be printed and circulated;
- a bank may be paid to process share applications;
- the company must insure against the possibility of some shares remaining unsold, therefore a fee is paid to an *underwriter* who must buy any unsold shares;
- there are advertising and administrative expenses;
- it must have a minimum of £50,000 share capital.

Figure 14.4 lists the advantages and disadvantages of public limited companies.

Joint ventures

A *joint venture* is where two or more companies share the cost, responsibility and profits of a business venture. Most joint ventures involve two firms and the costs and profits are shared equally. What are the advantages of joint ventures?

- They allow companies to enjoy some of the advantages of mergers, such as higher turnover, without having to lose their identity.
- Businesses can specialise in aspects of the venture to suit their expertise.
- Takeovers are expensive. Heavy legal and administrative costs are often incurred.
- Mergers and takeovers are often unfriendly. Most joint ventures are friendly. The companies commit their funds and share responsibility. This may help to improve the success of the venture.
- Competition may be eliminated. If companies cooperate in a joint venture they are less likely to compete with each other.

There are some disadvantages to joint ventures:

- Some joint ventures do not work out. There may be control struggles. For example, who should have the final say in a 50:50 joint venture?

- Disagreements may occur about the management of the joint venture. As with any partnership, there may be different views on which direction to take.

- The profit from the venture is split between the investors. This obviously reduces profit potential.

Key terms

Flotation – the process of a company 'going public'.
Limited company – a business organisation which has a separate legal entity from that of its owners.

QUESTION 2

Fiat, the Italian car company, is to make cars and engines in China from 2011. It has formed a joint venture with Guangzhou Automobile Group (GAC). Each will invest €400m in a 50:50 joint venture. They plan to build a large production plant in Hunan province. Fiat and GAC have said the plant will produce 140,000 cars and 220,000 engines per year. However, it could be expanded to produce up to 250,000 cars and 300,000 engines. The venture with GAC will launch Fiat into a highly competitive market with more car manufacturers than the US.

Source: adapted from www.ft.com

(a) Using this case as an example, explain what is meant by a joint venture.

(b) Outline two advantages of joint ventures.

Chapter review – homeofficeplus.com

Nathan Edwards is the majority shareholder in Nathan's Home Offices Ltd. Three other shareholders are family members. They all work in the business. The company is based in Australia and serves the Brisbane area. It specialises in office fitting for people that work at home. The business was started in 2001 when Nathan operated as a sole trader. However, in 2004 he invited family members to take a stake in the business and formed Nathan's Home Offices Ltd. They contributed some capital and the business expanded. The family is now considering raising more money by 'going public'. Nathan wants to expand the business further and needs $10 million. This will be used to:

- develop an online business;

- build two warehouses as distribution centres;

- develop a fleet of delivery vehicles to serve the whole of Eastern Australia;

- buy stock to supply a full range of office equipment and accessories.

The company also plans to change its name to homeofficeplus.com.

(a) What evidence is there to suggest that Nathan's Home Offices Ltd is a private limited company? (2 marks)

(b) When Nathan's Home Offices Ltd was formed, Nathan had to produce a Memorandum of Association. What information would this contain? (2 marks)

(c) What is the purpose of a prospectus? (2 marks)

(d) Share issues have to be underwritten. What does this mean? (2 marks)

(e) Why is going public expensive? (4 marks)

(f) Do you think Nathan should convert his business to a public limited company? (8 marks)

Chapter 15

Multinational companies

Getting started...

In the last 30 years or so, some businesses have developed large operations in many different countries. They serve global markets and provide jobs and other benefits for the countries in which they locate. They are called **multinationals**. Look at the example below.

The global car industry

The global car industry is dominated by a few large multinationals such as Toyota, General Motors (GM), Ford, Volkswagen, Honda and Nissan. All of these firms produced over 3 million cars in 2007. Two of them, Toyota and GM, produced over 9 million. These companies have a global outlook. They sell their cars anywhere and set up production wherever costs can be minimised. For example, Ford has factories in many countries such as the US, UK, Spain, Brazil, Mexico, France and Thailand.

Fifty years ago the three US car makers, GM, Ford and Chrysler, dominated the global car industry. Now their market share has fallen as new, leaner producers such as Toyota have entered the market. GM and Ford are cutting thousands of jobs and closing plants. In contrast, Toyota is building one new plant each year. Toyota is worth 10 times as much as GM and is now the world's largest car maker.

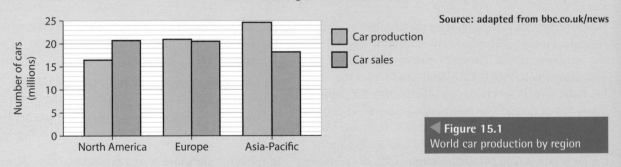

Source: adapted from bbc.co.uk/news

◀ **Figure 15.1**
World car production by region

(a) What do you think is meant by a global market?

(b) Look at Figure 15.1. (i) Which particular car markets are becoming more important in the world?
(ii) What might account for your answer to (i)?

(c) What evidence is there to suggest that the US is becoming less important in the global car industry?

Globalisation

Many markets today are global. This means that some firms expect to sell their products anywhere in the world. Firms and people are behaving as though there is just one market in the whole world. This development is called **globalisation**. What are the key features of globalisation?

- Products are traded freely across international borders. There are no government restrictions that prevent firms from selling in overseas markets.

- People are free to live and work in any country they choose. People from many different nations often live and work in the same city.

- There is a high level of interdependence between nations. This means that events in one economy are likely to affect other economies. For example, the financial crisis in the US in 2008 had an impact in many economies all over the world.

- Capital can flow freely between different countries. This means, for example, that a firm or consumer in Australia can put their savings in a bank in the US. It also means that firms and investors can buy shares in foreign companies.

DID YOU KNOW?

It is not unusual for a firm to have a head office in London, borrow money from a Japanese bank, manufacture goods in China, deal with customers from a call centre in India and sell goods to countries in Europe and the Americas.

The importance and growth of multinationals

Multinationals play a large and growing role in the world economy. They contribute about 10% to world GDP and about two-thirds to global exports.

Figure 15.3 provides a summary of information about the world's five largest multinationals.

KEY FACT

The number of multinationals in the world has increased from about 7,000 in 1970 to about 78,000 in 2005. Between them they employ about 73 million workers, that is, around 3% of the global workforce.

	Company	Sector	Turnover	Year	HQ
1	ExxonMobil	Oil & gas	$390.3 billon	2007	US
2	Wal-Mart Stores	Retailing	$374.5 billon	2008	US
3	Royal Dutch Shell	Oil & gas	$355.8 billon	2007	UK/Netherlands
4	British Petroleum	Oil & gas	$292.0 billion	2007	UK
5	Toyota	Automotive	$264.8 billion	2008	Japan

◀ **Figure 15.2**
The world's five largest multinationals

Why have multinationals been created?

Economies of scale Multinationals can exploit economies of scale. This is because they are so large. Firms that sell to global markets will produce more than those who just sell to domestic markets. They can therefore lower costs. Multinationals are powerful and can put pressure on suppliers to lower their prices. Also, multinationals have access to cheap global resources such as labour, capital and commodities.

Marketing Some firms have become multinationals by relying on effective marketing. Firms such as Starbucks and McDonald's are good examples. These are low-tech firms that have developed a successful brand at home and then exploited it globally. They have protected their brand with patents and use heavy advertising and innovative marketing to attract customers globally.

Technical and financial superiority Most multinationals have developed into large businesses over a period of time. They have developed advanced technologies and built up a huge bank of knowledge. They can also afford to invest heavily in R&D. They are experienced and can afford to employ the most talented people available. They also have the resources to take risks and are often diversified. As a result they can take on business ventures that small firms could never dream of.

 QUESTION 1

HSBC is one of the largest banks in the world. It has around 9,500 offices in 86 countries in Europe, the Asia-Pacific region, the Americas, the Middle East and Africa. HSBC has an international network linked by advanced technology. It also makes increasing use of e-commerce. HSBC provides a wide range of financial services for individuals, commerce, corporations and investors. In 2008, HSBC had a turnover of nearly £50 billion and employed over 300,000 people.

Source: adapted from www.hsbc.com

(a) What evidence is there to suggest that HSBC is a multinational?

(b) In common with many other banks, HSBC offers an online banking service. How would this help the company to reach the global market?

KEY FACT

According to an IBM database, a report said that around 10,000 new foreign business projects created 1.2 million jobs around the world in 2007. Local suppliers are also likely to get work when a multinational arrives.

Advantages of multinationals

Increase in income and employment When multinationals set up operations overseas income in those countries rises. Multinationals create new jobs in developing countries.

Increase in tax revenue The profits made by multinationals are taxed by the host nation. This increases tax revenue for the government that can be spent improving government services.

Increase in exports The output produced by multinationals abroad is recorded as output for that country. Therefore, if this output is sold out of the host country, it is counted as an export. This helps less developed countries to increase their foreign currency reserves.

Transfer of technology Multinationals often provide foreign suppliers with technical help, training and other information. They may also help local suppliers to purchase resources and modernise production facilities.

Improvement in the quality of human capital Multinationals provide training and work experience for workers in less developed countries. Also, governments in less developed countries often spend more on education to help attract multinationals. This happened in India where the government invested heavily in IT education and training.

Enterprise development The arrival of multinationals has encouraged more people to set up businesses in less developed countries. Multinationals may have provided the skills and motivation needed for enterprise. For example, a new multinational may encourage locals to supply services such as transport, accommodation, maintenance, cleaning and leisure activities.

 QUESTION 2

Coca-Cola is a multinational and the world's largest beverage company. Along with Coca-Cola, the world's most valuable brand, other brands include Diet Coke, Fanta, Sprite, Coca-Cola Zero, Vitaminwater and Powerade. People in more than 200 countries consume nearly 1.6 billion servings a day. Coca-Cola has more than 300 bottling partners around the world which manufacture, package, distribute and merchandise their brands. In 2008, Coca-Cola had a turnover of $31.9 billion and made a profit of $7.4 billion.

Source: adapted from www.thecoca-colacompany.com

(a) How might: (i) residents; (ii) the government, benefit from Coca-Cola locating one of its production facilities in its country?

(b) To what extent do you think Coca-Cola is able to exploit economies of scale?

Disadvantages of multinationals

Environmental damage Many environmentalists are wary of multinationals because they may cause environmental damage. One reason is because multinationals are heavily involved in the extraction industries such as coal, oil and gold mining. Mining is often destructive.

Exploitation of less developed countries It is sometimes argued that multinationals may exploit developing nations:

- Some multinationals may encourage developing countries to rely on producing primary products. This is risky because the prices of primary products can change sharply, which causes variations in income. Relying on one industry also makes them vulnerable.

- Multinationals often pay low wages. They may also employ child labour and working conditions are often very poor.

- Resources are extracted and sold with little money going to the host nation.

- Taxes paid to the host nation are often minimal.

It must be remembered that although such exploitation does occur, many multinationals have good records when developing business interests in less developed countries.

Repatriation of profit The profits made by multinationals abroad are often **repatriated**. This means that profits are returned to the country where the multinational is based. As a result the host country loses out. This suggests that developed countries benefit more from multinationals than developing nations. This is because most multinationals are based in developed countries.

 DID YOU KNOW?

Oil spills and waste dumping have seriously damaged agricultural land in the Niger Delta, Nigeria.

Key terms

Globalisation – the growing integration of the world's economies.
Multinational – a large business with markets and production facilities in several different countries.
Repatriation of profit – where a multinational returns the profits from an overseas venture to the country where it is based.

Lack of accountability Some argue that because multinationals are so large and powerful they lack accountability. This means they may be able to evade the law – especially in countries where the government is weak or corrupt. Also, multinationals may be keener to operate where regulation is inadequate or non-existent. However, multinationals may be monitored by pressure groups. This helps improve accountability.

Chapter review – Newmont Mining Corp

Newmont Mining Corporation is mainly a gold producer. Based in Colorado, the company has 34,000 employees worldwide.

Newmont owns mines in Indonesia and claims that over a seven-year period one mine (now shut) paid the Indonesian government $500 million. Another Newmont mine currently pays $35.90 million a year in taxes and other fees to the government. Newmont says it buys $183 million of goods and services from Indonesian businesses. It also pays $55 million to Indonesian employees and spends $2.3 million in community development.

However, there have also been some negative impacts, which include:

- loss of life in mining accidents;
- contamination of lakes in Sulawesi;
- loss of water for farming;
- damage to the forests.

In 2006, some protestors were shot by police near one of Newmont's mines. The protests centred on Newmont's activities in forests near Sumbawa. Local people wanted the company to leave. They said Newmont had caused environmental damage and loss of livelihood. Locals were prevented from collecting honey, candlenut and palm sugar from the forests. The water supply has decreased, and crops such as rice and cucumber have failed because of drought.

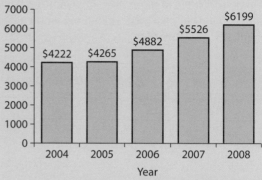

Source: adapted from dte.gn.apc.org and en.ce.cn

▲ **Figure 15.3**
Newmont revenue 2004–2008 (millions)

(a) Using this case as an example, explain what is meant by a multinational. **(2 marks)**

(b) How do you think Newmont's shareholders have benefited from its involvement in other countries in the world? **(2 marks)**

(c) State two reasons why multinationals such as Newmont are created. **(2 marks)**

(d) How has Indonesia benefited from Newmont's business ventures in the country? **(4 marks)**

(e) Analyse the disadvantages to Indonesia of Newmont's business developments in the country. **(10 marks)**

Chapter 16

Relationship between objectives, growth and business organisation

Getting started...

There is a relationship between the objectives of a business and the type of business organisation. This is because it may be necessary for a business to change its legal status in order to achieve a particular objective. Generally, as a business grows the legal status of the business changes. Look at the examples below.

Marco Valdez

Marco Valdez is a self-employed taxi driver. He works in Mexico City and owns his own vehicle. He operates as a sole trader and made a profit of 150,000 Mexican peso in 2008. Marco is happy with his current business situation and does not want to expand. He likes operating as a sole trader. He likes to make all the decisions and keep all the profit. He works six days a week and has some regular business customers. His business earns enough profit to keep him and his family comfortable.

▲ **Figure 16.1** A taxi in Mexico City

Cemex

Cemex is a large Mexican multinational. The company was founded in 1906 and supplied the north of Mexico with cement. Today Cemex is a global building materials company. It produces and sells cement, ready-mix concrete and other building materials in more than 50 countries. Cemex has 64 cement plants, 2,200 ready-mix factories, 493 quarries, 253 distribution centres and 88 marine terminals.

Source: www.cemex.com/tc/tc_gl.asp

(a) Do you think that Marco Valdez can achieve his business objectives operating as a sole trader?

(b) Explain why Cemex could not really operate as a sole trader.

(c) Why might businesses in general be forced to change their legal status as they grow?

The type of business organisation and growth

Many businesses start small and grow over a period of time. Most businesses change their legal status when growing. This is because they need to raise more capital. For example, sole traders often find it difficult to raise more finance. However, by taking on a partner, or becoming a private limited company, more money can be raised. This is because more owners can generate more capital. Similarly, if private limited companies want to raise large amounts of capital they may have to go public.

Many small businesses are sole traders or partnerships. Public limited companies are much larger, with thousands of employees and huge turnovers. It could be argued that a very large business could only be run if it were a limited company. For example, some business activity, such as oil processing and chemical manufacturing, requires large-scale production. This could not be managed effectively by sole traders or partnerships.

Other factors affecting the choice of business organisation

The need for finance Finance is the main reason why owners change the legal status of their businesses. Quite often the only way to get more money is to change the type of organisation. Additional finance can only be raised if the business has more owners. This helps to explain why sole traders often form partnerships or private limited companies. Also, some private limited companies 'go public' because they need to raise very large amounts of money.

Degree of control Some owners like their independence. They like to have complete control of their business. This is why many owners remain as sole traders. Once new partners or shareholders join the business, some control is lost because it is shared with the new owners. It is possible to keep control of a limited company by holding the majority of shares. However, even if one person holds 51% of shares in a limited company, the wishes of the other 49% cannot be ignored.

Limited liability Owners can protect their own personal financial position if the business is a limited company. Sole traders and partners have unlimited liability. They could be forced to use their own money to meet business debts. Therefore, some owners become limited companies to give themselves more financial protection.

The nature of the business The type of business activity may influence the choice of legal status. For example:

* household services such as plumbing, decorating and gardening tend to be provided by sole traders;
* professional services such as accountancy, legal advice and surveying are usually offered by partnerships;
* relatively small manufacturing and family businesses tend to be private limited companies;
* large manufacturers and producers of consumer durables, such as cookers, computers and cars, are usually plcs.

It must be remembered that there are many exceptions to these general examples.

Chapter review – ADgirlsport.com

Amanda Duval has run her sports shop business, ADgirlsport.com, as a sole-trader, a partnership and a limited company. Founded in 1999, the business first traded from a back bedroom where she supplied sportswear for girls by mail order. But now it has a shop and a growing internet business. Amanda says: 'When I started, I started small, operating from home, and never needing outside funding, so being a sole trader seemed the simplest option.'

Three years later Amanda decided to open a shop. However, she needed money for premises, stock and marketing. After a few months there was a strain on cash flow. Therefore she decided to take on her best friend as a partner. This helped to share the burden of running the business and raised $20,000 much needed cash. However, after 18 months Amanda fell out with her partner, who wanted to take more profit from the business, whereas Amanda wanted to use it for expansion. The break-up of the partnership was bitter and Amanda ended up having to pay her friend off. Amanda said: 'I was a fool really. I should have drawn up a Deed of Partnership in case we fell out.'

Immediately after the break-up Amanda formed a private limited company. Amanda had 51% of the shares because she wanted control. Her mother bought 29% and she allowed two of her staff to buy the remaining 20%. She wanted to reward them for their loyalty and also keep them motivated. Some of the money raised from selling shares was used to set up an online business. This is now expanding fast and Amanda also thinks she could develop a small chain of shops. A major sports retailer has recently put a number of stores up for sale. However, to buy, convert and stock them would cost $5m. The only way she could raise this is by going public.

(a) Why was a sole trader organisation suitable for Amanda's business when she first started? (2 marks)

(b) (i) Explain why Amanda changed her business to a partnership? (2 marks)
(ii) Outline briefly the importance of drawing up a Deed of Partnership when forming a partnership. (2 marks)

(c) Do you think it was appropriate for Amanda to form a private limited company after the break-up of the partnership? (4 marks)

(d) Do you think Amanda should become a public limited company to buy the shops? (10 marks)

◀ **Figure 16.2** Interior of a sports shop

Chapter 17

Control and responsibility

Getting started...

As businesses grow they need to be formally organised. This means that workers must be placed into groups, teams or departments. Each group must be led by someone who is responsible for the whole group and is able to control its activities. Every person must understand their role in the organisation and be accountable to someone. Look at the example below.

Cerrillos Auto Hire

Cerrillos Auto Hire is a car hire business based in Santiago, Chile. It is an established business and serves local business people. The business has 65 vehicles, employs nine staff and is divided into four departments. The business is organised as follows (see Figure 17.1):

- **General manager:** Carlos is in charge of the whole business. His main task is to buy and sell the cars. He works closely with Juan, the mechanic. Carlos is accountable to the owners.

- **Bookings and administration:** Gabriela runs this department but is helped by Gina and Patricia. It deals with customers when cars are booked, collected and returned. It deals with all the paperwork and provides customer service.

- **Car maintenance and preparation:** Two people are employed in this department to maintain and prepare the cars. Juan is a mechanic and is in charge while Jesus valets the cars.

- **Finance and accounts:** Charles is in charge of accounts. He also processes wages, deals with staff problems, carries out purchasing and deals with complaints. Julia is his part-time assistant.

- **Marketing:** Veronica is responsible for promoting the business and tries to develop new customers. She has recently designed a questionnaire to gather feedback from customers.

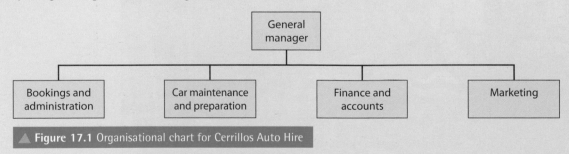

▲ **Figure 17.1** Organisational chart for Cerrillos Auto Hire

(a) Who is in control of Cerrillos Auto Hire?

(b) Describe briefly how Cerrillos Auto Hire is organised.

(c) What is Gabriela's role in the organisation?

(d) To whom is (i) Veronica; (ii) Jesus accountable?

Formal organisation

Running a business involves planning, decision making, coordination and communication. These tasks are easier if workers are organised into a structure made up of different departments. The internal structure of a business is known as its **formal organisation**. Small businesses rarely need a formal organisation. This is because the workforce is small and everyone will know what the others are doing. They will all be accountable to the same person – probably the owner. However, businesses that employ thousands of people need formal organisation. Without it the business is difficult to control. Communications may break down, mistakes may occur and staff may become confused about their roles.

The formal organisation can be represented by an **organisation chart** that shows:

- how the business is split into divisions or departments;
- the roles of employees and their job titles;
- who has responsibility;
- to whom people are accountable;
- communication channels;
- the relationships between different positions in the business.

An organisation chart for Denham plc, a manufacturer, is shown in Figure 17.2. It is a traditional organisation chart and the person in charge is the chairperson. The chairperson, at the top of the **hierarchy**, is accountable to the shareholders. The roles played by all other employees in the chart are outlined below.

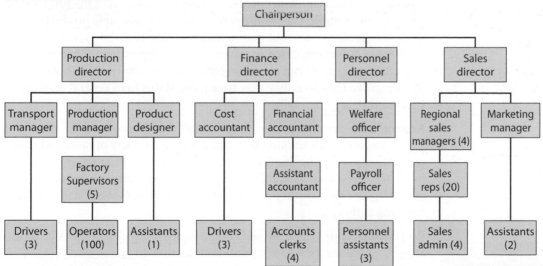

▲ **Figure 17.2**
Organisation chart for Denham plc

Employee roles

The roles played by employees vary depending on the size and nature of the business. The roles at Denham plc are as follows:

Directors Directors are appointed by the owners to run the business. With the chairperson they form the *Board of Directors*. They make all the important decisions in the business. Figure 17.2 shows that Denham plc is divided into four departments: production, finance, personnel and sales. Each of these departments is run by a director. These four directors are accountable to the chairperson. They also have **authority** over the managers in the layer below them.

Managers Managers are responsible for controlling and organising. They make the day-to-day decisions in the business. The manager in each department is accountable to the departmental director. The role of managers is discussed in Chapter 18. In Figure 17.2 there are a number of managers in each department:

- The production department has a transport manager and a production manager. There is also a product designer who has the same *status* as a manager in the chart. They are on the same level in the hierarchy.
- In the finance department the cost and financial accountants both have managerial status. This is because they are responsible for the work of others.
- The welfare officer in the personnel department also has managerial status. He or she is responsible for the work of the payroll officer and three assistants.
- The sales department has four regional sales managers and a marketing manager. Each regional manager has five sales staff working for them.

Supervisors Supervisors monitor the work in their area. They have authority over operatives and general workers. At Denham plc five factory supervisors are employed in the production department. Each of them has authority over 20 operatives. Supervisors may carry out managerial duties, but at a lower level. For example, Figure 17.2 shows that the assistant accountant, the payroll officer and the sales reps are all at the same level in the hierarchy.

Operatives These are skilled workers. They are involved in the production process. For example, they may operate machines, assemble products, work with tools or carry out maintenance. Figure 17.2 shows that there are 100 operatives employed in the production department. They are accountable to supervisors or managers. They are shown at the bottom of the hierarchy. However, they may have more status than general workers because they are often skilled.

General staff Businesses often employ staff that do not have any specific skills. However, with training they can perform a variety of tasks and gain promotion to other positions. Examples of general staff in Figure 17.2 include drivers, assistants, accounts clerks and people with administration jobs. They are shown at the bottom of the hierarchy. General staff do not have any authority.

Professional staff These are skilled and highly trained. Examples include lawyers, accountants, doctors, pilots and dentists. In places where lots of professionals are employed organisation charts may be different.

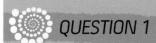

QUESTION 1

Chittagong Textiles Ltd manufactures towels and related products in Bangladesh. The company employs 200 staff and serves retailers, hotels, hospitals and other customers. The factory is based in Green Valley, Chittagong and operates three production lines: A, B and C. Each line produces a 'family' of products. Figure 17.3 shows part of the company's organisation chart.

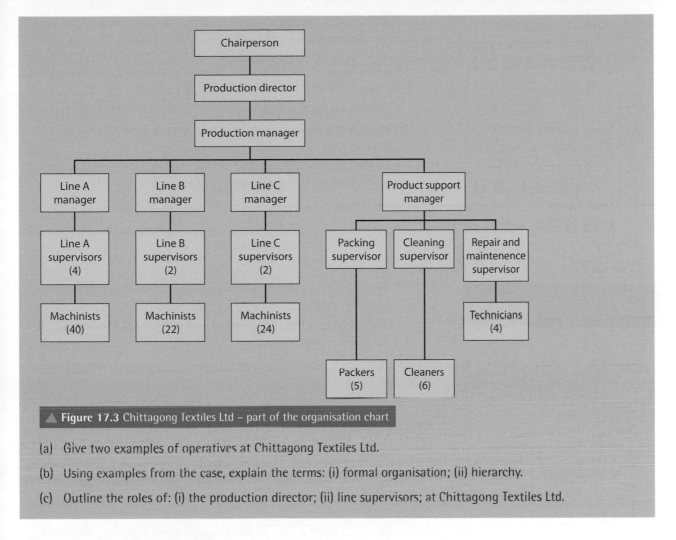

Figure 17.3 Chittagong Textiles Ltd – part of the organisation chart

(a)   Give two examples of operatives at Chittagong Textiles Ltd.

(b)   Using examples from the case, explain the terms: (i) formal organisation; (ii) hierarchy.

(c)   Outline the roles of: (i) the production director; (ii) line supervisors; at Chittagong Textiles Ltd.

Features of organisational structures

Chain of command Organisation charts show the **chain of command** in a business. This is the route through which orders are passed down in the hierarchy. In Figure 17.2 above, each layer in the hierarchy is like a link in a chain. Orders will pass down through the layers from the top to the bottom. Information may also flow back from the bottom to the top. If the chain of command is too long:

• messages may get lost or confused as they pass up and down the chain;

• making changes might meet with resistance lower down the chain, so, if there are lots of links in the chain, resistance is more likely.

Span of control The number of people, or **subordinates**, a person directly controls in a business is called the **span of control**. For example, in Figure 17.2 above, the finance director is responsible for two people – the cost accountant and the financial accountant. Therefore the director's span of control is two. In the sales department each regional manager is responsible for five sales reps. Their span of control is five.

If a business has a *wide* span of control it means that a person controls relatively more subordinates. Someone with a *narrow* span of control controls fewer subordinates. If the span of control is greater than six, difficulties may arise.

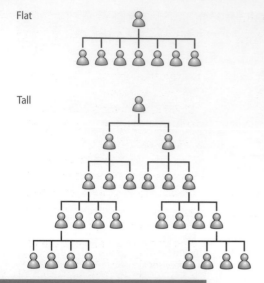

Flat

Tall

▲ **Figure 17.4**
Flat and tall organisational structures

Flat and tall structures Organisation structures may be flat or tall. Examples are shown in Figure 17.4. A flat structure means there are a fewer layers in the hierarchy. In Figure 17.4 the flat structure only has two layers in the hierarchy. The chain of command is short but the span of control is wide. With flat structures:

- communication is better because the chain of command is short;
- management costs are lower because there are fewer layers of management;
- control may be friendly and less formal because there is more direct contact between layers.

With tall structures:

- communication through the whole structure can be poor because there is a long chain of command;
- management costs will be higher;
- there may be a clear route for promotion that might help to motivate staff;
- control tends to be more formal and less friendly because of all the layers in the hierarchy.

QUESTION 2

Marks & Spencer has over 800 stores in more than 40 countries. It sells clothing, food, homeware, furniture and some electrical goods. In recent years the company has struggled financially. Marks & Spencer developed a reputation as an ageing and bureaucratic company. Critics said it was losing touch with younger customers. As a result, in 2004, Marks & Spencer began a review of the business and made some changes. These changes created a business with a flatter organisational structure. Marks & Spencer lost a number of layers of authority. This meant that employees had more accountability than before.

Source: adapted from www.thetimes100.co.uk

(a) Explain what is meant by a flatter organisation structure.

(b) Why did Marks & Spencer adopt a flatter structure?

Delegation In some situations a manager may hand a more complex task to a subordinate. This is called **delegation**. The manager will still have responsibility. However, time can be saved if a subordinate completes the task. Sometimes delegation can motivate workers. This is because they feel as though they are being trusted to carry out a more difficult work.

Relationships across organisational structures

Organisation charts often suggest that each department is independent. However, departments must work together. This means that there must be communication between departments. With reference to Figure 17.2, examples are as follows:

- The product designer may communicate with the marketing manager. The marketing manager may have information about customer needs that would be used when designing products.

- The welfare officer from the personnel department may have to meet the sales director to discuss customer complaints about one of the sales reps.
- The cost accountant may have to communicate with the product designer to ensure that new designs are profitable.

There are many more examples of interaction between departments in a business. A business may struggle if there is no cooperation between departments.

Organisational charts and business expansion

As businesses expand the formal organisation is likely to change. One change in recent years has been a switch to flatter structures. This has helped to cut managerial costs. It has also given more responsibility to other workers that may help to motivate them.

Key terms

Authority – the right to command and make decisions.
Chain of command – the way authority and power is structured in an organisation.
Delegation – authority to pass down from superior to subordinate.
Formal organisation – the internal structure of a business as shown by an organisation chart.
Hierarchy – the order or levels of responsibility in an organisation from the lowest to the highest.
Organisation chart – a diagram that shows the different job roles in a business and how they relate to each other.
Span of control – the number of people a person is directly responsible for in a business.
Subordinates – people in the hierarchy who work under the control of a senior worker.

Chapter review – Ceylan Pumps

Ceylan Pumps makes pumps and checkvalves. It is a family business based in Ankara, Turkey. Emre Ceylan is the chairman of the company. It has a traditional structure and the following information is given about the finance department:

- The finance director is in charge of the finance department.
- The department is divided into four sections each of which is run by a manager. These are the financial accountant, the cost accountant, the purchasing manager and the credit controller.
- The financial director has two assistant accountants each of which have three accounts clerks working for them.
- The cost accountant has one assistant cost accountant but no clerks.
- The purchasing manager has one supervisor and two purchasing clerks.
- The credit controller has no supervisor or assistant but does have two clerical officers.

(a) Draw an organisationtal chart for the finance department. **(6 marks)**

(b) What is the span of control for: (i) the credit controller; (ii) the cost accountant? **(2 marks)**

(c) Using this case as an example, explain what is meant by the chain of command. **(2 marks)**

(d) State two possible reasons why the finance department would interact with other departments in the business. **(2 marks)**

(e) The financial accountant often delegates work to the assistant accountants. What does this mean? **(2 marks)**

(f) Explain how having a formal organisational structure helps to control a business. **(6 marks)**

Chapter 18

Internal organisation and the role of managers

Getting started...

As businesses grow, they need to employ managers. This is because the burden of running a larger business needs to be shared. Managers are employed to take responsibility. Their job is to 'get things done', often by other people. Not all managers are the same, though. Look at the examples below.

Hotel manager

The Benguerra Island Hotel is located on an island off the coast of Mozambique. The general manager is Maria Mendes. She runs the hotel on behalf of the owners, a Portuguese travel company. Maria says: 'I have to do everything. I work with the chef, the housekeeper, the entertainments officer, the bar stewards, the transport manager, the gardener, the pool attendant and the cashier. I have to organise the staff, agree the menus, check the cleanliness of the rooms and get up in the night when someone is ill.'

▲ Figure 18.1
A beach on Benguerra Island

Marketing manager

Kim Jung-Nam is the marketing manager for a large South Korean electronics company. His main job is coordinating and motivating the sales team. He works closely with four regional sales managers. He agrees sales targets and reports every week to the chief executive. He also works with the promotions team. He has to make sure the advertising budget is not wasted. Kim Jung-Nam says: 'Too much of my time is spent dealing with paperwork – sales reports and more sales reports. There is not enough variety in my job any more.'

(a) State two specific tasks for which each of the above managers are responsible.

(b) What is the main difference between the two managers in the above cases?

The role of managers

Managers are employed by businesses for one of the following two reasons:

- The owners are absent and someone is put in charge of the business. For example, shareholders who own plcs employ directors and managers to run businesses on their behalf.

- The owners need help running the business because it has grown too big for one person to manage. As businesses grow, the burden of running them has to be shared.

Managers have a number *functions*. However, their overall *role* is to achieve the aims of the owners. They are employed to 'get things done' using the resources of the business as effectively as possible. They are also leaders and help to guide and shape the business.

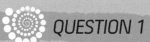

QUESTION 1

The **co-operative** pharmacy

'To deliver and exceed the profit and sales targets for the pharmacy branch by leading, managing and coordinating all aspects of the day to day operation of a community based pharmacy'.

Figure 18.2
The role of a branch manager at the Coop Pharmacy

Source: adapted from www.co-operative.coop

(a) Using the case in Figure 18.2 as an example, describe the role of managers in a business.

The functions of managers

Managers have several functions. In large businesses managers at different levels in the hierarchy will perform different functions. For example, senior managers spend more of their time planning than commanding.

Planning Senior managers plan strategy. They have to predict what is likely to happen in the future. They set objectives and decide which strategies are needed to achieve the objectives.

For junior managers planning might involve setting out a production schedule for the next month, or planning how many workers will be needed to meet production targets. In the marketing department planning might involve scheduling all the different aspects of a 12-month promotional campaign.

Organising 'Getting things done' in a business involves a lot of organising.

Commanding and controlling This involves giving instructions to subordinates. The manager has the authority to make decisions and must ensure that tasks are carried out. Staff may act on their own initiative. However, in some firms workers may lay 'idle' if they are not given instructions. Managers also measure and correct the work of subordinates.

Coordinating This involves bringing together of the activities of people within the business. Individuals and groups will have their own goals. These may be different from those of the business. Management must make sure that workers have a common approach. It is the company's goals that are important.

DID YOU KNOW?

Examples of organisational tasks carried out by a manager are:
- prioritising work;
- deciding which tasks are necessary to complete an order;
- allocating work to different employees;
- ensuring that resources are available when needed;
- making sure that deadlines and targets are met.

Decision making Managers have to make decisions. This might mean making choices between alternatives or committing to a particular course of action. For example, senior managers may have to decide whether to:

- launch a new product or re-launch an existing one;
- build an extension to the factory;
- outsource marketing to a specialist;
- close down a loss-making branch.

Leading and motivating Managers are leaders. Subordinates expect them to set an example and 'show them the way'. They may also have to motivate workers because they lack motivation. They may have to be given incentives and encouragement to carry out their tasks effectively. Managers are also expected to resolve conflict. For example, two workers competing for the same resources may ask the manager who should have them.

The difference between ownership and control

Sometimes those that own and control businesses are the same people. For example, a sole trader who employs two other staff will own the business and have complete control. However, in some large businesses, such as plcs, the shareholders, may not be in complete control. Control is handed over to the directors who are elected by the shareholders. Directors make all the key decisions and managers lower down in the hierarchy ensure that the board's objectives are achieved.

In some businesses there may be a *divorce of ownership and control*. This means that those who control the business start to pursue their own aims rather than those of the owners. For example, directors and senior managers may increase their own salaries and benefits at the expense of profit.

Chapter review – AirCater (Oman)

AirCater (Oman) is a branch of AirCater Arabia, a provider of airline meals in the Middle East. AirCater (Oman) serves airlines operating from Muscat International Airport. The business employs 120 staff and has three departments. Each department is led by a manager who is accountable to the general manager. The general manager has to report to the board of directors in Dubai every month. The three departments are described below:

- **Production** – responsible for preparing thousands of airline meals every day.
- **Finance** – responsible for recording transactions, payroll, credit control and producing branch accounts.
- **Sales and distribution** – responsible for processing daily orders, liaising with customers and ensuring that meals are packed and transported to the airport.

(a) To whom is the: (i) production manager; (ii) general manager accountable? **(2 marks)**

(b) State two organisational tasks that the production manager may have to carry out in this case. **(2 marks)**

(c) State two decisions the sales manager may have to make. **(2 marks)**

(d) Why are managers responsible? **(2 marks)**

(e) How might the planning tasks of the board of directors and the finance manager in this case be different? **(4 marks)**

(f) Managers are said to be leaders and motivators. Describe what this might involve for the sales and distribution manager at AirCater (Oman). **(4 marks)**

(g) Explain the difference between ownership and control. **(4 marks)**

Chapter 19

Communication 1

Getting started...

People in businesses exchange information all the time:

- A sales manager may telephone the production manager to ask if a customer order is ready.
- A credit controller may write to a customer explaining that their account is overdue.
- An operative may ask a technician to repair a fault with a machine.

Look at the examples of communication in Figures 19.1 and 19.2.

A team meeting

We have to increase sales this month. Every person who meets their sales target will get a bonus of $200.

Figure 19.1 ▶
A team meeting

Customer email

Customer Service Centre
Apollo Airways
12/10/08

Dear Mr Husain,
Please note that the time of your flight from London to Dubai has been brought forward by one hour. The new flight itinerary is shown below. We apologise if this causes any inconvenience.

Outward
London Flight A102 Dep:13.05   12.11.08
Dubai   Flight A102 Arr: 21.25 12.11.08
Return
Dubai   Flight A103 Dep: 14.05   19.11.08
London Flight A103 Arr: 22.55   19.11.08

Please remember to arrive at the airport three hours before departure.

Yours sincerely

Waleed Abbas (customer services)

Figure 19.2 ▶
A customer email

(a) Identify the: (i) sender; (ii) receiver(s); (iii) message in Figures 19.1 and 19.2.

What is communication?

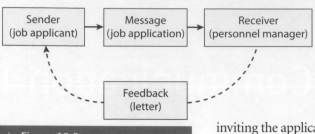

▲ **Figure 19.3**
The process of communication

Communication is about sending and receiving information. Figure 19.3 shows how communication might work in business. It shows who is involved, the message and the feedback. Communication begins with a *sender*. In Figure 19.3 the sender is an applicant for a job. The *message* being sent is a job application form. The *receiver* is the personnel manager. The *feedback* is a letter inviting the applicant for an interview. Note that the personnel manager becomes the sender when the interview invitation is sent back. Therefore, the applicant now becomes the receiver.

All sorts of information may be communicated by a business. Messages may be verbal or written and may contain words, numbers or images. Some examples of communication in a business are given below.

How does communication take place?

Inside a business messages can be passed vertically (upwards or downwards) and laterally. Figure 19.4 shows the different routes along which communication takes place. These routes are called **channels of communication**.

Downward communication This often involves managers giving information or instructions to their subordinates. Downward communication is important because:

• subordinates look to their managers for leadership and guidance;
• it allows the decisions made by management to be carried out by employees;
• it allows managers to command, control and organise.

Upward communication This often involves workers giving feedback to managers. However, it might also involve requests by workers. They may need more resources, for example. Upward communication is helpful because it:

• helps managers to understand the views and needs of subordinates;
• may alert managers to problems;
• helps staff to feel that they are valued;
• provides managers with information to help make decisions.

Horizontal (or lateral) communication This occurs when workers on the same level in the hierarchy exchange information. Inside a department horizontal communication is common. For example, operatives are likely to discuss their work with each other.

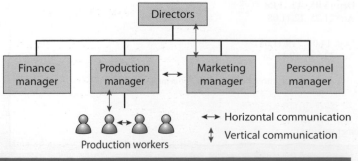

▲ **Figure 19.4** The process of communication

The importance of communication in business

If internal communication is poor problems can arise. As a result efficiency and profitability may suffer. Poor communication can lead to mistakes, wasted resources and confusion.

Poor external communication can make the business look foolish and cost money. For example, if prices on a company's website are set too low by mistake, this could lead to a flood of online orders. These may have to be accepted at a loss.

QUESTION 1

Didier Bonnet is the regional manager of La Femme, a French clothes retail chain. He is responsible for the performance of six stores in the south of France. The table in Figure 19.5 contains financial information about the performance of the stores in June 2009. The table has been sent to the finance director who is compiling a report for a board meeting.

	Nice	Marseille	St Tropez	Cannes	Toulon	Nimes	Total
Turnover	98,500	133,400	87,600	94,900	76,900	83,400	574,700
Profit	23,200	34,600	21,400	19,700	-1,200	16,800	114,500

▲ **Figure 19.5** Financial information for La Femme

(a) Who is the sender of the information in this example?

(b) Using this case as an example, explain what is meant by vertical communication.

(c) What sort of information is being sent in this example?

(d) Explain why upward communication is helpful.

Barriers to communication

Communication is only effective if a message is sent and understood by the receiver. Things that get in the way of good communication are called **barriers to communication**. Some examples are given below.

Message is unclear If a message is not clear it may be misinterpreted or ignored.

Technological breakdown A lot of business communication is done electronically. If technology is faulty, communication may be distorted or break down. For example, emails cannot be sent if broadband connections are lost. Mobile telephone conversations can often be distorted by a weak signal. Sometimes mobile phones cannot be used because there is no signal.

KEY FACT

Information is more likely to be understood if:
- there is not too much information;
- clear and precise language is used;
- it is delivered at a reasonable pace;
- the receiver is familiar with the sender and method of communication;
- the message only contains relevant information.

Poor communication skills Some people may have poor communication skills. For example:

- when communicating verbally, some people may have a limited vocabulary or may not be able to make themselves understood;
- some people may be poor listeners and switch off during communication;
- written messages may contain poor spelling or weak grammar.

Jargon Sometimes people use jargon when communicating. Jargon is terminology that is used and understood by people in a specific group. However, outside that group it may be meaningless. Clearly, jargon should not be used when communicating with people outside such a group.

Long chain of command If there are too many layers in the organisational hierarchy, the chain of command will be longer. This means messages take longer to pass through the chain and may become distorted on the way.

Using the wrong medium The different methods by which messages can be sent are called **communication media**. These are discussed in the next unit. However, if a sender uses an inappropriate medium an important message may be missed.

Different countries, languages and cultures In multinationals people may be working in different countries where languages and cultures vary. Such differences may hamper communications. There may also be time differences between countries.

DID YOU KNOW?

In Arabian countries it is common to spend time discussing trivial matters before a business meeting gets under way. This may not be acceptable in the West and may slow down communication.

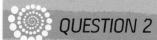

QUESTION 2

Eric Demsey left school and got a job as an apprentice in a market research agency. On his first day he asked about lunch arrangements. He was told that most team members ate at El Desco. At 1.00pm Eric spent a fruitless 45 minutes looking for a restaurant by the office called El Desco. When he returned he discovered that El Desco was not a restaurant but meant eating at your desk.

On the fourth day when Eric arrived at work, he was asked by his team leader why he missed the team briefing the previous afternoon. Eric explained that he did not know about it. His leader said that the notice was quite clear on the staff notice board.

(a) (i) Using this case as an example, explain what is meant by jargon.
(ii) Why should jargon be avoided when communicating?

(b) Do you think the communication medium used to notify people about a meeting in this case was effective?

(c) What steps can be taken to ensure that messages are clear?

Overcoming the barriers to communication

Training Businesses must overcome barriers to communication. One way is to train staff in communication. For example, training can be used to improve verbal communication skills, such as when dealing with customers on the telephone.

Recruitment Businesses should recruit staff with good communication skills. The quality of people's written communication in job applications may provide some guide. Also, people's verbal communication skills can be assessed in interviews.

Technology If communication barriers result from faulty technology, a business may have to repair or replace equipment.

Chain of command If this is too long, a business may decide to remove some of the management levels in the organisation. A shorter chain of command means that information can pass through an organisation more quickly.

Social events Internal communication may improve if social events are organised for staff. These provide opportunities for workers from different departments to come together, which may be helpful.

Key terms

Communication – the sending and receiving of messages.
Communication barriers – things that get in the way of communication.
Communication channels – routes along which information might travel in a business.
Communication media – the different methods by which information can be sent.

Chapter review – SASB

SASB is a South American satellite television broadcaster based in Lima, Chile. It broadcasts programmes to Chile, Argentina, Uruguay and Peru. Recently, many customers have cancelled their subscriptions because of poor customer service. SASB lost $15 million in subscriptions in a single month. There are two problems:

- As a result of a technical fault on the switchboard, customers hang up because they cannot get through to a helpline. Some of the equipment is too old.

- Workers employed in one call centre based in Argentina have complained that they are not equipped to give out the information wanted by customers. This was the result of inadequate training.

Generally, communications at SASB are poor. It has been suggested that the chain of command is too long. Also, people are not given enough opportunities to mix with their colleagues. Workers at SASB do not know each other very well. As a result staff turnover is high and money is being wasted on constant recruitment. An urgent meeting was organised for all Level 6 divisional managers to discuss communication at SASB.

(a) Using an example from this case, explain what is meant by communication. **(2 marks)**

(b) Explain what is meant by horizontal communication. **(2 marks)**

(c) Describe two communication barriers at SASB. **(4 marks)**

(d) How does this case highlight the importance of good communication in business? **(4 marks)**

(e) Discuss the measures that might be taken to overcome the communication problems at SASB. **(8 marks)**

Chapter 20

Communication 2

Getting started...

Businesses use a variety of methods to communicate information. For example, communication might be verbal or written. Information can be sent electronically or distributed using the postal system. Communication may also be formal or informal. Look at the examples below.

Case 1

A business wants to inform a customer that an order will be delayed due to an item being out of stock.

Case 2

A member of staff has to be informed that they have been promoted to a senior position and will be entitled to higher pay.

Case 3

A general worker needs permission from a supervisor to finish work 15 minutes early to take her daughter for a hospital appointment.

▲ **Figure 20.1**
Examples of communication

(a) Suggest suitable methods of communication for each of the above cases.

Internal and external communication

Internal communication takes place inside a business between employees. Examples include:

- a manager giving a verbal warning to a subordinate for poor punctuality;
- a board meeting where directors are discussing a possible acquisition.

External communication occurs when businesses exchange information with people and organisations outside the business. Examples include:

- a statement from a credit card company;
- a focus group where people from the marketing department discuss a product with members of the public.

Formal and informal communication

Formal communication in a business is when people use recognised channels. **Informal** communication is through non-approved channels. Most informal communication is done through the *grapevine*. This means that unofficial information is passed on through gossip and rumours.

Methods of communication

Face-to-face communication This takes place when spoken information is exchanged by people who can see each other. Face-to-face communication is effective. Some examples of face-to-face communication in business are given below:

- In an interview where a candidate is being interviewed for a job.

- At a training session where people are being taught new skills.

- Giving customer service over a counter or in reception.

Written communication Businesses communicate written information using a variety of methods. Each of them has their own advantages and disadvantages:

- **Letters** are a common way to send written information. They are flexible because they can be sent to a variety of different people such as customers, employees and suppliers. The information in each letter can also be tailored to the needs of the message. Letters can also be used for confidential information and provide a record of the communication.

- **Reports** are used to communicate important written information that may be complex or detailed. However, reports should be concise, structured and presented using a formal format. Reports can contain numerical data and images. The main disadvantage of reports is that they take time to write.

- **Memorandums (memos)** are used for internal communications. They contain brief messages and are flexible. They are often used to remind people of events, confirm telephone conversations and pass on simple instructions.

- **Forms** are used to communicate routine information. Examples are application forms for jobs, loans or licences, claim forms for expenses and other entitlements, order forms for ordering goods and time sheets for recording time spent on an activity.

- **Noticeboards** are cheap to use and can pass on information to a large number of people. However, they can become untidy, are open to abuse and often overlooked.

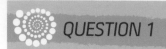

TRM Finance Ltd
127 Bone St
London
WE4 5TY

9 April 2009

Dear Mrs Kumar,
RE: Loan No. FR266421H

Our records show that the last instalment for £132.65 was not paid by your bank on the 1 April 2009. If this is an oversight, please could you arrange for the payment to be made immediately.

If you are unable to make this payment, please telephone 0200 239 9987. May we remind you that according to the terms of the loan agreement an interest rate of 34.5% will be charged on late payments. This will be included in your next statement.

Yours sincerely
Alan Nutter (Senior Loan Controller)

▲ **Figure 20.2** A letter sent by a finance company to a customer

(a) Explain whether the message in Figure 20.2 is an example of internal or external communication.

(b) Explain the advantages of using a letter as a means of communication in this case.

Online communication is not without problems:
* people can only use the Internet if they have access to a computer;
* in some areas it is not possible to get a broadband connection;
* connections can be lost when using the Internet;
* email inboxes get 'clogged up' with electronic junk mail called spam;
* computer viruses can result in the loss of files;
* computer hackers may get hold of sensitive and confidential information.

▲ **Figure 20.3**
Problems with online communication

Electronic communication

Most businesses use electronic communication media. It is possible to deliver messages instantly, all over the world and to a number of people all at the same time using electronic methods. Here are some examples.

Email This is one of the most common methods of communication. It allows businesses and individuals to communicate text or images instantly using a computer. Email can be used to send letters, memos, reports, photographs, film, sound and any other image – even when people are not there to receive them.

Internet The Internet can be used for internal and external communication. Many businesses use their own website to provide a wide range of information.

The Internet can be used to:

* market products by displaying them on shopping sites;
* allow customers to buy products with credit and debit cards;
* provide general information about the history and nature of the business;
* advertise jobs to people inside and outside the business;
* obtain information about other companies and products for market research;
* deal with customer queries online.

Other methods Other methods of electronic communication include mobile phones, intranets, video conferencing, Tannoy systems and electronic noticeboards.

Using methods appropriately

Quite often the same information can be sent using different communication media. A business must use the most appropriate method. Generally, methods should be used that minimise costs. For example, mobile telephones should not be used if a landline is available. A number of other issues are also important:

- Confidential information, such as people's personal details, should be communicated securely – using a letter for example.

- Sensitive information, such as that regarding a staff disciplinary matter, should be communicated face to face.

- Some communications, such as a job offer, must be supported by a document such as a letter.

- If immediate feedback is required, verbal communication will be needed.

- Standard information is best communicated using forms.

- Complex and detailed information is best communicated in a report.

 QUESTION 2

Li Shanshan is a finance manager for a Chinese toy manufacturer. When she arrived at the office one morning she identified a number of tasks that required communication:

- Send a copy of the marketing budget to the marketing manager.

- Contact a sales rep in Japan to find out whether a large order has been clinched.

- Interview two candidates for a job in the finance office.

- Explain to all staff in the department a new system for recording sales data.

(a) In each of the above examples, suggest the most appropriate method of communication. In each case explain your answer.

(b) Li wants to know whether staff in her department would be interested in a social evening at her apartment. How might she find out informally whether such an event would be popular?

External communication – communication between the business and those outside, such as customers, investors or the authorities.

Formal communication – the use of recognised channels when communicating.

Informal communication – the use of non-approved channels when communicating.

Internal communication – communication between people inside the business.

The need for effective internal communication

Chapter 19 discussed the importance of communication in business. However, it will be helpful to understand the consequences of a breakdown in communications.

Mistakes occur When internal communication breaks down mistakes are likely to occur. For example, when there is a misunderstanding, defective goods might be produced which have to be scrapped.

Costs rise Breaks in communication often result in lost time. In business lost time costs money. For example, if a construction project is delayed due to a break in communication, financial penalties might be incurred.

Staff motivation suffers Poor communication can frustrate employees. This will affect their motivation and could result in a higher staff turnover. Employees like to be kept informed and consulted when changes are made.

Decision making slows down If information takes too long to reach its destination, there may be a delay in decision making. This could result in the business missing out on an important opportunity.

Chapter review – Honda

Many businesses have their own website. These provide a wide range of information and some allow people to buy products online. The information on websites is available 24/7. It can be accessed anywhere in the world and easily updated. Visit www.honda.com and answer the following questions.

(a) Who is the sender in this communication? **(2 marks)**

(b) State two stakeholders that might be interested in this website. **(2 marks)**

(c) Explain whether this is a formal or informal method of communication. **(2 marks)**

(d) Describe two pieces of information that can be obtained by receivers using this method of communication? **(4 marks)**

(e) Discuss the advantages and disadvantages of the Internet as a method of communication. **(10 marks)**

▲ **Figure 20.5** A car produced by Honda

Chapter 21

Use of funds

Getting started...

No business can get started or survive without adequate funding. This means that money is needed to set up a business and to keep it running. Funds are also needed to help a business expand. Sometimes businesses need emergency funding to meet unexpected costs. Look at the examples below.

Lobamba Cattle Ranch

Albert Dlamini runs the Lobamba Cattle Ranch in Swaziland. The business employs 23 workers and is successful. However, Albert is ambitious and wants to expand. He hopes to diversify into poultry and export to South Africa. Here demand for meat is growing. Albert plans to use some of the profit made by the business to help build a poultry house and set up a poultry processing plant. However, he will need to raise a further $80,000.

Emily Robinson

Emily Robinson received $40,000 in redundancy pay when she lost her job as an investment banker in Chicago. She now plans to set up an employment agency to supply staff in financial services. She believes that when the economy picks up the financial services sector will recover quickly. Therefore financial institutions will need to recruit staff again. However, she needs an office, office furniture and computers. She also plans to spend a lot on advertising to establish the business. Emily reckons this will all cost $100,000. She needs to find another $60,000 to set up the agency.

▲ **Figure 21.1** Poultry farming

(a) Explain why funds are needed in the above examples.

(b) How might funds be raised by Albert Dlamini and Emily Robinson?

The need for funds

Start-up capital Funds are most needed when first setting up a business. This is because a lot of resources are needed before trading can begin. Some of these resources are 'one-off' items. For example, a new restaurant would need to buy cookers, refrigerators, utensils, furniture, glassware, cutlery, crockery and other equipment. Once these one-off costs have been met, they may not be repeated for many years. Other start-up costs might include research, converting premises, legal fees, licences, website design and marketing.

Working capital Once a business starts trading it will get revenue. This money can be used to meet the day-to-day running costs of the business such as wages, raw materials, components, utility bills and administration. However, sometimes the revenue from sales may not cover all expenditure – at the end of the month, for example, when lots of bills have to be paid. This is when a business will need to borrow money. The money needed to fund the day to day expenditure is called *working capital* (see Chapter 47).

Expansion Once a business is established the owners often want to expand. They may:

• want to expand capacity to meet growing orders;

• develop new products;

• branch into overseas markets;

• diversify.

These activities often require large amounts of money. Most businesses have to find extra funding to expand. This is because internal sources, such as profit, are not adequate.

Emergency funding Businesses often get unexpected bills – in the UK a tax demand from HM Revenue and Customs perhaps. If the business does not have enough money it will need to get some very quickly. Businesses have to manage their *cash flow* (see Chapter 43) carefully. If businesses run out of cash they will collapse. Consequently, businesses are often forced to raise money quickly when cash runs short.

QUESTION 1

Al-Sayed Raouf wants to set up a pest control business in Giza, Egypt. He plans to help hotels and restaurants in Giza to deal with pest control problems such as rats and cockroaches. He has found some premises and has produced a list of resources that will be needed to start the business. This is shown in Figure 21.2.

(a) (i) Calculate the total amount of start-up capital that the business will need in this case.

(ii) Al-Sayed Raouf has £500 of his own money. How much more will he need to raise in start-up capital?

(b) Why is the need for funds probably at its greatest when businesses are first set up?

(c) Explain why Al-Sayed Raouf will need working capital.

Start-up costs	
	EGP
Van	320
Mobile phone	25
Lease on premises	400
Pest control manual	80
Rat traps	200
Cockroach traps	300
Safety boots	25
Disposable gloves	40
Bait gun	25
Sewer bait depositor	150
Pesticides	200
Pesticide storage locker	95
Rechargeable hand lamp	40
Other equipment	200
Other set-up costs	300

▲ Figure 21.2
Start-up costs for Al-Sayed Raouf's pest control business

Short-term capital needs

Businesses often need to borrow money for a short period of time. This is called **short-term finance** and is money borrowed for *one year* or less. Short-term finance is often used to boost working capital. Here are some examples:

- Some businesses have seasonal trade. A farmer, for example, may need to borrow money for a few months until more revenue comes in from selling the harvest.

- A textiles manufacturer may need short-term finance to pay for raw materials and wages to meet a large order.

- A firm might need a short-term loan because it is waiting for a customer to pay.

Short-term finance is also likely to be used to meet emergency expenditure. For example, if a machine breaks down unexpectedly, the repair costs might have to be met by a short-term loan.

Long-term capital needs

Long-term finance is money borrowed for more than one year. However, long-term sources can vary in length. For example, a five-year bank loan is a long-term source but so is a 25-year mortgage. Money raised by selling shares is *permanent capital*. It is never repaid if the company continues trading.

Long-term finance is used to meet start-up costs and business expansion. When a business needs large amounts of money, long-term sources are more suitable. This is because large amounts of money take a lot longer to repay. Long-term sources are often used to fund *capital expenditure*. This is spending on resources such as land, property, plant, machinery, equipment and vehicles.

Key terms

Long-term finance – money borrowed for more than one year.
Short-term finance – money borrowed for one year or less.

Chapter review – Tata Steel

Tata Steel is the world's sixth largest steel company. It is a multinational with interests in over 50 European and Asian markets. In 2009 the company said it might need to raise funds for expansion. The company recently raised $500 million. The funds, if raised, will be used to increase production capacity to 16 million tonnes by 2014. For example, the company has a capacity of 6.8 million tonnes in Jamshedpur, which it plans to take up to 10 million tonnes by 2011.

(a) Why does Tata Steel need to raise funds? **(2 marks)**

(b) Some of Tata Steel's capital is likely to be permanent capital. What does this mean? **(2 marks)**

(c) Do you think Tata Steel will be raising short-term or long-term finance? Explain your answer. **(4 marks)**

(d) Discuss reasons why Tata Steel might need to raise short-term finance. **(6 marks)**

(e) Why do you think some businesses run short of working capital? **(6 marks)**

Chapter 22

Sources of funds

Getting started...

Nearly all businesses have to raise finance from time to time. They may be able to choose from a wide range of sources. Look at the examples below.

Dabengwa Crafted Furniture Ltd

Henry Dabengwa runs a small business making furniture and other wooden products. He rents a workshop in Harare, Zimbabwe and specialises in teak products such as doors, chairs, bar stools, staircases and window frames. He employs four people and serves both business and residential customers. He has just been given a $500 bank overdraft for six months. This is to help meet the cost of completing a big order for a hotel in Harare.

▲ **Figure 22.1** A carpenter working in a workshop

Billington Logistics

Malcolm Billington runs a haulage company in Canada. He owns five lorries and has a contract with a Canadian supermarket chain. He distributes grocery products from suppliers to a network of supermarkets. In 2009, he needed $30,000 to replace one of the older lorries. He considered a number of sources but decided to take out a three-year bank loan. The interest rate was 9.5% per annum.

(a) (i) Describe the sources of finance used in the above examples.
    (ii) In each case state whether the source is short term or long term.

(b) Calculate the total interest charge on Malcom Billington's three-year loan.

Internal and external finance

Sources of finance may be internal or external and are summarised in Figure 22.2 overleaf. Internal sources can only be used by an established business. This is because new businesses are usually short of cash. There are three internal sources of finance.

Profit Retained profit is profit that has not been returned to the owners. It is the most important source of finance for a business because it is cheap. There are no charges such as interest, dividends or administration. However, if profit is used by the business it cannot be returned to the owners. Some owners might object to this.

Working capital It may be possible to 'squeeze' working capital to provide extra finance for the business. This can be done by:

- Reducing the trade credit period, say from 90 to 60 days. This means that customers have to pay for their goods sooner.
- Reducing the amount of stocks held. This means money is released and can be used to boost cash reserves.
- Delaying payments to suppliers so that the business holds on to its cash for longer.

Sale of assets An established business may be able to sell some unwanted *assets* (see Chapter 45) to raise finance. For example, machinery, land and buildings that are no longer required could be sold off. Large companies can sell parts of their organisation to raise finance.

Short-term sources of finance

Bank overdraft This is a common source of finance for most businesses. A bank overdraft means a business can spend more money than it has in its account. It can go overdrawn. An overdraft limit will be set and interest is only charged when the account is overdrawn. Bank overdrafts are simple and flexible.

Bank loan (unsecured) A loan is a fixed agreement between a business and the bank. The amount borrowed must be repaid in regular instalments over a clear time period. Bank loans can be short term or long term. The main advantage of a bank loan is that a business will know exactly what it has to pay every month.

Hire purchase Small businesses often use **hire purchase (HP)** to buy tools, equipment, vehicles and machinery. What are the features of a HP agreement?

- A business usually makes a down payment.
- The remainder is paid in monthly instalments.
- The goods bought do not legally belong to the buyer until the very last instalment has been paid.
- If the buyer falls behind with the repayments, the goods can be repossessed.
- HP agreements can be short term and long term.

Trade credit Businesses often buy resources and pay for them at a later date. Usually within 30–90 days. This is called *trade credit* and is a cheap way of raising finance. It means a business holds on to its cash for longer.

However:

- many suppliers encourage early payment by offering discounts;
- the cost of goods is often higher if firms buy on credit;
- delaying payment may result in conflict with suppliers.

Credit cards Credit cards are popular because they are convenient, flexible and avoid interest charges if accounts are settled within the credit period. They can be used by executives to meet expenses when travelling on company business. Small businesses use credit cards to buy materials from suppliers. However, interest rates on credit cards are high if accounts are not settled within the credit period.

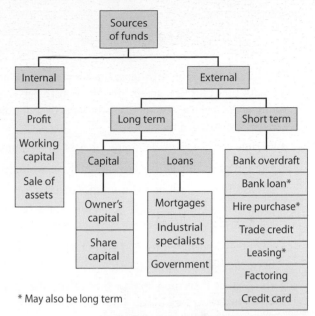

▲ **Figure 22.2**
Sources of finance

* May also be long term

QUESTION 1

Stratton Finance is an Australian finance company that provides funds for HP agreements. Many customers use their funds to buy vehicles. Some of the benefits of using their services are outlined below:

- flexible contract terms ranging from 24 to 60 months;
- fixed interest rate with a fixed monthly repayments;
- deposit (either cash or trade-in) may be used;
- a tax deduction is available when the vehicle is used for business purposes;
- customers registered for GST (sales tax) can claim back the GST;
- the finance is secured against the vehicle, allowing lower interest rates.

Source: adapted from www.strattonfinance.com.au

(a) Explain what is meant by a HP agreement.

(b) Under what circumstances might a business consider HP as a source of finance?

(c) How might a business benefit from taking out a HP agreement with Stratton Finance?

▲ **Figure 22.3**
Stratton Finance homepage

KEY FACT

Share capital is *permanent* capital. This means that it is not repaid (as long as the company is still trading).

Key terms

Hire purchase – buying specific goods with a loan.
Retained profit – the profit held by a business rather than returning it to the owners.
Share capital – money raised from the sale of shares in a limited company.
Venture capitalists – specialist financial institutions which provide funds for businesses, usually in exchange for an equity stake.

Long-term sources of finance

External long-term funds can be in the form of capital or loans. Capital is the money put in by the owners and loans are borrowed money.

Owner's capital Small businesses are often set up using money belonging to the owner. For example, sole traders or partners may put their savings or money raised from friends and relatives into a business. Once this money is put in it is not likely to be taken out.

Share capital For limited companies **share capital** is an important source of finance. The sale of shares can raise very large amounts of money.

Loan capital Loan capital is money that is borrowed, usually from banks and other financial institutions. It may come from a number of sources.

- **Mortgages:** A mortgage is usually a long-term loan and the borrower must use land or property as security. This means that if the borrower fails to make the repayments, the lender can repossess the property. Mortgages are popular because the interest rates are much lower than those on unsecured bank loans.

- **Industrial specialists**: Some institutions specialise in lending money to businesses. They sometimes lend to businesses that have difficulty in raising funds from other sources. **Venture capitalists** provide funds for companies that have some potential, but are considered too risky by other investors. They usually take a stake in the business, which means they can influence decision making.

- **Government assistance**: In some countries governments give financial help to businesses. Governments prefer to give money to businesses that set up in regions which suffer from heavy unemployment.

 ## QUESTION 2

Tune Hotels is a budget hotel chain with five hotels in Malaysia. It claims to offer a 5-star service at 1-star prices. It now wants to set up a franchising operation and develop more hotels in other Asian countries. Tune Hotel's CEO Mark Lankester said 'We are looking at 20 franchised hotels in India, 20 in Indonesia, Singapore and Malaysia and possibly 20 more in Thailand'. The company is considering raising $25 million by issuing shares.

Source: adapted from www.btimes.com

(a) Why is Tune Hotels planning to raise $25m?

(b) Using this case as an example, explain what is meant by a long-term source of capital.

(c) Explain one advantage of raising capital by selling shares.

Chapter review – Propshore Ltd

Propshore Ltd is a boat manufacturer. The business is established and was successful up until 2009 when it made a small loss. In 2008, the business made a profit of $2.1 million but in 2009 the loss, as a result of the global recession, was $79,000. Wally Spencer, the main shareholder in the business said: 'Trading conditions are very difficult now and will be for at least the next 18 months.'

However, despite these difficulties Wally is optimistic that the company will recover quickly. Indeed, Wally is now designing a new boat, which will come to the market in 2011. To develop the design the business needs a total of $1 million. Half of this will come from retained profit, but Wally can't decide whether to take out a mortgage or get a venture capitalist to provide the rest.

(a) Explain why retained profit is an internal source of finance. **(2 marks)**

(b) What is the main advantage to Propshore Ltd of using retained profit to fund business activity? **(2 marks)**

(c) Propshore uses trade credit to buy raw materials. Outline one advantage and one disadvantage of this source of finance. **(4 marks)**

(d) Discuss whether Propshore Ltd should use a mortgage or a venture capitalist to provide the remaining $500,000 for the new product development. **(12 marks)**

Chapter 23

Choice of funds

Getting started...

Businesses have to decide which source of funds is best for their needs. Businesses are often faced with a choice between alternative sources of finance. Also, most businesses are likely to use several different sources. Look at the example below.

Yanbu Cement Company

The Yanbu Cement Company (YCC) is one of Saudi Arabia's biggest cement companies. It recently built a new production line at the Yanbu Site and new HQ offices in Jeddah. Demand for cement is expected to rise mainly because the Saudi government is developing some new cities. A number of commercial and residential construction projects are planned along with some infrastructure developments. As a result, Yanbu said it would spend SAR1.5 billion to raise capacity by 48%. YCC will fund the expansion through internal sources and a loan from the National Commercial Bank.

The company has issued share capital of SAR1,050 million. At the end of June 2009, YCC had a bank overdraft of SAR2.94 million, owed SAR8.03 million to suppliers and owed SAR7.4 million in other bank loans.

Source: adapted from www.yanbucement.com

(a) How did the Yanbu Cement Company raise its capital?

(b) How is the company going to raise SAR1.5 billion to expand capacity?

(c) Identify other sources of funds used by the company.

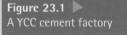

Figure 23.1 ▶
A YCC cement factory

Business funding decisions

Choosing a suitable source of funds is an important decision for a business. Many businesses struggle to raise funds. This often slows down growth. In some cases, businesses collapse because they are not able to raise enough money. Businesses need to choose a suitable and cheap source of funds. What factors affect the choice of funds?

Cost Businesses prefer cheap sources of finance. They have to consider both the interest payments and administration costs. For example, share issues can carry high administration costs while the interest payments on bank overdrafts tend to be relatively low. Interest rates on mortgages are also competitive. Other factors may also be important. For example, if venture capitalists provide funding, they usually want a stake in the business. This means that the owners lose some control.

Use of funds Spending on resources such as plant, machinery and equipment is usually funded by long-term sources. For example, a new factory may be financed by a share issue or a mortgage. Money needed for working capital is usually financed by short-term sources. For example, the purchase of raw materials may be funded by trade credit or a bank overdraft.

Status and size Sole traders are usually limited in their choices of finance. For example, long-term sources may be mortgages or personal capital. Limited companies tend to have a lot more choice. This is because they are larger and considered more secure. They may get lower interest rates from lenders. They may also be able to exploit financial economies of scale (see Chapter 26).

Financial situation The financial situation of businesses is likely to change. When a business is in a poor financial situation, raising more funds can be very difficult. At the same time, the cost of borrowing rises. Financial institutions are more willing to lend to secure businesses that have more *collateral* (assets which provide security for loans).

 QUESTION 1

D'Souza Ltd, a family business, is a food wholesaler based in Ahmadabad, India. It supplies more than 400 stores, some of which it owns. Its wholesale arm supplies fresh and frozen food from a 230,000 sq ft warehouse in Ahmadabad. Other operations include the D'Souza corner shop chain and shop developer D'Souza Group Property. Sales in 2008 reached Rs27.8 billion, when the group opened 27 new stores. A further 28 are planned for this year. D'Souza employs 1,847 staff and made a profit of Rs755 million in 2008.

(a) State whether the following expenditure by D'Souza Ltd would require long-term or short-term funding: (i) buying land for new stores; (ii) paying wages; (iii) buying food from farmers and other suppliers; (iv) buying new lorries.

(b) What sources of finance might be suitable to fund the building of a Rs350 million warehouse for D'Souza Ltd?

Risk Sometimes businesses have to choose between loans or capital when raising money. Taking out a loan may be more risky because interest has to be paid. Increasing loans also places a burden on businesses. In contrast, if money is raised using capital, there is no interest to pay and the business will have less debt. However, whoever puts in the capital will want a share of the profit and perhaps some influence on decision making.

Availability of finance

Some sources of funds are not available to all businesses. For example, sole traders and partnerships cannot sell shares or debentures. Small businesses may be refused funds because they are too risky. Also, during 2008 and 2009 there was a banking crisis that resulted in a 'credit crunch'. This meant that banks and other institutions lacked the confidence to lend to businesses.

Chapter review – Gulf Oil Supplies

Gulf Oil Supplies makes engineering equipment for the Emirate's oil industry. It has AED1,000,000 of share capital. This is owned equally between Ali Ibrahim and Yousef Maaded. A bank loan for AED250,000 and an AED50,000 government grant was also used as start-up capital. Yousef, who studied Business Management at university, insisted that the business should be properly funded at the start. He knew that small businesses that lacked funding at the start would struggle. The company rents a factory unit and leases about 80% of its plant, machinery and equipment.

Helped by the rising oil price, the company has done well since starting up. Most of the company's growth has been funded from retained profit. Ali and Yousef have been happy to retain around 90% of the profit for investment. This has avoided the need to borrow large amounts of money. However, in 2006, Ali and Yousef decided it was time to move to a larger factory. They reckoned that AED1,200,000 would be needed to move and update their technology. Half of the money would come from retained profit but the rest would have to come from other sources.

(a) Draw a pie chart to show the start-up capital of the business. **(4 marks)**

(b) What is the main advantage of using a government grant as a source of finance? **(2 marks)**

(c) Many new businesses struggle because they do not have enough capital when they start trading. How did Gulf Oil Supplies overcome this problem? **(4 marks)**

(d) What is the advantage to Ali and Yousef of funding much of the expansion from retained profit? **(4 marks)**

(e) How do you think Ali and Yousef should raise the rest of the money for the new technology? **(6 marks)**

▲ **Figure 23.2** An oil drilling platform

Role of marketing

Getting started...

Most businesses operate in competitive markets. Customers will only buy products if the products:

- meet their needs;
- are fairly priced;
- are conveniently located;
- are brought to their attention.

Businesses are aware of this and understand that to be successful their products have to be **marketed** effectively. There are different ways of doing this. Look at the examples below.

Coca-Cola

There is a huge range of choice in the global market for soft drinks. However, Coca-Cola is the most recognised brand in the world. Coca-Cola uses a number of different marketing approaches to help maintain its position as market leader.
For example:

- It has developed over 3,000 different brands such as Coke, Diet Coke, Coke Zero, Fanta, Dr Pepper, Sprite, Lilt, Powerade and Dasani.
- It spends hundreds of millions of dollars on advertising all over the world.
- It promotes its brandname by supporting sporting events. For example, Coca-Cola was one of the main sponsors of the 2008 Olympic Games in Beijing.

▲ **Figure 24.1**
A Coca-Cola production line

Nike

Some businesses use mobile phones to market their products. For example, Nike, the sports multinational, erected a large interactive billboard in Times Square, New York. Passers-by could use their mobile phones to text in their own design and receive a free pair of Nike ID trainers. After designing a trainer on the screen, the user received a text message within seconds. That message contained an image of the design. Nike gave away 3,000 pairs of shoes in this promotion. It was suggested that users were just as excited by their design on the billboard as they were by the free trainers.

Source: adapted from www.christine.net

(a) Describe the approaches used in the above examples to help sell products.

(b) How important do you think marketing is to Coca-Cola and Nike? Explain your answer.

What is marketing?

Marketing involves a range of activities that help a business to sell its products. However, marketing is not just about selling, it involves:

- identifying the needs and wants of consumers;
- designing products that meet these needs;
- understanding the threats from competitors;
- telling customers about products;
- charging the right price;
- persuading customers to buy products;
- making products available in convenient locations.

Marketing can be defined as 'a management process involved in identifying, anticipating and satisfying consumer requirements profitably'.

Satisfying customer needs

Businesses have to satisfy customer needs and wants. To do this they have to identify what consumers want. Businesses do this by carrying out *market research*. Market research is one of the most important marketing activities. It is the first step in satisfying customer needs. Market research is discussed in the next chapter.

KEY FACT

If possible, businesses need to anticipate customer needs. This means they try to predict what customers want in advance and respond to changes very quickly. Businesses have to keep up with the latest designs, trends, fashions and technology.

QUESTION 1

Catalina Gomez is the manageress of the Hotel El Prado, a 4-star hotel in Mendoza, Argentina. She is always keen to improve the hotel service and aims to exceed the expectations of guests. Catalina uses a questionnaire left in the guests' rooms to gather feedback. If guests complete the questionnaire they can collect a free gift when they check out. An extract from the questionnaire is shown in Figure 24.2.

(a) How is Hotel El Prado attempting to identify customer needs?

(b) How might the hotel use the information it gathers?

HOTEL EL PRADO – MENDOZA

Please take a moment to rate our services.
Thank you for giving us the opportunity to serve you.

	Excellent	Good	Average	Below average	Poor N/A
Menu variety	○	○	○	○	○
Value for price paid	○	○	○	○	○
Quality of service	○	○	○	○	○
Quality of food	○	○	○	○	○
Quality of beverage	○	○	○	○	○

	Excellent	Good	Average	Below average	Poor N/A
Overall, how would you rate our staff's hospitality? (friendliness, courtesy, responsiveness)	○	○	○	○	○
Overall, how would you rate our hotel's public areas?	○	○	○	○	○
Overall, how would you rate the value for the price paid?	○	○	○	○	○
Overall, how would you rate the hotel's ability to provide a relaxing atmosphere ?	○	○	○	○	○

Comments

Figure 24.2 ▶
An extract from a questionnaire used by Hotel El Prado

The marketing mix

The activities which businesses use when marketing their products are known as the **marketing mix**. The marketing mix emphasises four particular elements, often referred to as the 4Ps:

- **Product**: Businesses need to design high-quality products that meet customer needs and present them attractively.

- **Price**: Products must be priced so that customers think they are getting value for money. However, the price charged must also generate a profit for the business.

- **Promotion**: Customers must be given information about products and encouraged to buy them.

- **Place**: Products must be available in convenient locations at times when customers want to buy them.

The marketing mix is discussed further in Chapter 28.

Marketing objectives

Although the general role of marketing is to help sell products, it is possible to identify specific marketing objectives. Theses are the goals that a business is trying to achieve through its marketing. However, they may differ between organisations. Also, objectives will change according to a firm's marketing needs at the time. Examples of marketing objectives might be:

- Increase market share by 10%.

- Increase weekly sales by $10,000.

- Re-brand an existing product – this usually means giving it new name.

- Increase the number of outlets by 50.

Marketing strategies

A **marketing strategy** is a set of plans that are drawn up so that a specific marketing objective can be achieved. For example, a business may decide to target a small segment of the market. Its strategy to achieve this objective might be to:

- adapt an existing product;

- improve the packaging;

- raise the price;

- advertise in exclusive magazines;

- distribute through exclusive outlets.

Notice that the strategy involves all aspects of the marketing mix. Marketing strategies are discussed in more detail in Chapter 33.

Key terms

4Ps – product, price, promotion and place.
Marketing – identifying customer needs and satisfying them profitably.
Marketing mix – the key elements in a firm's marketing strategy, commonly known as the
Marketing strategies – a set of plans designed to achieve marketing objectives.

Chapter review – Marketing in the car industry

Many car manufacturers use focus groups. This involves inviting a small group of customers to discuss products. In a recent focus group the following ideas emerged:

- **Low maintenance car**: People said that dealerships provide bad service and cars are too complicated for consumers to repair themselves. Therefore, why not design a car that requires limited maintenance.

- **Safe car for teenagers**: Teenagers are often at risk when driving, which worries parents. Participants agreed that a sporty car should be designed that appeals to teenagers but also includes safety features. This would appeal to parents.

- **A more durable car**: Participants felt that cars were not built to last. Also, frequent design changes do not make any sense in a world of scarce resources and rising car prices. Thus, manufacturers should design and introduce 5-year or 10-year models.

Car manufacturers are one of the largest spenders on advertising. In 2007, $9.42 billion was spent on advertising cars. Figure 24.3 shows the advertising spend on different media by car makers.

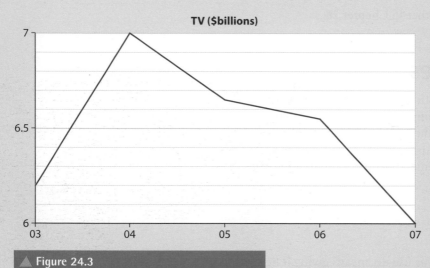

TV ($billions)

Source: GM roars forward into digital ad channels, *Advertising Age* (Halliday, J. 17 March 2008), with permission from Wright's Media

▲ Figure 24.3
Car manufacturers' expenditure on TV advertising

(a) What is the role played by marketing in business? **(2 marks)**

(b) What are focus groups used for in the car industry? **(2 marks)**

(c) Why do you think so much money is spent on advertising in the car industry? **(2 marks)**

(d) Outline one possible reason for the pattern of TV advertising shown in Figure 24.3. **(2 marks)**

(e) Using this case as an example, explain what is meant by the marketing mix. **(4 marks)**

(f) What might be a future marketing objective of the car manufacturer in this case? Explain your answer. Hint: use the information gathered from the focus group. **(8 marks)**

Chapter 25

Market research

Getting started...

One of the most important marketing activities is gathering information. Businesses have to find out what customers need and want. This will help them to design products which people will buy. Information is also needed about the market. Businesses need to find out about their competitors, what sort of people buy the product and the size of the market. Look at the example below.

Eurostar

Eurostar provides a high-speed rail service through the Channel Tunnel linking London with mainland Europe (see Figure 25.1). It employed a market research agency, Maritz Research, to carry out a survey. Maritz assessed the customer experience in the following key areas:

- the Eurostar Call Centre
- on-board Eurostar
- customer relations
- the catering facilities
- the Eurostar ticket offices
- customer relationship management
- the terminals
- frequent traveller service.

In order for Eurostar to respond quickly to problems, Maritz developed an online reporting tool. This allowed Eurostar's managers to examine customer responses to the survey. Maritz also discussed the findings with managers in workshops. This helped Eurostar to identify customer problems quickly and make immediate improvements.

▲ **Figure 25.1** A Eurostar train

Source: adapted from www.maritz.com

(a) What sort of information was gathered by Eurostar in this case?

(b) How did the information help Eurostar?

(c) Eurostar employed a market research agency to gather information. State one possible advantage and disadvantage of this approach.

Product and market orientation

In the past many businesses were **product orientated**. This meant that businesses were most concerned about the quality of their products. Their efforts concentrated on the design and manufacturing of the product itself. They then tried to persuade people to buy it. Some businesses today are still product orientated. For example, in the pharmaceuticals industry companies such as Pfizer, Bayer and AstraZeneca focus most of their attention on the development of a new drugs and medicines. They already know that a need exists.

In contrast, most firms today are **market orientated**. They are led by the market and their focus is on the customer. They do not make products until they know what people want. Market-orientated firms spend a lot of their resources on identifying, reviewing and analysing the needs of customers. As a result they attach a lot of importance to **market research**.

The uses of market research

Market research involves gathering, presenting and analysing information about the marketing and consumption of goods and services. Businesses spend money on market research because it helps to reduce the risk of failure. Products that are well researched are more likely to be successful. However, there are some specific uses of market research. Some examples are shown in Figure 25.2.

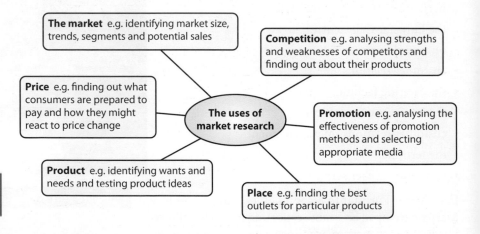

Figure 25.2 ▶
The uses of market research

Primary research

Businesses use **primary** or **field research** to gather information that does not already exist. It involves collecting new information from new sources. Primary data is usually gathered by asking questions or observing people's behaviour. The main advantage of primary research is that it is original and the information gathered can be tailored to the needs of the business. However, primary research is often time consuming and expensive. Some businesses, like Eurostar in the above example, employ a *market research agency* to carry out research. Agencies are experts in gathering, presenting and analysing information. However, they may be too expensive for many businesses.

QUESTION 1

In 2008, Wang Zhi opened the Cathay Garden, a new Chinese takeaway restaurant in Dubai. However, before he started trading he gathered information about the market for Chinese takeaway food in the city. He spent a lot of time finding out about competitors. He found out about the:

- number and location of Chinese takeaways in Dubai;
- menus and prices charged;
- opening times;
- advertising and promotions used;
- additional services offered, such as delivery;
- speed of service;
- types of customers who bought Chinese takeaways.

The information gathered by Wang Zhi was very helpful. For example, he discovered that one of the main criticisms of current restaurants was the slow speed of service. When Wang Zhi opened the Cathay Garden his speed of service was a unique selling point.

(a) Wang Zhi used primary research when gathering information about the Chinese takeaway market in Dubai. Explain what this means.

(b) Do you think Wang Zhi's business is product or market orientated?

(c) How might the research carried out by Wang Zhi benefit his new business?

Secondary research

Businesses use **secondary** or **desk research** to collect information that already exists. It has been collected by someone else and may be available for other users. The information collected may be *internal*, which means that it already exists inside the business. It may also be *external*, which means it exists outside the business. Figure 25.3 shows some different sources of secondary data.

Secondary research is quick and easy to gather. For example, internal data may be immediately available on intranets. Also, a lot of external data is available online. However, the main problem with desk research is that the data collected might not be exactly what the business needs. It may also be dated and inaccurate.

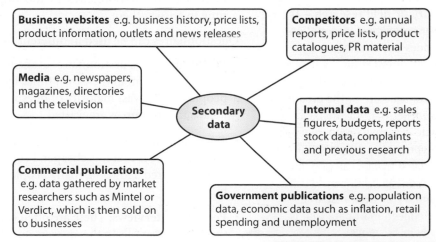

Figure 25.3
Sources of secondary data and the type of information

Sampling

Ideally, information could be gathered from every single person in a market. However, this would take too long and cost too much money. To overcome this problem businesses use a **sample** of people. A sample is a much smaller group. However, their behaviour and views must be *representative* of the whole population.

DID YOU KNOW?

Online surveys may be more sophisticated because they can use a wider range of images. They are cheaper to administer and can be made available to respondents 24/7. However, many people still ignore them.

Key terms

Consumer panels – groups of customers are asked for feedback about products over a period of time.

Market orientation – where a business focuses on the needs of consumers when developing products.

Market research – the collection, presentation and analysis of information relating to the marketing and consumption of goods and services.

Primary or field research – the gathering of 'new' information that does not already exist.

Product orientation – where a business focuses on the design and manufacture of the product itself rather than the market.

Sample – a small group of people that represents a proportion of a total market when carrying out market research.

Secondary or desk research – the collection of data that is already in existence.

There are different ways of choosing samples. The most common approach is to choose a *random sample* where every single person in a population has the same chance of being chosen. 'Picking names out of a hat' would generate a random sample. Samples may also be subdivided according to age, gender or income for example. This will help to get representation across different groups and is called a *stratified sample*.

Methods of research

Some of the main methods of gathering data are discussed briefly below.

Questionnaires A questionnaire is a list of written questions. They are very common in market research and are used to record the views and opinions of respondents. A good questionnaire will:

- Have a balance of *open* and *closed* questions. Closed questions allow respondents a limited range of responses. An example would be: 'How many times have you flown with Emirates this year?' The answers to closed questions are easier to analyse. Open questions let people say whatever they want. They do not have to choose from a list of responses. Open questions are best used if there are a large number of possible responses. An example would be: 'How would you improve the quality of service provided by Emirates?'

- Contain clear and simple questions, without jargon, poor grammar or bad spelling.

- Not contain leading questions. Leading questions are those that 'suggest' a certain answer. They should be avoided because otherwise the results will be biased.

- Be concise. If questionnaires are too long, people will not give up their time to answer them.

Questionnaires can be used in different situations:

- **Postal surveys:** Questionnaires are sent out to people and they are asked to complete them in their own time. They may be more convenient for people, but the vast majority of questionnaires are never returned. This means that resources are wasted.

- **Telephone interviews:** The main advantage of interviewing people over the telephone is that it is cheaper. People from a wide geographical area can be covered. However, many people do not like being telephoned by businesses.

- **Personal interviews:** These are often carried out in the street and the interviewer fills in the answers on a form. The advantage is that questions can be explained if a respondent is confused. It may be possible to collect more detailed information. However, many people do not like being approached in the street.

- **Online surveys:** As access to computers increases around the world, so does the use of online surveys. These are similar to postal surveys except respondents may be directed to a questionnaire – after ordering something on the Internet, for example.

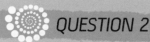

QUESTION 2

Some businesses use online surveys to gather data. This involves providing a link to a questionnaire on a company website and inviting people to complete it. An online questionnaire can be completed quickly and responses can often be analysed immediately. Survey costs are lower because there is no printing and postage. Online surveys can be interactive and may be fun to complete. They can also be accessed at any time and be completed when it is convenient. However, there are problems. The sample used may not be representative. This is because online surveys are only presented to Internet users. The views of others will be neglected even though they may be a potential customer.

Improving Staff Communication

Q3 To what extent do you agree or disagree with the following statements?

	Strongly agree	Agree	Neither agree nor disagree	Disagree	Disagree strongly	Don't know
Communication within my team is good	○	○	○	○	○	○
Communication between my team and other parts of the company are good	○	○	○	○	○	○
I feel well informed about what is happening within the company	○	○	○	○	○	○
I have a good understanding of the future direction of the company	○	○	○	○	○	○
I have attended a team meeting in the last month or so	○	○	○	○	○	○

Back   Restart   Next

Powered by **snap**

▲ **Figure 25.4**
A survey on www.snapsurveys.com

(a) Discuss the advantages and disadvantages of online surveys.

(b) Explain whether an online survey would benefit a company selling to: (i) customers in isolated areas; (ii) less developed countries such as Bangladesh, Sudan and Vanuatu.

Focus groups or consumer panels If a business wants very detailed information from customers it might use **focus groups** or **consumer panels**. A focus group is where a number of customers are invited to attend a discussion led by market researchers. The group must be representative of the whole population and be prepared to answer detailed questions. This is a relatively cost-effective method of collecting information, but the group may be a little small.

Consumer panels are similar to focus groups except that groups of customers are asked for feedback over a period of time. This approach allows businesses to see how consumers react to changes in their products.

Observation This is where market researchers 'watch' the behaviour of customers. This approach might be used in retail outlets. Observers might record the amount of time customers spend looking at particular products and displays in the store. However, because there is no feedback using this method a lot of questions go unanswered.

Test marketing This involves selling a new product in a restricted geographical area to test it before a national launch. After a period of time feedback is gathered from customers. The feedback is used to make modifications to the product before the final launch. This reduces the risk of failure.

Limitations of market research

Although carrying out market research can reduce the risk of products failing in the market, it is not entirely dependable:

• Market research data may be biased. For example, if the sample used by a business is not representative, any conclusions drawn on the basis of the sample will be inaccurate.

- Human behaviour is unpredictable. Although people may indicate their intentions in a questionnaire, what they do in reality might be quite different. People might change their minds or misunderstand the question. They might also give answers that they think the interviewers wanted to hear.

- Research technique may be poor. If questionnaires are poorly designed or interviewers have not been trained, the quality of the research carried out will be poor.

Chapter review – Manzini Safari Tours

Manzini Safari Tours supervises trips around the Mlilane Wildlife Sanctuary, located between Manzini and Mbabane in Swaziland. Animals found in the park include zebra, giraffe, antelope, crocodile, hippo and a variety of birdlife. Walking, cycling and horse riding is permitted in the reserve and there are many vehicle and walking trails. However, visitors to the park have fallen from 21,400 in 2004 to 9,400 in 2009. A survey was carried out by Manzini Safari Tours

using telephone interviews. A total of 1,000 telephone numbers were chosen at random from a list of potential customers provided by a research agency.

Figure 25.5 shows answers to five key questions from the survey and Figure 25.6 shows a selection of comments made by the people

1. Have you ever been on a Manzini Safari Tour?
   YES 7% NO 93%
2. Have you ever been on any other safari tour?
   YES 61% NO 39%
3. Would you go on a Manzini Safari Tour if it was cheaper?
   YES 44% NO 56%
4. Have you seen any adverts for the Manzini Safari Tours?
   YES 7% NO 93%
5. Would a holiday in Swaziland appeal to you?
   YES 46% NO 54%

▲ **Figure 25.5**
Answers to five questions from the survey

'The tours appear too strictly supervised.'

'There aren't any tigers in the park.'

'I've never heard of Swaziland.'

'It's too expensive – it would cost me and my family over £300 to go for the day.'

▲ **Figure 25.6**
Comments made by some of the people surveyed

(a) Explain whether the research carried out by Manzini Safari Tours is primary or secondary. **(2 marks)**

(b) Explain one advantage and one disadvantage of using telephone surveys. **(4 marks)**

(c) Using examples from the case, explain the difference between open questions and closed questions in a survey. **(4 marks)**

(d) What limitations might there be in the survey carried out by Manzini Safari Tours? **(4 marks)**

(e) Analyse the data for Manzini Safari Tours and suggest reasons why the number of visitors have fallen in recent years. **(6 marks)**

▲ **Figure 25.7** A game reserve

Chapter 26

Presenting and using market research data

Getting started...

Once market research information has been gathered, the results have to be presented and interpreted. A number of methods can be used to present information, such as graphs, charts and diagrams. These methods help to make the presentation more attractive and easier for users to interpret the information. Look at the example below.

The Indian Premier League

The Indian Premier League (IPL) is a Twenty20 cricket competition. It started in 2008 with the Rajasthan Royals beating Chennai Super Kings in the final. The tournament generated huge interest in India. Some of the world's finest cricketers such as Shane Warne, Sachin Tendulkar, Daniel Vettorri and Mahendra Dhoni played.

A feature of the IPL has been the huge amounts of money involved. The tournament was expected to generate $1.6 billion over the next five to ten years. The TV rights to broadcast the IPL were sold for US $1.026 billion.

As part of its coverage of the event an Indian newspaper carried out some market research. The newspaper wondered how much supporters in India would pay for a ticket at the final. It also wanted to know if there was much interest in England.

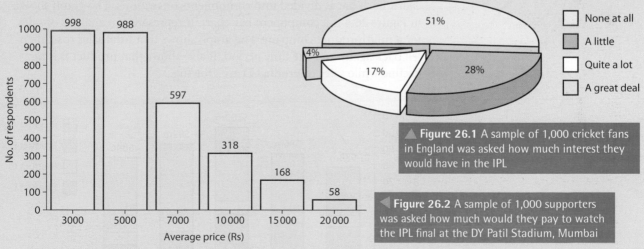

Figure 26.1 A sample of 1,000 cricket fans in England was asked how much interest they would have in the IPL

Figure 26.2 A sample of 1,000 supporters was asked how much would they pay to watch the IPL final at the DY Patil Stadium, Mumbai

(a) What might be the advantages of presenting the market research information using the methods shown in Figures 26.1 and 26.2?

(b) How might the information in Figure 26.1 be used by the BCCI (the body setting the prices for the final)?

(c) How might the information in Figure 26.2 be of interest to a TV company considering buying the rights to broadcast IPL in England?

Presenting market research data visually

Market research data is more useful if it is presented clearly and attractively. It is often better to present it visually because it:

- might be easier to understand;
- can be studied more quickly and have a bigger impact on the reader;
- might make it easier to detect trends;
- can be used to make a good impression;
- can be more concise than text.

Some examples of the different methods used to present data are outlined briefly below.

Bar charts

A **bar chart** is one of the simplest methods of presenting data. Numerical information is shown as 'bars' or 'blocks'. These can be drawn vertically or horizontally. The longer the bars, the more important the data. The bar chart in Figure 26.3 shows the responses to a question in a male lifestyle survey. It shows that style is important when men buy clothes.

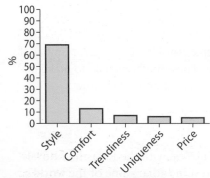

Source: adapted from uk.askmen.com

▲ **Figure 26.3**
Answers to the question 'what is the most important factor governing your clothing purchases?'

Component bar charts

A **component bar chart** shows more information than a standard bar chart. Each bar is divided into components or sections. The graph shown in Figure 26.4 is a component bar chart. It represents an analysis of sales for a multiproduct company. The graph shows that total sales rose, then fell back again over the time period. It also shows that product B is in decline while sales of product D are growing.

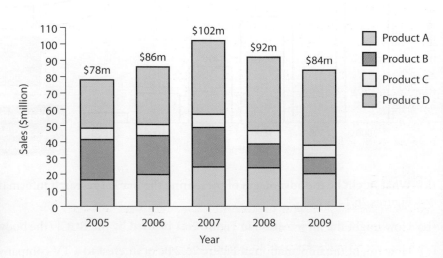

Figure 26.4 ▶
A component bar chart showing the sales of four products for a company between 2005 and 2009

114

QUESTION 1

A bus company in Egypt operates a service between Cairo and Alexandria. The owners of the business have been worried recently because passenger numbers have fallen. As a result some market research was carried out to see if there was a problem with the service. The results are shown in Figure 26.5.

(a) Construct a component bar chart to show the information in Figure 26.5.

(b) Using the information shown by the bar chart drawn in (a), discuss briefly why you think passenger numbers are falling.

2009	May	June	July	August
No. of complaints	342	359	388	432
Complaint type:				
Bus fares	48%	51%	49%	53%
Bus frequency	29%	31%	31%	30%
Punctuality	12%	10%	11%	10%
Overcrowding	11%	8%	9%	7%

▲ **Figure 26.5**
The number and nature of passenger complaints for an Egyptian bus service

Pie chart

In a **pie chart** all the data is represented by a circle. The circle is divided into segments. Each segment (or piece of pie) represents part of the total data. The pie chart in Figure 26.6 shows the market shares enjoyed by supermarkets in the UK – clearly Tesco has the largest share.

The easiest way to draw a pie chart is to use a computer program such as Microsoft Excel. The main advantage of pie charts is that readers get an immediate impression of the various parts. They can also be used to make comparisons in different time periods.

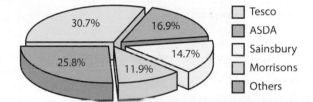

▲ **Figure 26.6**
Market shares in the UK supermarket industry

Line graphs

Line graphs are common in business. They show the relationship between two variables. One set is shown on the vertical axis and the other on the horizontal axis. The values of the variables can be joined by straight lines or a smooth curve. The line graph in Figure 26.7 shows the relationship between sales levels and the amount spent on advertising by a business. The graph shows clearly that sales rise as the business spends more on advertising. The advantage of this type of graph is that readers can see quickly the relationship between two variables.

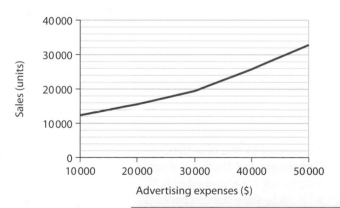

▲ **Figure 26.7**
The relationship between sales and advertising expenditure for a business

Tables

Tables are used to present many forms of data. They may be used:
• if data contains both numbers and words;
• where several variables need to be shown at the same time;
• where detailed data need to be shown.

115

Criteria	US	Europe	Australia	Middle East	South America
Fuel economy	3.4	6.8	5.6	2.3	5.6
Style	5.1	6.1	5.7	6.3	5.4
Power	6.7	7.6	5.6	6.7	5.3
Reliability	7.7	7.9	7.1	6.9	6.1
Price	7.8	8.9	9.1	7.8	8.3
Safety record	8.9	8.9	9.8	9.1	7.1

Figure 26.8 ▶
Car survey results

Figure 26.8 contains a table of results from a survey. In each region 1,000 people were asked what was important to them when buying a car. For each criteria respondents had to give a score out of 10. In the table the average scores are given for each criteria in each region. For example, in Australia the most important feature when buying a car was safety. At 9.8 this was the highest rated criteria. In the Middle East, the least important feature was fuel economy at 2.3 – probably because fuel is so cheap.

 QUESTION 2

Figure 26.9 shows some market share information for internet search engines.

(a) Construct a pie chart using the data in Figure 26.9.

(b) What does the pie chart show about the market for search engines?

(c) State one advantage of using pie charts to represent data.

Search engine	Per cent
Google	72.4
Yahoo	17.8
MSN/live	6.6
Ask	2.3
AOL	0.9

Source: adapted from blog.compete.com

▲ **Figure 26.9**
Search engine market shares – February 2009

Key terms

Bar chart – a chart where numerical information is represented by blocks or bars.
Component bar chart – a chart where each bar is divided into sections to show the components of a total.
Line graph – a line that shows a link between two sets of variables.
Pie chart – a circular chart where segments represent the data.
Trends – patterns in data.

Using market research data

Market research data can by used in a number of ways.

Trends Market researchers may look for **trends**. Trends are patterns that might occur in data. For example, a restaurant owner looking at annual sales data might notice that sales in the fourth weekend of every month drop by 23%. This might be because people are running out of money before they get paid again. After noticing the trend, the owner might take measures to boost sales in this fourth weekend.

Decision making One of the main reasons why market research data is gathered is to help businesses make decisions. For example, the information in Figure 26.1 might help the BCCI to decide what price to charge for the IPL final in Mumbai. The BCCI might decide to charge an average price of Rs5,000. This is because at Rs7,000 the number of supporters who would buy a ticket falls sharply.

Recommendations Market research data may be used to draw conclusions and make recommendations. For example, a business using a variety of different advertising media might carry out some research to find out how effective they are. As a result, researchers might recommend that the business switches spending from radio adverts to online advertising.

Chapter review – Tourism in India

India has been a popular destination with tourists for a number of years. The country is rich in culture, has attractive coastal and mountain scenery and is populated by very friendly people. Some data relating to the Indian tourist industry is shown in Figures 26.11 and 26.12.

	2001	2002	2003	2004	2005	2006	2007
Tourists	2,282,738	2,073,025	2,726,214	3,457,477	3,918,610	4,447,167	4,977,193

▲ **Figure 26.11** The total number of tourists entering India 2001–2007

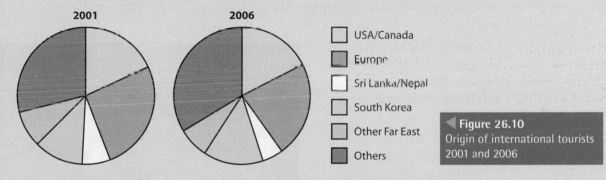

2001   **2006**

- ☐ USA/Canada
- ◩ Europe
- ☐ Sri Lanka/Nepal
- ☐ South Korea
- ☐ Other Far East
- ◩ Others

◀ **Figure 26.10**
Origin of international tourists 2001 and 2006

Source: adapted from www.itopc.org/travel-requisite/inbound-tourism-statistics.html

(a) (i) Draw a line graph to show the data in Figure 26.11. (3 marks)
   (ii) State one advantage of using line graphs to present data. (1 mark)

(b) Outline two other ways a business might use market research data. (4 marks)

(c) Discuss how the information in Figures 26.11 and 26.12 might be helpful to businesses in the Indian tourist industry. (6 marks)

(d) What are the advantages of using visual methods to present market research data? (6 marks)

Chapter 27

Market segmentation

Getting started...

One reason for market research is to gather information about customers. If businesses have detailed information about customer needs, they can target their products at different customer groups more effectively. Some businesses produce several products that are targeted at different customer groups. Look at the example below.

Etihad Airways

Etihad Airways was set up in 2004. Like most other airlines it provides services for different customer groups. For example, a return flight from Dubai to Mumbai in September 2009 offered three different services:

- **Coral Economy (Price = AED1,775):** This services offers spacious seats, the best entertainment and a very warm welcome from in-flight hosts.

- **Pearl Business (Price = AED3,025):** This business class service offers a comfortable 73-inch bed. Each self-contained seat is equipped with individual lighting and a reading lamp. There's also a built-in massage facility.

- **Diamond First (Price = AED5,495):** This is a luxury service. Each suite has its own wardrobe as well as a 23-inch wide-screen LCD TV. Meals are served on an extra large wood finished table.

Source: adapted from www.etihadairways.com

(a) Describe the different groups of customers targeted by Etihad in this example.

(b) How might Etihad benefit from offering three different services?

▲ **Figure 27.1**
First-class seating

What is meant by market segmentation?

Markets can be divided into different sections or **segments**. Each segment is made up of consumers that have similar needs. Businesses recognise this and target particular market segments with their products.

- Some businesses concentrate on producing one product for one particular segment. For example, Rolls-Royce, which produces luxury cars, targets a very wealthy market segment in the car market.

- Some businesses produce a range of different products and target them at several different segments. In the above example, Etihad targets three different market segments with its different classes of airline service.

- Some businesses aim their products at nearly all consumers. For example, large food manufacturers such as Heinz are likely to target their brands at everyone.

However, by dividing markets into segments businesses can more easily supply products that meet customers' needs.

Methods of market segmentation

Geographic segmentation Different customer groups are likely to have different needs depending on where they live. For example, groups living in very hot climates such as the Middle East will have different needs from groups living in temperate climates such as Germany. There might also be differences between groups living in different parts of the same country. For example, in India different regions have slightly different tastes in cuisine.

Demographic segmentation It is common for businesses to divide markets according the age, gender, income, social class, ethnicity or religion of the population:

- **Age**: Infants, teenagers, young adults and the over 65s are all likely to have different needs because of their age. Quite a lot of products are targeted to different consumer groups on the grounds of age. For example, clothes are produced in different sizes and styles for people in different age groups.

- **Gender**: Males and females are likely to be targeted by businesses with different products. For example, producers of clothes, cars, magazines, toiletries and drinks target different products to different genders.

- **Income**: Incomes in most countries vary considerably. As a result businesses target products at certain income groups. For example, Rolex the luxury watchmaker, targets its products at very high income groups. In contrast, Lidl, the low-cost European supermarket chain, targets lower income groups.

- **Social class**: Businesses pay a lot of attention to different **socio-economic groups**. Such groups are usually based on occupations. These can be used by businesses to target products.

- **Ethnicity**: Many countries in the world are becoming more cosmopolitan. This means that people from different ethnic groups are likely to live in the same country. This is important for businesses because different ethnic groups are likely to have different needs as a result of their different cultures. For example, in Canada, where there are over 200 different ethnic groups, Chinese consumers are likely to spend more on leather goods, furniture, appliances and electronic equipment.

- **Religion**: Different religious groups often have different tastes. For example, Muslims do not eat pork or drink alcohol. In the US the market for Kosher food is thought to be worth $100 billion.

DID YOU KNOW?

It is suggested that people in the A and B groups are more likely to use the Internet. So, businesses that want to target these groups might use online advertising.

Other methods of segmentation Some businesses group customers according to how they purchase products. Some customers are *repeat customers*. They are loyal and keep returning. A business might target such a group in a different way from other customers. For example, supermarkets offer regular customers loyalty cards that entitle them to discounts. Some customer groups use products or services at different times of the day. For example, commuters often use transport at 'peak' times. These might be targeted differently from those who travel 'off peak'.

Benefits of market segmentation

Generally a business is more able to meet the needs of different customer groups if the market is segmented. However, some specific advantages include the following.

- Businesses that produce different products for different market segments can increase revenue. In the above example, Etihad was able to charge first-class passengers more than double that of the economy passengers for the same flight. This helped to increase revenue.

- Customers may be more loyal to a business that provides products that are tailored specifically to them.

- Businesses may avoid wasting promotional resources by targeting products at customers that do not want them.

- Some businesses can market a wider range of goods to different customer groups.

Mass and niche markets

Some businesses sell their products to *mass markets*. This is when a business sells the same products to all consumers and markets them in the same way. Fast-moving consumer goods such as crisps, breakfast cereals, McDonald's and Coca-Cola are sold in mass markets. The number of customers in these markets is huge. This means that businesses can produce large quantities at a lower unit cost by exploiting economies of scale (see Chapter 36). This might result in higher sales and higher profits. However, there is often a lot of competition in mass markets and therefore businesses often spend a lot of money marketing these products.

A *niche market* is a small market segment – a segment that has sometimes gone 'untouched' by larger businesses. Niche marketing is the complete opposite of mass marketing. It involves selling to a small customer group, sometimes with specific needs. Small firms can often survive by supplying niche markets because they can avoid competition. It is also a lot easier to focus on the needs of the customer in a niche market.

Key terms

Market segment – part of a whole market where a particular customer group has similar characteristics.
Socio-economic groups – division of people according to social class.

QUESTION 1

Nomads is an online clothing retailer. It produces quality clothing from a variety of designs including Celtic, tie dye, ethnic and hippy. All of its products use fair trade materials and suppliers who both give and receive a fair rate of pay.

Source: adapted from www.nomadsclothing.com/pages/help.htm#1

(a) Using this case as an example, explain what is meant by a niche market.

(b) Outline two advantages of serving a niche market.

Chapter review – Toyota

Toyota is the largest auto manufacturer in the world. It currently produces 14 models in many different countries. In 2008, the company sold 8.97million vehicles. Four of Toyota's models are described below.

- **Prius $27,700*:** The Toyota Prius has become the byword for eco-conscious driving. It is a hybrid car, which means that it runs on both electricity and petrol. It is considered environmentally friendly because it does not use much petrol. It has very low CO_2 emissions. Many car manufacturers are launching hybrids, but Toyota was the first.

- **Hiace $24,500*:** The Hiace is a commercial vehicle. It has a strong load capacity and a space-efficient cargo area. The Hiace is said to deliver functionality, driveability and comfort. Its powerful engine supports an impressive workload while maintaining good economy.

- **AYGO $13,500*:** The AYGO is small, low-priced and described by Toyota as the ultimate city car. It is nimble, easy to handle and made for narrow gaps and tight parking. It is also very economical – achieving over 60 miles per gallon (mpg).

- **Land Cruiser $48,900*:** The Land Cruiser is described as a Sports Utility Vehicle (SUV). It can be driven 'off-road' and is said to offer premium levels of comfort. Toyota claim that the Land Cruiser has led the way in 4 × 4 technology for more than 50 years.

Source: adapted from www.toyota.co.uk

(a) Describe the types of customer (market segment) that Toyota is likely to target with the vehicles described here. **(4 marks)**

(b) Do you think any of these products are likely to be targeted at particular: **(i)** geographical areas; **(ii)** income groups? Explain your answer. **(4 marks)**

(c) Do you think Toyota relies on mass marketing or niche marketing? Explain your answer. **(4 marks)**

(d) Analyse the benefits to Toyota of market segmentation. **(8 marks)**

*Prices are approximate.

Chapter 28

The marketing mix

Getting started...

Businesses use marketing to help sell their products. However, marketing involves using a number of activities or approaches to encourage people to buy products. Look at the examples below.

Sony

After months of rumours and anticipation, Sony slashed the price of the PlayStation 3 by $100 in hopes of boosting sales ahead of the important holiday season. Sony said it would cut the price of the 80 gigabyte (GB) PlayStation 3, to $299. Sony also cut the price of its existing 160 GB PlayStation 3 by $100, to $399. All price cuts apply worldwide. When the Sony PlayStation 3 was launched in 2006 it cost around $600.

Source: adapted from finance.yahoo.com

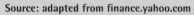
Figure 28.1 A Sony PlayStation 3

LG (Egypt)

LG is a multinational based in South Korea employing around 177,000 people. It produces electronic goods, chemicals and provides telecommunications services. An advert designed to look like a new TV program, using the TV model name as the series name, Scarlet, was used in Egypt to promote the company and a new range of high definition (HD) TVs.

Source: adapted from eg.lge.com

McDonald's (India)

McDonald's is a world famous burger chain. In 1996, the first McDonald's was opened in India – Delhi. However, in order to appeal to Indian consumers around 75% of the menu items had to be 'Indianised'. Some of the products on the Indian menu include McVeggie, McAloo Tikki, Paneer Salsa Wrap and Veg McCurry.

(a) Describe the marketing methods used in the above examples to help sell the products.

What is meant by the marketing mix?

A good marketing strategy is one that meets customers' needs. This means that a business must:

- design and produce high-quality *products*;
- charge a *price* that is acceptable to consumers;
- let consumers know about products through *promotion*;
- make products available in the right *place* at the right time.

This is called the **marketing mix** and often referred to as the 4Ps. To achieve marketing objectives a business must find the right balance or mix between product, price, promotion and place.

Product Products have to fulfil or exceed customer expectations. Products have certain features that businesses must get right:

- **Functional**: This means that products must perform the function for which they were bought. For example, a waterproof anorak must keep the rain out.

- **Appearance**: Products should look good. The shape, size and colour of products must be appealing to consumers. For some products such as jewellery, fashion items and cars this is vitally important.

- **Unique selling point (USP)**: Products will be more successful if they have a USP. This means that the product has a particular characteristic that makes it different from those of rivals.

- **Product life cycle**: Many products have a limited life. During that life sales will rise and then fall. A business will need to modify products or create new ones when they decline.

The importance of each of these features will vary according to the nature of the product. For example, a garage selling petrol does not have to consider the appearance of the product because it is never seen. The product is discussed in Chapter 29.

Price Consumers want value for money. This means that the price charged is important. The price charged by a business depends on a number of factors. These include:

- the quality of the product;

- the costs of production;

- the prices charged by competitors;

- how much consumers are prepared to pay.

Businesses can choose from a number of *pricing strategies* when setting the price of products. These are discussed in Chapter 30.

Promotion Businesses have to make sure that consumers know about their products. This means they have to provide consumers with information. This may include details about the nature and range of products, the prices charged and where products can be purchased. Businesses might also try to persuade people to buy their products. Businesses do this by promoting their products. Promotion is discussed in Chapter 32.

Place Part of the marketing mix involves the distribution of products to customers. Products must be made available in convenient locations at times when consumers want to buy them. Businesses can use a number of different distribution channels. For example, some manufacturers choose to sell their products using retailers such as supermarkets or wholesalers. However, others try to sell their products directly to consumers using mail order. Distribution is discussed in Chapter 31.

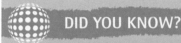

DID YOU KNOW?

Head and Shoulders shampoo is meant to remove dandruff. The removal of dandruff is the product's USP.

Choosing the right mix

Businesses have to find the right balance between product, price, promotion and place. In some markets price is the most important element. For example, supermarkets often emphasise the prices they charge. Some supermarkets display the prices charged by rivals for some lines in their stores. This is to show that competitors are more expensive. The marketing mix may be influenced by the following:

- **Nature of the product**: For example, firms selling technical products might emphasise the quality and reliability of their products rather than price or place.

- **Competition**: In highly competitive markets price is likely to be very important.

- **Marketing budget**: Firms with more resources can spend more on promotion.

- **Competitors' mix**: Businesses often copy the marketing activities of competitors.

- **Technology**: For example, an increasing number of businesses are advertising and selling online.

- **Market research**: Some market research is designed to assess the effectiveness of a firm's marketing activities. If a survey suggests that consumers are responding well to a particular promotion, a business will make more use of that promotion.

Key terms

Marketing mix – the elements of a firm's marketing that are designed to meet the needs of customers. Often called the 4Ps, they are product, price, promotion and place.

Chapter review – Ryanair

Ryanair is an Irish, low cost airline with bases at Dublin and Stansted Airports. It is the third-largest airline in Europe in terms of passenger numbers. Details of its marketing mix are shown in Figure 28.3.

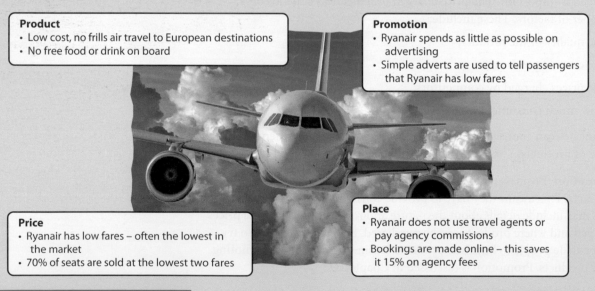

Product
- Low cost, no frills air travel to European destinations
- No free food or drink on board

Promotion
- Ryanair spends as little as possible on advertising
- Simple adverts are used to tell passengers that Ryanair has low fares

Price
- Ryanair has low fares – often the lowest in the market
- 70% of seats are sold at the lowest two fares

Place
- Ryanair does not use travel agents or pay agency commissions
- Bookings are made online – this saves it 15% on agency fees

▲ **Figure 28.3** Ryanair's marketing mix

Source: adapted from www.marketingteacher.com/case_study/ryanair_case_study.html

(a) Use this case as an example to explain what is meant by the marketing mix. (4 marks)

(b) Describe the product being sold by Ryanair. (2 marks)

(c) Ryanair sells tickets online. Outline the advantages of this approach. (4 marks)

(d) Explain two factors that are likely to affect the marketing mix chosen by a business. (4 marks)

(e) Which element of the marketing mix do you think is most important to Ryanair? Explain your answer. (6 marks)

Chapter 29

The product

Getting started...

The goods or services sold by a business have to be designed, named and packaged. Products also have to modified, improved and possibly replaced. This is because some products have a limited life cycle. Look at the example below.

Golf GTI

The Golf GTI is produced by Volkswagen, the German-based multinational car manufacturer. It was launched in 1975 and has sold 1.7 million. The Mk l GTI was unveiled at the Frankfurt Motor Show. The powerful hatchback could hit 60 mph in 9 seconds. Designed with the emphasis on fun, it had a tartan trim and an iconic golf ball gearshift.

The model has been updated several times since then. For example, in 2009 the New Golf GTI won the 'Best Compact Family Car' and the 'Best Hot Hatch' awards at the Auto Express New Car Awards. Testers complimented the sharp handling, impressive refinement and excellent comfort that make the latest Golf the best yet.

Source: adapted from www.seriouswheels.com

▲ **Figure 29.1** The Volkswagen Golf GTI

(a) What is the name of the product in the example?

(b) What is the length of the product's life cycle to date?

(c) Describe some of the measures taken by Volkswagen to extend the life of the Golf GTI.

(d) Do you think the Golf GTI will ever be withdrawn from the market?

Product design

Ideas for new products may come from business owners, customers, competitors, staff and *research and development* (R&D). Most products go through a design process that might involve a number of stages such as:

• producing a *design specification* (a precise description of what is needed);

• suggesting alternative solutions;

• selecting a particular solution;

- testing the product;
- modifying the product and then launching.

Market research data might be used to ensure that product designs meet the needs of customers. Some businesses use special *computer aided design (CAD)* programs to speed up the design process and improve the quality of designs. The Golf GTI, in the above example was designed by Volkswagen's chief designer Walter de'Silva. Figure 29.2 shows some important design features that might be considered by a business when designing new products.

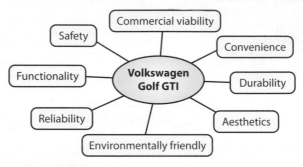

Figure 29.2 ▶
Important design features

Branding

Many businesses give their products a name. In the above example the Volkswagen car was called a Golf GTI. Names like these are called **brandnames**. A brand might be the name of a product, a product group or the business. Some brandnames are very well known and worth a great deal of money. For example, the Coca-Cola brandname is worth around $70 billion.

Branding is used to:
- differentiate the product;
- create customer loyalty;
- develop an image;
- raise prices when the image becomes strong.

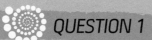 QUESTION 1

Google is a search engine and widely recognised worldwide. In 2009, it was suggested that the Google brand was worth around $100 billion. In the last two years the value of shares, property, pensions and other assets have fallen because of the global recession. However, the value of many brandnames has continued to rise. Figure 29.3 shows the top 10 brands in the world.

(a) Using an example from this case, explain what is meant by a brandname.

(b) Explain three reasons why businesses use brandnames.

Brand	Brand Value 09 ($M)
Google	100,000
Microsoft	76,300
Coca-Cola	67,600
IBM	66,600
McDonald's	66,600
Apple	63,100
China Mobile	61,300
General Electric	59,800
Vodafone	53,700
Marlboro	49,500

▲ **Figure 29.3** Top ten world brands

Packaging

One aspect of the product is its packaging. Businesses should consider packaging carefully. This is because consumers often link the quality of packaging with the quality of the product itself. With some products such as perfume, confectionery and make-up, packaging is vital because it says so much about the product. It also helps people to recognise it when placed next to rival products. Figure 29.4 summarises the factors that may be considered when a business designs its packaging.

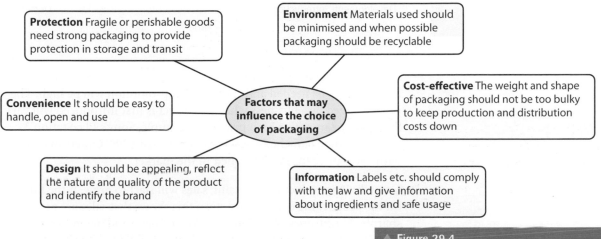

Figure 29.4
Factors that may influence the choice of packaging

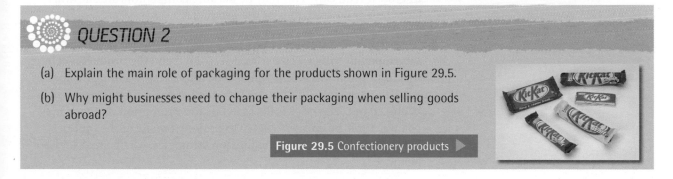

QUESTION 2

(a) Explain the main role of packaging for the products shown in Figure 29.5.

(b) Why might businesses need to change their packaging when selling goods abroad?

Figure 29.5 Confectionery products ▶

Product life cycle

Marketing may be more effective if businesses understand the **product life cycle**. This shows the level of sales at the different stages through which a product passes over time. Figure 29.6 shows that a product might pass through five stages over its life:

1. **Development**: During the development stage sales are zero. This is because the product is being researched, designed and tested. It is not yet on the market. This may be an anxious time for businesses because many products do not make it beyond this stage. Consequently, money invested in product development is lost. Development costs are also high and can damage the cash flow of a business.

2. **Introduction**: Businesses often introduce new products with an official *launch*. There may be a presentation or a party to give a new product a

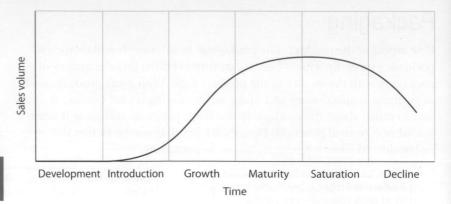

Figure 29.6 ▶
The product life cycle

lift when it is launched. Costs will continue to be high. New production facilities may be needed and spending on promotion will be high. The price charged by a business when a product is first introduced will vary. Some may start with a high price. For example, Sony's PlayStation 3 was $600 when launched in 2006. It is now just $299. Others may start with a low price to get established in the market.

3. **Growth**: If a product is successful, sales will start to grow. If the line on the product life cycle is very steep this shows that sales are growing sharply. The business will now get some revenue and begin to recover the costs of development. Costs are likely to fall and the product may start to make a profit. Towards the end of this stage sales may start to grow less quickly. This may be because competitors are starting to launch their own versions of the product.

4. **Maturity and saturation**: Eventually sales will start to level off. Development costs will have been recovered and the product will be making a profit. Cash flow will also be improving. As more businesses enter the market it will become saturated and some businesses will be forced out. The price is likely to fall and promotion methods may change. Some businesses will try to prolong the life of the product before it declines. They use **extension strategies**, which are discussed below.

5. **Decline**: Sales of many products decline and they are eventually withdrawn. This is because consumer tastes change, new technology emerges or new products appear in the market. Where possible a business will replace declining products with a new ones. In the above example, the Golf was introduced to replace the Volkswagen Beetle, which was withdrawn from the market (although the Beetle was reintroduced at a later date). Examples of products that are on the decline include typewriters, cheques and faxes.

Extension strategies

Extension strategies, which prolong the life of a product before it starts to decline, are popular with businesses. This is because the costs of product development are high and extension strategies help a product to generate more cash. Examples of extension strategies include:

- Finding new markets for the product – selling abroad for example.

- Finding new uses for a product – such as Ralph Lauren extending its Polo brand for clothes into towels and bedding.

- Modifying the product – in the above example, Volkswagen did this several times with the Golf GTI.

- Developing the product range – like a crisp manufacturer bringing out new flavours.

- Changing the appearance or packaging – like Coca-Cola selling coke in cans, glass bottles and different-sized plastic bottles.

- Encouraging more frequent use of the product – like Kellogg's persuading people to eat cornflakes for supper as well as for breakfast.

Key terms

Brandname – the name of a product that consumers see as being different from those of rivals.

Extension strategies – methods used to prolong the life of a product.

Product life cycle – the level of sales at the different stages through which a product passes over time.

Chapter review – GlaxoSmithKline

GlaxoSmithKline (GSK) is a pharmaceuticals company. One of the features of this industry is the huge amount of money spent researching and developing new products. For example, in 2008, GSK spent around £3.7 billion on R&D. The discovery and development of a new product can take many years. This is because drugs have to go through lengthy clinical trials to ensure that they are safe. However, companies can get patents that allow them to market a product for up to 20 years without any competition. This means that once a new drug is launched sales grow quickly and can remain high until the patent runs out. A product life cycle for a pharmaceutical product might look like the one shown in Figure 29.7.

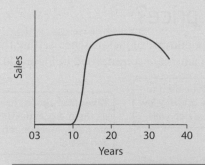

▲ **Figure 29.7**
Product life cycle for a pharmaceutical product

One of GSK's successful products is Requip. It is used to treat Parkinson's disease and was launched in 1997. After the initial growth stage, sales remained steady for many years. However, a new use for Requip was found by targeting the drug at another illness, the 'restless legs syndrome' (RLS). After this, the brand experienced strong growth. Sales of Requip grew from £120 million in 2004 to £268 million in 2007.

Source: adapted from www.icmrindia.org

(a) Use this case to explain what is meant by a product life cycle. **(2 marks)**

(b) Explain briefly why the development stage is so long for products in the pharmaceuticals industry. **(2 marks)**

(c) Explain why the prices of pharmaceutical products are likely to be high in the introductory and growth stages of the product life cycle. **(2 marks)**

(d) In what way will the packaging of products be important to GSK? **(2 marks)**

(e) Why do businesses use extension strategies? **(4 marks)**

(f) Comment on the nature and success of GSK's extension strategy in this case. **(6 marks)**

Chapter 30

Price

Getting started...

Setting the price of a product is a vital marketing decision. If the price is set too high, customers may not buy the product. On the other hand, if it is too low, this might suggest that the product is of a poor quality. The business might also struggle to make a profit. Businesses can use a number of methods to set their prices. Look at the examples below.

Dell Computers

When Dell Computers launched their personal computers the price was set lower than those of competitors. They were able to do this because their costs were lower. With a lower price Dell was able to penetrate the market effectively. For example, when Dell broke into the Chinese market in 2007, the price of PCs was set between 2,599 yuan to 3,999 yuan. The prices of rival PCs were around 5,000 yuan.

▲ **Figure 30.1** A Dell PC

Sanjay Stores

Sanjay runs a general store in Mylapore, Chennai. He uses a very simple method to calculate the prices of all products sold in the shop. He adds 20% to the cost of buying them in. So for example, a product that cost him Rs100 from a supplier is sold for Rs120 (100 + 20% × 100).

(a) Explain how the prices are set in the above examples.

(b) Outline one possible advantage of using the pricing method in each case.

What factors affect price?

Businesses have to take into account a number of factors when setting the price of products. Some of the important factors are summarised in Figure 30.2.

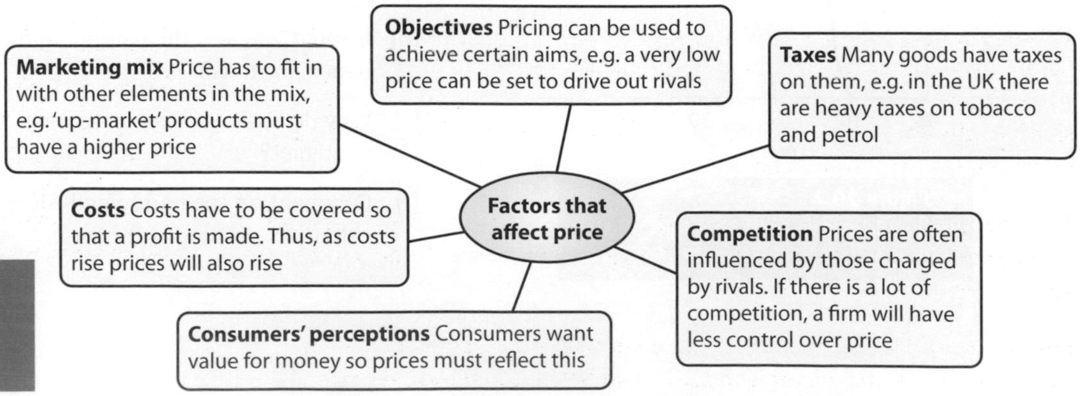

Objectives Pricing can be used to achieve certain aims, e.g. a very low price can be set to drive out rivals

Taxes Many goods have taxes on them, e.g. in the UK there are heavy taxes on tobacco and petrol

Marketing mix Price has to fit in with other elements in the mix, e.g. 'up-market' products must have a higher price

Costs Costs have to be covered so that a profit is made. Thus, as costs rise prices will also rise

Factors that affect price

Competition Prices are often influenced by those charged by rivals. If there is a lot of competition, a firm will have less control over price

Consumers' perceptions Consumers want value for money so prices must reflect this

Figure 30.2 ▶ Factors that affect the prices charged by a business

Pricing methods

Businesses can choose from a range of different methods when setting the prices.

Cost-based pricing

Businesses have to set prices that generate a profit. One method that ensures all costs are covered is **cost plus** or **cost-based pricing**. It is simple and involves adding a **mark-up** to total costs. For example, the cost to a manufacturer of making a bicycle is $60. The manufacturer adds a mark-up of 25% to get the price. Therefore the price of the bicycle is $75 ($60 + 25% × $60). This method is common with retailers. However, one of the drawbacks of this method is that it ignores market conditions. For example, the $75 price set by the cycle manufacturer may be far too high in relation to the prices of other bicycles in the market. This might result in low sales.

Market-orientated pricing

One of the drawbacks with cost plus pricing is that it completely ignores conditions in the market. **Market-orientated pricing** involves setting the price of a product after looking at market conditions. There are several pricing strategies that adopt this approach:

Skimming or creaming Some businesses may launch a product into a market charging a high price for a limited time period. This is called *skimming* or *creaming*. The main aim is to generate high levels of revenue with a new product before competitors arrive.

Pharmaceuticals companies also use this method. They sell new drugs for high prices when they are first launched. However, when patents run out competition emerges and prices fall. Charging a high price initially helps such companies recover high development costs.

Penetration pricing Sometimes a business will introduce a new product and charge a low price for a limited period. This is called *penetration pricing*. The aim of this strategy is to get a foothold in the market. Businesses using this strategy hope that customers are attracted by the low price, and then carry on buying it when the price rises.

Psychological pricing One common method is to set the price slightly below a round figure – charging $99.99 instead of $100. This is called *psychological pricing*. Consumers are 'tricked' into thinking that $99.99 is significantly cheaper than $100. Of course it is not, but this psychological effect often works for businesses.

Loss leaders Some products are sold at a low price below cost. These are called **loss leaders**. The aim of this strategy is to draw customers into a store where they will buy the loss leader.

Discounts and sales Businesses often cut prices for a short period of time. They have *sales* where goods are sold below the standard price.

Key terms

Competition based pricing – where prices are influenced by rivals' prices.

Cost plus or cost-based pricing – adding a mark-up to the costs of producing a product to get the price.

Loss leader – a product sold below cost to draw in customers.

Market orientated pricing – where prices are based upon the conditions in the market.

Mark-up – the percentage added to costs that makes a profit.

Price elastic demand – where a price change will result in a significant change in demand.

Price elasticity of demand – measures the responsiveness of demand to a change in price.

Price inelastic demand – where a price change will result in much smaller change in demand.

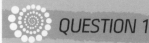
SmithKline Beecham (now GlaxoSmithKline (GSK)) introduced an anti-ulcer drug in 1978. The drug, called Tagamet, was priced at $10 per unit in the US. By 1990 the price came down to less than $2 and by 1994 it had fallen to 60 cents. Tagamet lost its patent protection in the US in 1995. As a result, other producers launched their versions of the drug onto the American market. Today a unit of Tagamet can be purchased for 29 cents.

(a) What pricing strategy is being used by GSK for its product Tagamet?

(b) Why did the price come down so sharply in 1994?

(c) What was the main advantage of this pricing strategy to GSK?

Competition-based pricing

Some businesses take a very close look at what their rivals are charging when setting their prices. This approach is called **competition-based pricing** and is likely to be used by businesses operating in a fiercely competitive market. One approach is to charge the same price as competitors. The advantage of this strategy is that a price war is likely to be avoided. It is considered to be a safe pricing strategy. Another approach is for the market leader to set the price and all others follow. This is called *price leadership*.

Sometimes a business might lower its price to drive out competition. This is called *destroyer* or *predatory pricing*. In 2008 Amazon.com, the online book retailer, was accused of predatory pricing in France where it was selling books without charging for shipping.

Eduardo Urondo runs a busy coffee shop in the centre of Rosario, Argentina. However, in 2009 a multinational coffee chain opened a branch directly opposite Eduardo's shop. The thing that upset Eduardo the most was the pricing policy of the new rival. The prices charged by the multinational were around half of what Eduardo was charging. Naturally, customers started to drift away. Eduardo said 'I know what will happen. Eventually I will be forced out of business. And then when I'm gone their prices will rise. I can't win. The multinational has huge resources and can afford to trade at a loss until I leave the market.'

(a) Explain the pricing strategy being used by the multinational.

(b) How can the new rival afford to trade at a loss?

Price elasticity of demand

The prices charged by businesses will also be affected by **price elasticity of demand**. Price elasticity of demand measures how responsive demand is to price changes. Most goods fall into one of two categories:

- **Goods with price elastic demand**: The demand for most products is **price elastic**. This means that a price change will result in a significant change in demand for the product. For example, if a business lowered the price by 10%, demand would rise by a greater proportion, say, 20%. Goods that have price elastic demand tend to be non-essentials or those with lots of substitutes. Businesses that sell goods with price elastic demand can increase total revenue by lowering the price. However, if they raise the price, demand and revenue will fall because customers can easily switch to other brands.

- **Goods with price inelastic demand**: For a minority of goods demand is **price inelastic**. This means that a price change will have little impact on the amount demanded. For example, if a business lowered the price by 10%, demand might only increase by 3%. Goods that have price inelastic demand tend to be essential goods or goods with very few substitutes. Tobacco and petrol are examples. If a business sells goods with price inelastic demand, revenue can be increased if prices are increased. However, a price cut will result in lower revenue because demand will not increase significantly after a price cut.

Chapter review – The Sharjah Tile Centre

The Sharjah Tile Centre is located in Industrial Area 2 in Sharjah, UAE. The business, which is owned by Faris Mubarak, has done very well recently. Tile sales in the UAE market exceeded €393.2 million in 2008, representing a 29% increase from the previous year. The outlet sells wall and floor tiles for a wide range of applications. To ensure that the business returns a profit Faris Mubarak uses cost plus pricing. He adds 50% to the cost of tiles that he buys direct from manufacturers. The Sharjah Tile centre serves both residential and trade customers.

(a) (i) Using this case as an example, explain what is meant by cost plus pricing. (2 marks)

(ii) Calculate the price Faris would charge for a pack of ceramic tiles costing AFD30. (4 marks)

(iii) Explain advantages and disadvantages of cost plus pricing. (4 marks)

(b) What is meant by competition-based pricing? (2 marks)

(c) (i) The products sold by The Sharjah Tile Centre have price elastic demand. What does this mean? (4 marks)

(ii) What is likely to happen to demand and revenue from sales if Faris lowers prices in his store? Explain your answer. (4 marks)

Chapter 31

Distribution channels

Getting started...

One important activity in the marketing mix is making sure that products are in the right place at the right time. Consumers are more likely to buy products if they are available in convenient locations. Businesses can distribute their products using a number of methods. Look at the examples below.

Mars

Mars is a worldwide manufacturer of confectionery, pet food and other food products. It had sales of $21 billion in 2008. The company is most famous for brands such as Mars Bar, Snickers, Skittles, Twix and Milky Way. Products such as these are sold in as many outlets as possible. They can be bought in newsagents, sweet shops, supermarkets, petrol stations, bars, cinemas, sports venues and vending machines.

▲ **Figure 31.1** Mars products

Loot Online

Loot Online Ltd is an online retailer serving the residents of South Africa. It began trading in 2003 and has been growing steadily ever since. At first Loot sold only books but added DVDs, games and music to the site in 2005. Loot's product range includes over 1.5 million different books and thousands of CDs, DVDs and games.

Source: adapted from www.loot.co.za/shop/welcome

(a) Explain the methods of distribution used in the above examples.

(b) State two advantages to Mars of selling goods through vending machines.

(c) Is Mars likely to use the Internet to distribute confectionery? Explain your answer.

What is place?

Place is one of the 4Ps in the marketing mix. It refers to the location where people can buy products. If products are not available in convenient locations, consumers may not have the time to search for them. For example, if motorway service stations were located two or three miles from the motorway, they may struggle to survive. Also, food producers in the UK would have limited sales if they did not make groceries available in supermarkets.

Distribution channels

The route taken by a product from the producer to the customer is called a **distribution channel**. Businesses can choose from a number of different distribution channels. Some of the main ones used for consumer goods are shown in Figure 31.2. One approach is to sell goods directly to consumers, but others involve using *intermediaries* such as retailers and wholesalers. These are businesses that provide links between producers and consumers. Figure 31.2 shows that some producers may use more than one channel of distribution.

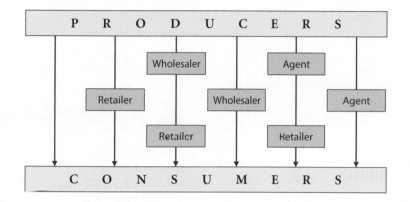

Figure 31.2
Distribution channels for consumer goods

Direct selling

Some producers market their products directly to consumers. **Direct selling** can take a number of forms. These are summarised in Figure 31.3.

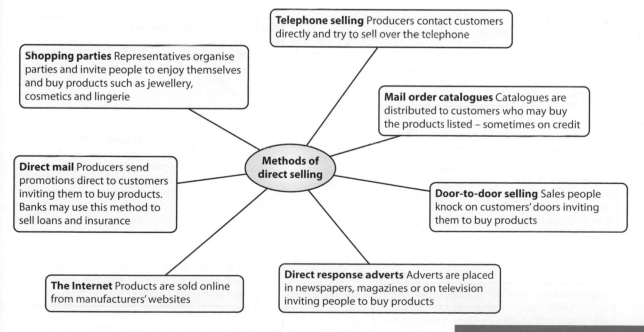

Figure 31.3
Methods of direct selling

QUESTION 1

Dove Chocolate Discoveries sells chocolate products direct to customers. The company, owned by Mars, sells at shopping parties organised by chocolatiers. At the parties, guests learn about chocolate while sampling the products. According to the company's president, there is a growing interest in chocolate. People can learn where chocolate is grown, how it is harvested and other interesting facts. At the end of the party they may have a fun quiz that tests what they have learned. Chocolate prizes are given to the winners.

Chocolatiers learn about the business from their kits. These contain a training manual and a DVD showing a sample party and the basics of hostess coaching. Dove provides further training and support through conference calls, as well as face-to-face meetings.

Source: adapted from www.dovechocolate.com

(a) Using this case as an example, explain what is meant by direct selling.

(b) Outline the advantages to Dove Chocolate Discoveries of direct selling.

(c) State four other methods of direct selling.

Retailing

Figure 31.4 shows that most distribution channels use **retailers**. These are businesses that buy goods and sell them straight to consumers.

▼ **Figure 31.4** Types of retailer

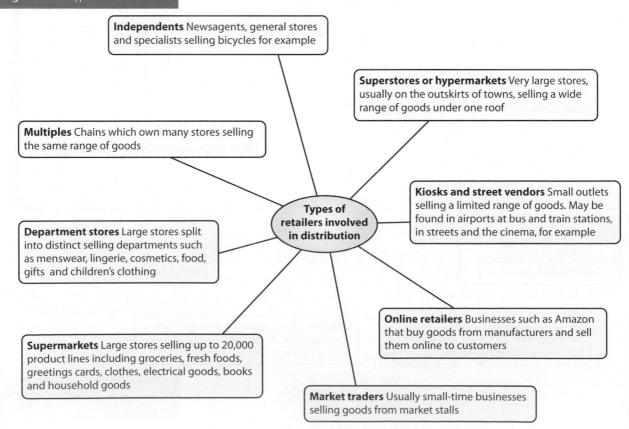

Wholesaling

Some producers use **wholesalers** to help distribute goods. Wholesalers usually buy from manufacturers and sell to retailers. Some wholesalers are called *cash-and-carries*. This is because customers come to the store, buy goods, pay cash and take goods away with them. Wholesalers may break bulk, repack goods, redistribute smaller quantities, store goods and provide delivery services. A wholesaler stocks goods produced by many manufacturers. Therefore retailers get to select from a wide range of merchandise.

Agents or brokers

The role of **agents** or **brokers** is to link buyers and sellers. They are used in a variety of markets. For example, travel agents sell holidays and flights for holiday companies, airlines and tour operators. Estate agents sell properties on behalf of vendors. Agents are also used to sell insurance, life assurance and other financial products. Manufacturers may also use agents when exporting. Agents can reduce the risk of selling overseas. This is because they have knowledge of the country and the market.

QUESTION 2

The use of online selling is growing rapidly all over the world. Shopping online is particularly favoured by those who:

- live in rural and isolated locations;
- do not have the time to go shopping;
- dislike going to shops;
- have mobility problems.

Online shopping can be cheaper because business costs are lower. It can be done 24/7 and there is generally a lot of choice. People can also shop from different locations such as at work, at home or travelling on a train. All they need is access to the Internet. Figure 31.5 shows the pattern of online retail spending in the US between 2001 and 2008.

Category	Online retail spending ($bn)				
	2001	2005	2006	2007	2008 (proj)
Computer hardware and software	11.0	18.1	21.2	24.1	26.7
Consumer electronics	1.5	4.7	6.8	8.4	10.0
Books, music and videos	3.8	7.5	9.0	9.8	11.1
Tickets	1.8	4.6	5.5	6.3	6.8
Consumer health	0.4	2.6	3.4	4.2	5.3
Apparel, accessories, footwear and jewellry	4.7	14.0	19.1	23.2	27.1
Grocery and pet food	0.8	4.1	5.6	7.4	9.1
Toys and video games	1.0	2.9	4.1	5.2	5.9
Sporting goods	0.7	2.0	2.3	2.5	2.8
Flowers and speciality gifts	1.2	3.1	3.9	4.3	4.9
Home	1.8	10.0	15.0	18.8	22.7
Office products	0.6	3.2	4.1	4.7	5.1
Other	1.8	6.7	8.1	9.1	10.1
Total	**31.0**	**83.6**	**108.1**	**128.1**	**147.6**

Source: adapted from www.census.gov/compendia/statab/tables/09s1016.pdf

▲ **Figure 31.5**
Online retail spending 2001 to 2007 and 2008 projections

(a) Outline two advantages to producers of selling online.

(b) Calculate the percentage increase in total online spending between 2001 and 2008.

(c) Briefly account for the pattern in (b).

(d) Which products are the most popular with online shoppers?

Choosing appropriate distribution channels

The nature of the product Different types of products may require different distribution channels. Some examples are given below:

* Most services are sold directly to consumers. It would not be appropriate for window cleaners, gardeners and hairdressers, for example, to use intermediaries.

* Fast moving consumer goods like breakfast cereals, confectionery, crisps and toilet paper cannot be sold directly by manufacturers to consumers. Wholesalers and retailers play an important role in the distribution of these goods because they break bulk.

* Businesses producing high quality 'exclusive' products such as perfume and designer clothes will choose their outlets very carefully. The image of their products is important so they are not likely to use supermarkets, for example.

* Some products need explanation or demonstration. For example, technical products or complex financial products might need to be sold by expert sales people. These products are likely to be sold by specialists.

Cost Businesses will choose the cheapest distribution channels. They will also prefer direct channels. This is because each time an intermediary is used they will take a share of the profit. Large supermarkets will try to buy direct from manufacturers. This is because they can bulk buy and get lower prices. Independents are more likely to buy from wholesalers. They have to charge higher prices as a result. Many producers now sell direct to consumers from their websites. This helps to keep costs down.

The market Producers selling to mass markets are likely to use intermediaries. In contrast, businesses targeting smaller markets are more likely to target customers directly. For example, a building contractor in a small town will deal directly with customers. Producers selling in overseas markets are likely to use agents because they know the market better. Businesses selling goods to other businesses are likely to use more direct channels.

Control For some producers it is important to have complete control over distribution. For example, producers of exclusive products do not want to see them being sold in 'down market' outlets. This might damage their image. Some products, such as heating systems, require expert installation to comply with health and safety legislation. Producers of such products might prefer to handle installation themselves and deal directly with customers. They can ensure safe installation more easily.

Key terms

Agent or broker – an intermediary that brings together buyers and sellers.
Direct selling – where producers sell their products directly to consumers.
Distribution channel – the route taken by a product from the producer to the customer.
Retailer – a business that buys goods from manufacturers and wholesalers and sells them in small quantities to consumers.
Wholesaler – a business that buys goods from manufacturers and sells them in smaller quantities to retailers.

Chapter review – Distribution channels

Banking services

Figure 31.6 A bank ▶

Electricity

▲ **Figure 31.7**
A power station

Agricultural goods

▲ **Figure 31.8**
A farm

(a) Look at Figures 31.6 to 31.8. What distribution channels might be used by these producers? Explain your answer. **(6 marks)**

(b) Outline the main disadvantage to farmers of using an intermediary to help distribute produce. **(2 marks)**

(c) Explain why banks are making increased use of online services. **(4 marks)**

(d) Explain why a producer selling overseas might use an agent. **(4 marks)**

(e) Analyse two factors that a producer is likely to take into account when choosing an appropriate distribution channel. **(4 marks)**

Chapter 32

Promotion

Getting started...

Businesses have to make consumers aware of their products. They have to give them details about the features of the products, their prices and where they can be purchased. However, many businesses go further than this. They use a variety of methods to encourage people to buy their products. Look at the examples below.

Supermarkets

One of the methods used by supermarkets to keep customers informed is to distribute leaflets to people's homes (see Figure 32.1). These leaflets are generally used to promote the latest special offers available in the stores.

▲ **Figure 32.1** Supermarket leaflet

La Villa Des Orangers

La Villa Des Orangers is a luxury hotel located in Marrakech, Morocco (see Figure 32.2). The hotel is a palace in the style of a classic riad: an exquisite home built around a courtyard. The 5-star property is visually stunning. The hotel has its own website that is used to promote the Villa.

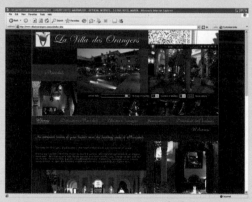

◄ **Figure 32.2** The Villa Des Orangers website

Source: adapted from www.villadesorangers.com/uk/navigation.php

Greenhouse Bonanza

Greenhouse Bonanza sells a range of garden products such as greenhouses, greenhouse accessories, cold frames, fencing, bird tables, nest boxes, trellis and plant racks. One of the methods the business uses to promote its products is placing adverts in magazines. The advert in Figure 32.3 appeared in a gardening magazine.

(a) Describe the methods used by these businesses to promote their products.

(b) Which of these businesses is most likely to use TV advertising?

(c) How is Greenhouse Bonanza targeting customers?

Figure 32.3 Greenhouse Bonanza advert ▶

Greenhouse **BONANZA**
Factory Direct Greenhouses
10 x 12 Highline Package £450

Offer features
- Aluminium Finish
- Roof Vents x4
- Auto Openers x4
- Louvre
- Eaves Height 6ft 1ins

0897 2634 278 (24/7)
www.greenhouses4sale.co.uk
Greenhouse Bonanza
Tweed Industrial Estate
Suite B33, BE14 4GF

What is promotion?

Businesses have to communicate with their customers. They use two different methods of promotion to draw attention to their products.

- **Above-the-line promotion**: This approach is to advertise in the media. Advertising in newspapers and magazines, advertising on the television and the radio and banner adverts on websites are all examples.
- **Below-the-line promotion**: This is any form of promotion that does not involve using the media. Examples might include, point-of-sale displays, merchandising, coupons and direct mailing.

What are the aims of promotion?

Generally, businesses use promotion to obtain and retain customers. However, promotion is likely to be used to achieve some specific aims:

- Tell consumers about a new product.
- Remind customers about an existing product.
- Reach a widely dispersed target audience.
- Reassure customers about products.
- Show consumers that rival products are not as good.
- Improve or develop the image of the business.

Above-the-line promotion

Above-the-line promotion involves **advertising** in the media. Businesses pay television companies or newspapers, for example, to have their adverts broadcast or printed. Figure 32.4 shows the advantages and disadvantages of the main media.

▼ **Figure 32.4**
The advantages and disadvantages of the main media

Media	Advantages	Disadvantages
Television	Huge audiences can be reached The use of products can be demonstrated Creative adverts can have great impact Scope for targeting groups with digital TV	Very expensive Message may be short lived Some viewers avoid TV adverts Delay between seeing adverts and shopping
Newspapers and magazines	National and local coverage Reader can refer back Adverts can be linked to articles and features Scope for targeting with specialist magazines Relatively cheap	No movement or sound Individual adverts may be lost in a sea of adverts Rivals' products may be advertised as well
Radio	Sound can be used Minority audiences allow targeting Cheap production Can target youngsters	Not visual May be ignored May lack impact Can be intrusive when listening
Posters and billboards	Can produce national campaigns Seen repeatedly Good for short sharp messages Large posters can have big impact	Posters can get damaged by vandals Only limited information can be shown Difficult to evaluate effectiveness
Internet	Can be updated regularly Can be targeted Hits and response can be measured Cheap and easy to set up	Some adverts such as pop-up adverts are irritating Possible technical problems

QUESTION 1

The amount of money spent on advertising is huge. For example, in the US around 2% of GDP is spent on above-the-line promotion every year. Between 1997 and 2007 the amount spent on total advertising media rose from $187,529 million to $279,612 million. An analysis of the expenditure is shown in Figure 32.5.

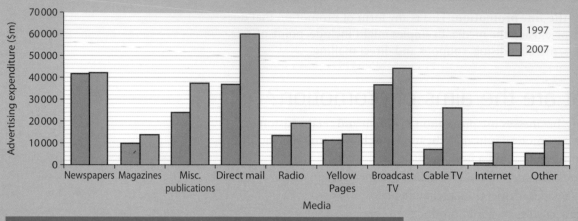

▲ **Figure 32.5** US advertising expenditure by media 1997 and 2007 ($million)

(a) Explain what is meant by above-the-line promotion.

(b) Outline the key changes in advertising expenditure shown by Figure 32.5.

Below-the-line promotion

Below-the-line promotion is usually designed and produced by a business 'in-house'. It refers to any form of promotion that does not involve advertising. There is a huge range of promotions that might be used.

Sales promotions These are incentives to encourage people to buy products. They are used to boost sales in the hope that if new customers are attracted they will continue to buy the product. Sales promotions include:

• free gifts;

• coupons;

• loyalty cards;

• competitions;

• money off deals.

DID YOU KNOW?

Sales promotions are popular. They might be used to break into a new market or encourage new customers to try the product. They may also be used to reward loyal customers and allow businesses to measure the impact of promotion (by counting the number of returned coupons, for example).

Public relations Some businesses communicate with stakeholders using public relations (PR). The main purpose of PR is to increase sales by improving the image of the business. A number of approaches might be used to attract publicity:

- press releases;
- press conferences;
- sponsorship;
- charitable donations.

The main advantage of PR to businesses is that it is often a cheap method of promotion.

Merchandising and packaging Some businesses may arrange the point of sale so that it is attractive and likely to encourage sales. This is called *merchandising*. Some examples are:

- product layout in a store;
- display material;
- well stocked shelves.

Direct mailing This is where certain types of businesses send leaflets or letters to households. Figures 32.1 and 32.3 are examples.

Direct selling or personal selling This might involve a sales rep calling at households or businesses hoping to sell products. It could also be a telephone call from a call centre where an 'army' of sales staff are employed to sell over the telephone.

Exhibitions and trade fairs Some businesses attend trade fairs or exhibitions to promote their products. Businesses set up a stall and promote their products face-to-face.

▲ **Figure 32.6** A trade fair

Gifts India 2009 is India's largest trade fair for corporate and personal gifts. It claims to be the number one marketing vehicle for business in Indian and international markets. Around 20,000 visitors are expected to attend representing distributors, catalogue houses, gift buyers and many other commercial buyers. Exhibits at the trade fair will include gift wrapping, souvenirs, handicrafts, promotional toys and jewellery.

Source: adapted from www.biztradeshows.com/gifts-india/

(a) Using this case as an example, explain what is meant by a trade fair.

(b) Discuss the advantages to a Chinese toy manufacturer of attending Gifts India.

Key terms

Above-the-line promotion – placing adverts using the media.

Advertising – communication between a business and its customers where images are placed in the media to encourage the purchase of products.

Below-the-line promotion – any promotion that does not involve using the media.

Merchandising – Arranging the layout of products in a store so that it is stimulating and engaging to encourage people to buy.

Sponsorship – making a financial contribution to an event in return for publicity.

Choosing methods of promotion

Many businesses use a range of different promotional methods. However, they must be coordinated so that they support each other. Small businesses often have limited resources so careful consideration is needed when choosing a method of promotion. What affects the choice of promotion?

- **Cost**: Many businesses are forced to use cheaper promotions because advertising on TV and in national newspapers is too dear.

- **Market type**: Local businesses often rely on adverts in local newspapers and the *Yellow Pages* business telephone directory. In contrast, businesses aiming their products at mass markets are more likely to use TV and national newspapers or specialist magazines.

- **Product type**: Certain products are better suited to certain methods of promotion. For example, car manufacturers are not likely to use sales promotions such as coupons, BOGOF deals or loyalty cards. Indeed, their favoured method is TV advertising. Similarly, supermarkets are unlikely to use personal selling.

- **Stage in the product life cycle**: It is common for promotional methods to change as a product gets older. For example, PR is often used at the beginning, but when the product matures other methods will be used.

- **Competitors' promotions**: It is common for businesses to copy the method of promotion used by a rival. Once one business comes up with a successful promotion, others soon bring out their own versions.

- **Legal factors**: In many countries legislation designed to protect consumers can affect the method and style of promotion. For example, in the EU tobacco products cannot be advertised on the TV.

Chapter review – UEFA Champions League

The UEFA Champions League is one of the most famous football tournaments in the world. It is contested every season by Europe's top football clubs such as Real Madrid, Barcelona, Inter Milan, Manchester United and Chelsea. The tournament is sponsored by multinationals including Ford, Sony, UniCredit, Mastercard, Adidas and Heineken. Each sponsor is allocated four advertising boards around the perimeter of the pitch. They get logo placement at pre- and post-match interviews and free tickets. They also get priority on TV adverts during matches to give them maximum exposure.

Source: adapted from BMRB Sport/TGI Sport+ survey 2008

(a) Using this case as an example, explain what is meant by sponsorship. **(2 marks)**

(b) Outline the advantages to the sponsors of their involvement in the UEFA Champions league. **(4 marks)**

(c) State two other methods of PR that businesses might use to promote their products. **(2 marks)**

(d) (i) What does the graph in Figure 32.7 show? **(2 marks)**

   (ii) Explain how the graph in Figure 32.7 might be helpful to the sponsors of the UEFA Champions League? **(4 marks)**

(e) Discuss the factors that might influence the choice of promotion for a company like Ford. **(6 marks)**

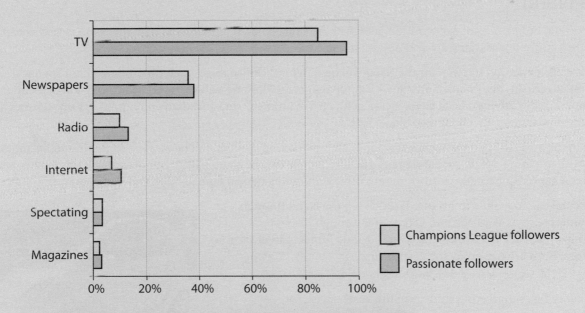

▲ **Figure 32.7**
Percentage of followers using each medium to follow the Champions League

Chapter 33

Marketing strategy

Getting started...

Businesses are likely to spend time making careful plans when marketing products. Once they have identified a specific marketing objective, they need to plan a course of action designed to achieve that objective. This will involve using different elements in the marketing mix. Look at the example below.

Tata Nano

In 2009, Tata, India's biggest car producer launched the Tata Nano. At a price of $2,421, the Nano is very cheap. It is also fuel-efficient, averaging around 92 mpg in the city.

Tata's overall marketing strategy for the Nano will be different. Unlike most small cars, Tata will not spend much on advertising the Nano. Nor will a TV campaign be used. Nano will be advertised through articles in newspapers, radio adverts, messages or ticker news on TV, online games and chatrooms, pop-ups on websites and Nano conversation on Facebook and blogspaces.

People in the advertising industry say that the Nano's marketing strategy will be creative so that Nano becomes linked with anything 'small, cute and brief'. The idea is to make the Nano part of our everyday language like 'see you after a nano'. It's a totally word-of-mouth campaign,' said a person familiar with the Nano marketing strategy.

To make the car accessible to people, Tata will sell the Nano through retail outlets such as Westside and Croma and through its own dealerships. Westside is a lifestyle retail brand and Croma is an electronic megastore. Both are owned by the Tata Group.

Source: adapted from www.businessweek.com and www.examiner.com

(a) What is Tata's marketing strategy in this case?

(b) Identify elements in the marketing mix (4Ps) used in the launch of the Tata Nano.

(c) What is the marketing objective in this case?

▲ **Figure 33.1** The Tata Nano

What is a marketing strategy?

A marketing strategy is a set of plans that aim to achieve a specific marketing objective. For example, a local car rental company might aim to become the market leader in the region. Its strategy to achieve this objective might be to:

• improve the quality of customer service by delivering cars to people's homes;

• contact all previous customers offering them a half-price deal;

- offer a three-day weekend rental for the price of two days;

- invest $5,000 in a local newspaper advert;

- donate a vehicle to a local community group to get some PR;

- set up a website to promote the business and take online bookings.

This strategy involves all aspects of the marketing mix and a number of different promotional methods.

Different businesses are likely to have different marketing strategies. This is because different products require different approaches. For example, the way healthcare and confectionery are marketed is likely to be different. However, businesses in the same industry may also have different marketing strategies. Also, small businesses will use different approaches from multinationals because they have fewer resources.

Using the marketing mix to influence consumer spending

The way in which elements in the marketing mix might be emphasised are outlined below.

Product In some markets the product sold by all competitors is very similar or exactly the same – in the petrol industry for example. If this is the case, other elements in the marketing mix, such as promotion, become much more important. However, in other markets the features of a product are crucial.

Price Price is important if there is a lot of competition. For example, when demand is elastic, a business can increase sales and revenue by lowering price. Businesses can charge higher prices if they can persuade customers that their product is of a superior quality. For example, Ferrari charges very high prices because their sports cars are perceived as very high quality. In markets where businesses copy the prices charged by rivals other elements in the marketing mix become important.

Promotion There are many ways in which businesses can promote products. Promotion is important for fast-moving consumer goods and in markets where prices are very similar. In other markets there may be very little promotion.

Place For most services place will be an important element in the marketing mix. This is because services have to be delivered direct to the customer. Businesses offering services must be prepared to locate conveniently close to customers. More and more businesses are taking their services into customer homes.

An increasing number of goods can be marketed using the Internet. The growth in online marketing has been huge in recent years. Most goods that we buy can now be bought online. Therefore, the role of place is changing.

 DID YOU KNOW?

Manufacturers of aircraft engines would not attach too much importance to promotion. Their marketing strategies are more likely to rely on the quality of the product and the price.

 DID YOU KNOW?

Most takeaway restaurants deliver meals to homes. Personal trainers, tutors, hairdressers, car rentals, financial advisors, garden designers and DVD rentals are examples of services that might be provided direct to customer homes.

Virgin Active is a chain of health clubs in South Africa, Italy, Spain, Australia and the UK. In 2007, it became one of the first companies to adopt a new marketing concept. The idea involved printing a miniature, removable magazine on a bottle. Virgin Active's on-bottle magazine was called *Move*. It featured competitions, celebrity fitness trends, fitness tips, special offers and discounts. The water bottles were given away to the public in the UK, in August 2007.

In 2009, Virgin Active ran its first brand campaign. It used the slogan 'More pleasure. Less pain'. The £1 million outdoor, radio and print strategy reflected a move away from the price-led sales campaigns often used by gyms. The adverts feature people wearing vibrant red clothing – Virgin's brand colour. Virgin Active claimed that it was the biggest outdoor drive to have been run by a health club. It is also considering a move to TV.

Source: adapted from www.marketingmagazine.co.uk

▲ **Figure 33.2** One of the Virgin Active adverts

(a) Outline briefly the role played by (i) promotion; (ii) price in the marketing of Virgin Active.

(b) Why do you think Virgin Active changed its method of promotion between 2007 and 2009?

The marketing mix and the product life cycle

The marketing strategies used by businesses are likely to change over the life of a product. The reason for this is because the marketing objectives change. Look at the examples below.

Launch strategies When a product is first launched, the main objective is to penetrate the market. This involves raising consumer awareness and getting them to try the product. Different businesses might do this in different ways:

- A new clothes boutique might have a launch party at the shop. It may provide refreshments, invite local dignitaries and potential customers and offer some products at a discount.

- A boat manufacturer might launch a new design at a boat show. It may rely on PR and interest from buyers at the show to get established.

- Producers of technical products often charge high prices when they are first launched. For example, when Apple launched its new iPhone in 2007 it was priced at $599. Three months later the price was reduced to $399.

Growth Once sales start to grow, the amount spent on marketing may fall. This is because marketing expenditure is high when a product is first launched. During the growth stage promotion may be designed to reassure customers that have bought the product. Or it may aim to encourage repeat purchases. When competitors join the market businesses may have to adjust their marketing strategies. For example, they may have to lower prices and take into account the marketing strategies used by rivals.

Maturity Once competitors have entered the market, marketing strategies are likely to change again. More and more attention will be paid to rivals' marketing activities. A business may start to consider new markets and other methods of promotion.

Extension strategies When a business thinks that a product is about to decline it may introduce extension strategies. This is likely to require a new marketing strategy and increased marketing expenditure. For example, the product may be modified or repackaged. Or the existing product may be launched in new markets.

QUESTION 2

Fresh Living was launched in 2007 on behalf of the South African supermarket chain Pick 'n Pay. The magazine is aimed at women who shop for their families. It had a circulation of 48,012 between July and September 2008. It contains features about everyday family food and recipes for entertaining. It also has information about seasonal food and health topics. At the same time it promotes food and other products sold at Pick 'n Pay. The magazine is cheap at R9.95 and contains R100 worth of discount vouchers.

Source: adapted from www.marketingmix.co.za/pebble. asp?relid=4441

(a) What is the target market for *Fresh Living*?

(b) Briefly describe the marketing strategy used when the magazine was launched.

(c) How might the marketing strategies change if the magazine becomes established?

▲ **Figure 33.3** *Fresh Living* magazine

Chapter review – Nokia

Nokia is the biggest manufacturer of mobile phone handsets in the world with a 46% market share. Some of its new mobiles include the BlackBerry and Apple's iPhone. How does it stay market leader? Will Harris, UK marketing director at Nokia, says what's important is to look after customers rather than worry about the competition. This year, Nokia has been focusing its marketing activities on games, maps and music (see Figure 33.4).

Source: adapted from www.utalkmarketing.com

(a) What is important to the success of Nokia? **(2 marks)**

(b) What was the aim of Nokia's online films? **(2 marks)**

(c) Why do you think social media campaigns are important to Nokia? **(6 marks)**

(d) Discuss which elements of the marketing mix are most important to Nokia. **(10 marks)**

In a TV campaign, Nokia promoted its 6220 handset. The advert featured a group of people creating a massive hand-drawn map, which appears to fill New York's Central Park. Harris said: 'We are concentrating our marketing on small things that work, like just doing a really creative TV campaign – that's where the ad world is going – you have to do less, well.'

An online campaign was used to raise awareness of its new maps service which uses GPS navigation to find places such as restaurants and cash machines. Five online films were used to promote the service on Nokia's website, a strategy Harris says 'is about doing less marketing channels better – rather than fitting one campaign across several different channels'.

Banner adverts on Facebook were used to recruit 200 people to show Nokia owners how to use the applications on their handsets. The campaign was so successful they had to stop recruiting. 'That social media campaign cost pennies compared to a TV campaign and yet the results were staggering', said Harris.

Harris also says that sponsorships are important. Consumers need to see a link between what their favourite brands put their names to. Nokia sponsored the Royal Parks half marathon in London in 2009. It aimed to communicate Nokia's guided maps product – free on all Nokia handsets.

▲ **Figure 33.4**
Nokia's recent marketing activities

Chapter 34

Resources and production

Getting started...

Businesses use a range of resources to make goods or deliver services. Examples include raw materials, components, buildings, energy, tools, equipment, machinery and people. Businesses will try to make the best use of these resources to reduce costs and improve efficiency. Look at the resources used by the business below.

JCB

JCB is one of the world's top manufacturers of construction equipment. The company employs around 7,000 people on four continents and sells products in 150 countries. JCB has a reputation for innovation and high quality products. It has some of the finest engineering facilities across the globe (see Figure 34.1). It produces a range of over 300 machines and has a reputation for high-quality customer service.

(a) Identify four resources that are likely to be used by JCB.

(b) How might JCB improve the efficiency of its workers?

Figure 34.1
An engineering facility

What is production?

Production involves converting resources into goods or services. These goods and services are provided to satisfy the needs and wants of people. Some examples of production might be:

• a baker using flour, yeast, salt and water to make bread;

• a large manufacturer using people to assemble components to make laptop computers;

• a dentist using surgical instruments to extract a diseased tooth;

• a taxi driver using a car to transport a family from their home to an airport.

All of these examples involve using resources to produce goods or provide services. These resources are called the **four factors of production**. They are summarised in Figure 34.2.

Land Businesses will need a 'plot of land' on which to locate their premises. For example, a large supermarket may need several acres of land on the outskirts of a town to locate a large store with car parking facilities. However, land also includes natural resources such as coal, oil, iron ore, rainwater, forests, rivers and fertile soil.

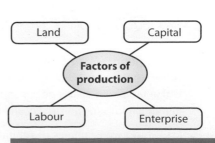

Figure 34.2
The four factors of production

- Some land resources are *non-renewable*. This means that once they have been used they cannot be replaced. Examples include coal, oil, diamonds and gold.

- *Renewable* land resources are those like fish, forests and water that are replaced by nature. These resources should not run out. However, there is a risk that if some of them are not protected they could disappear.

Labour The workforce in the economy is the **labour**. Manual workers, skilled workers and managers are all part of a nation's workforce. The quality of individual workers will vary considerably. Each worker is unique, possessing a different set of abilities, characteristics, skills, knowledge, intelligence and emotions.

Capital Capital is often said to be an artificial resource because it is made by labour. There are two types of capital.

- **Working capital** or **circulating capital** refers to stocks of raw materials and components that will be used up in production. It also includes stocks of finished goods that are waiting to be sold.

- **Fixed capital** refers to the factories, offices, shops, machines, tools, equipment and furniture used in production. It is fixed because it will not be converted into a final product. Fixed capital is used in production to convert working capital into goods and services.

Enterprise The people who set up and run businesses are **entrepreneurs**. Without them production would not take place. What is the role of entrepreneurs?

- They come up with a *business idea*. This might involve the production of a completely new product. However, most new businesses supply goods or services that are currently produced by others.

- They are business *owners*. They usually provide some money to help set up a business and are responsible for its direction.

- Entrepreneurs are *risk-takers*. For example, they risk their own money in the venture. If the business collapses, they may lose some or all of the money. However, if the business is successful they may make a lot of profit. But when they start up they do not know what will happen – they are taking a risk.

- Entrepreneurs are responsible for *organising* resources. They have to buy and hire resources such as raw materials, tools, equipment and labour. Entrepreneurs need to use skills such as decision making, people management, time management and financial judgment to organise resources effectively.

 QUESTION 1

Alonso Cortez set up a small bus company to provide an express passenger transport service from Madrid city centre to the airport. He invested €20,000 in the venture and recruited two drivers to help him out. He spent €10,000 on a 50-seater coach and rented a small office in the bus station. He also purchased a computer, mobile phones for his drivers and some office furniture.

(a) State two examples of capital that Alonso Cortez will use.

(b) Explain why Alonso Cortez is an entrepreneur.

Combining the factors of production

Businesses have to manage resources effectively. They have to choose a suitable combination of materials, tools, equipment, machinery and labour for production. Some businesses use **labour-intensive** production. This means that they use relatively more labour than capital. Labour-intensive production is common in Far Eastern countries such as China where labour is cheap. In contrast, some businesses use **capital-intensive** production methods. This means that production relies more on the use of plant and machinery.

Productivity

Businesses will want to use their resources as efficiently as possible. Output can be increased if **productivity** is raised. Productivity is the amount of output that can be produced with a given quantity of resources. It is common to measure the productivity of specific resources. For example, a business may measure labour productivity. This is output per worker. It can be calculated by:

$$\text{Labour productivity} = \frac{\text{Total output}}{\text{No. of workers}}$$

An example involving the calculation of labour productivity is shown in Figure 34.3.

A factory producing racing cycles employed 20 workers in 2008 During the year a total of 12,000 cycles were produced. In 2009 four more workers were employed and total production rose to 15,000. What has happened to labour productivity over the two years?

2008 Labour productivity $= \dfrac{12,000}{20} = 600$ cycles per worker

2009 Labour productivity $= \dfrac{15,000}{24} = 625$ cycles per worker

Over the two years labour productivity has increased at the cycle factory from 600 cycles per worker to 625 cycles per worker.

Figure 34.3
Calculating labour productivity

Increasing productivity

Businesses try to increase productivity because they will lower costs and make more profit. Productivity may be increased by firms in a number of ways.

Specialisation One feature of modern business is **specialisation**. This is the production of a limited range of goods by an individual, business, region or nation. For example, Coca-Cola specialises in soft drinks, Toyota makes cars and Emirates provides air travel. Specialisation inside a business is also common. Departments specialise in different activities such as marketing, production, finance, personnel and purchasing.

Division of labour Workers also specialise in certain tasks and skills. This is called the **division of labour**. It allows people to concentrate on a limited range of tasks. For example, in construction an architect will draw up plans, a bricklayer will build walls, a roofer will lay the roof, and so on. The division of labour will increase productivity because:

- workers concentrate on the task that they do best;
- workers' skills improve as they continually repeat the same task;
- time is saved because workers are not switching from one task to another;
- the organisation of production is easier.

Although specialisation is likely to improve productivity, it does have drawbacks. For example, work can become tedious and boring because of repetition. Also, when one stage of production depends on another, there may be delays if one stage breaks down.

Other factors that increase productivity

Productivity in a business can be increased in a number of ways:

- **Education and training:** The government can help improve the quality of labour by investing in education. This might involve providing more equipment for schools or improving the quality of teaching. Firms can also improve the productivity of their workers by providing their own training.

- **Improve the motivation of workers:** If people are motivated at work they will be more productive. Firms might use financial incentives such as piece rates (see Chapter 51). Workers who are not motivated by money may respond to other incentives. For example, job rotation might be introduced. This involves an employee changing jobs from

---

QUESTION 2

Dublin Construction Company is based in Ireland. It has 37 employees, eight of whom are general labourers. The remainder are skilled workers. Details of three are outlined below:

- **Brendan O'Hagan** is 26 years old and has worked for the company since leaving school. He is a bricklayer and learnt his trade from one of the experienced bricklayers in the company.

- **Mary O'Mara** is 27 years old and has only just started working for the company. She is a qualified electrician. She spent three years at college and got an NVQ Level 3 in Electrical Installation.

- **Ahab Patel** is a self-taught plumber. He spent time working with his father and then became self-employed. However, after doing some contract work for Dublin Construction Company, he was invited him to join them full time.

(a) Using examples from this case, explain what is meant by the division of labour.

(b) How might such specialisation benefit Dublin Construction Company?

time to time. If people are trained to do different jobs, their time at work may be more interesting because there is more variety.

- **Improve working practices:** The way labour is organised and managed can affect productivity. Working practices are the methods and systems that employees adopt when working. For example, productivity might be increased by changing the factory layout or increasing labour flexibility. This is discussed in Chapter 42.

- **Use more technology:** Productivity usually increases when new technology is introduced. This is because new technology is more efficient. Productivity is also likely to increase if production becomes more capital intensive. The impact of technology on productivity is discussed in Chapter 42.

Key terms

Capital-intensive production – production methods that make more use of machinery relative to labour.

Division of labour – specialisation in specific tasks or skills by an individual.

Entrepreneur – an individual who organises the other factors of production and risks their own money in a business venture.

Factors of production – the resources used to produce goods and services. They include land, labour, capital and enterprise.

Fixed capital – the stock of 'man-made' resources such as machines and tools used to help make goods and services.

Labour – the people used to produce in production.

Labour-intensive production – production methods that make more use of labour relative to machinery.

Production – the transformation of resources into goods or services.

Productivity – the amount of output in relation to the resources used.

Specialisation – in business, the production of a limited range of goods.

Working capital or circulating capital – stocks of raw materials and components to be used up in production. Also stocks of finished goods waiting to be sold.

Chapter review – Dragon Toys

Dragon Toys, a Chinese company, manufactures plastic toys such as pedal tractors. The company recently appointed a new production manager to improve productivity. In 2007 the company produced 25,000,000 units with a workforce of 50. In 2008 output fell to 24,000,000 units with the same number of people. As a result, Dragon Toys was losing its competitive edge. The new manager carried out a staff survey and found that they were bored and poorly motivated. The manager promised to improve productivity by introducing new technology. She believes that production should become more capital intensive.

(a) Explain the difference between production and productivity. **(4 marks)**

(b) What is meant by labour productivity? **(2 marks)**

(c) Calculate labour productivity in 2007 and 2008 to show that it has fallen. **(4 marks)**

(d) How might the Chinese government help to increase labour productivity? **(2 marks)**

(e) How might the production manager improve worker motivation? **(4 marks)**

(f) How might more capital-intensive production improve productivity? **(4 marks)**

Chapter 35

Production methods

Getting started...

Businesses can use different production methods when making products. For example, the method used by a jeweller is different from that used by a computer manufacturer. There may also be differences in the same industry. For example, some furniture is mass produced in large factories while smaller producers make furniture by hand. Look at the production methods used in the examples below.

Kellogg's

Kellogg's is a multinational producer of breakfast cereals and convenience foods such as cookies, crackers, cereal bars and frozen waffles. It is based in Michigan, US but has factories all over the world. Kellogg's produces millions of units of output to serve huge global markets. Its production methods are capital intensive and many of its brands are produced on automated production lines that run continuously.

▲ **Figure 35.1**
Kellogg's cornflakes

Mehreen Carpets

Mehreen Carpets make hand knotted oriental carpets and is based in Pakistan. It has its own looms and manufacturing facilities and can meet the needs of a wide range of customer designs. The business also produces high-quality rosewood handicrafts and furniture. All products are crafted by artisans and can be made to specific customer orders. Its factory is located in Chiniot, a town that is famous for its rich history in craftsmanship and skill.

Source: adapted from www.mehreencarpets.com/profile.htm

(a) Compare the two production methods used in the above examples.

(b) Explain two reasons why the two businesses use different production methods.

Job production

Job production is where a business produces one product from start to finish before moving on to the next. Each item produced is likely to be different. Job production is used when orders are small, such as 'one-offs'. Examples might include the construction of an office block, the making of a wedding dress, the drawing up of a person's will or the design of a television advert. The advantages and disadvantages of job production are summarised briefly in Figure 35.2.

Advantages
Quality is high because workers are skilled
Workers are well motivated because work is varied
Products can be custom made
Production is easy to organise

Disadvantages
High labour costs as a result of skilled workers
Production may be slow – long lead times
A wide range of specialist tools may be needed
Generally an expensive method of production

◄ **Figure 35.2** The advantages and disadvantages of job production

QUESTION 1

Henry Ndzima is a chartered accountant and runs a small business from an office in Mbabane, Swaziland. He produces final accounts for sole traders, partnerships and small private limited companies. He has around 110 business clients and employs a secretary and a young trainee accountant. In addition to preparing accounts he offers other services such as:

- completing tax returns;
- taxation planning;
- advice on the financial management of businesses and investment;
- auditing.

(a) Use this case as an example to explain what is meant by job production.

(b) Explain why job production might help to motivate Henry Ndzima and his trainee.

Batch production

Job production is suitable when demand is relatively low. However, when demand grows and orders for multiple units are placed a business might switch to **batch production**. This is where a business makes a number (a batch) of products to the same design or specification and then changes production to another product with different specifications. When products are made in batches production is usually divided into a number of operations or *processes*. Figure 35.3 gives an example of batch production.

Operation	Description
Laser cutting	The correct profile is cut from the metal sheet
Part marking	The armrest is marked with a number for identification
Punching	Holes are punched in the armrest to make it lighter
Folding	The armrest is folded into the correct shape
Assembly	Components and fasteners are put together
Plating	The armrest is coated in zinc plating
Packaging	The armrests are packed into cases for transit

Figure 35.3
Operations involved in the production of an armrest for an aircraft seat

Many products are made using batch production, particularly in engineering, the clothes industry and food processing. For example, in a canning plant, a firm may can several different batches of soup, each batch being a different recipe. Products can be produced in large or small batches depending on the level of demand. Larger production runs tend to lower the *unit* or *average cost* of production. The advantages and disadvantages of batch production are shown in Figure 35.4.

Figure 35.4
Advantages and disadvantages of batch production

Advantages

Workers are likely to specialise in one process
Unit costs are lower because output is higher
Production is flexible because different orders can be met
More use of machinery is made

Disadvantages

More complex machinery may be needed
Careful planning and coordination is needed
Less motivation because workers specialise
If batches are small costs will still be high
Money may be tied up in work-in-progress

Yalta Apparel make workwear, leisurewear and promotional clothing for European customers. In 2006, the company moved to a new factory in Colombo, Sri Lanka. The company has an excellent reputation in the industry. This is because it:

- provides a wide choice of quality clothing at low prices;
- provides excellent customer service;
- is flexible and can meet orders quickly.

Like most companies in the clothes industry, Yalta Apparel uses batch production. The company can meet a wide range of different orders because of the flexibility of its machinery and multi-skilled workforce.

(a) Use the clothes industry as an example to explain what is meant by batch production.

(b) Why is batch production common in the clothes industry?

(c) How do you think Yalta Apparel has overcome some of the typical problems associated with batch production?

Flow production

Flow production is an efficient method of production. It is organised so that different operations can be carried out, one after the other, in a continuous sequence. Products move from one operation to the next, often on a conveyer belt. What are the main features of flow production?

- Large quantities are produced.
- A standardised product is produced.
- A semi-skilled workforce, specialising in one operation, is often employed.
- Large amounts of machinery and equipment are used.

Flow production is used in the manufacture of products as varied as newspapers, food and cement. *Repetitive flow production* is the manufacture of large numbers of the same product, such as plastic toy parts or metal cans. **Process production** is a form of flow production that is used in the oil or chemical industry. Materials pass through a plant where a series of processes are carried out in order to change the product. An example might be the refining of crude oil into petrol. The advantages and disadvantages of flow production are summarised in Figure 35.5.

Figure 35.5 ▶
Advantages and disadvantages of flow production

Advantages

Very low unit costs because of economies of scale
Output can be produced very quickly
Modern technology can allow some flexibility
Production speed can vary according to demand

Disadvantages

Products may be standardised
Huge set-up costs before production can begin
Worker motivation can be very low – repetitive tasks
Breaks in production can be very expensive

Choosing an appropriate method of production

Businesses have to decide which production method is best for their needs. The method chosen might depend on a number of factors.

- **The nature of the product**: Products often require a specific method of production. For example, in the construction industry, projects such as bridges, roads, office blocks and schools must be produced using job production. Farming involves batch production. A plot of land undergoes several processes before it 'produces' a crop.

- **The size of the market**: Fast-moving consumer goods such as soap, confectionery and canned drinks are normally produced using flow production because the market is so big. When the market is small, flow production techniques are not cost-effective so batch or job production will be used.

- **The stage of development a business has reached**: When firms are first set up, they often produce small levels of output and employ job or batch production methods. As they grow and sell more they may switch to flow production.

- **Technology**: As technology advances, new materials and machinery become available. When technology changes firms often use new production methods. For example, the development of computers and robotics has changed the way in which cars are made.

Key terms

Batch production – a method that involves completing one operation at a time on all units before performing the next.
Flow production – large-scale production of a standard product, where each operation on a unit is performed continuously, one after the other, usually on a production line.
Job production – a method of production that involves employing all factors to complete one unit of output at a time.
Process production – a form of flow production where materials pass through a plant where a series of processes are carried out in order to change the product.

Chapter review – Saudi Aramco

Oil refining involves processing crude oil into several different products. It often starts with a fractional distillation column. Crude oil is heated and the different products are pulled out at different temperatures. For example, lubricating oil, used for motor oil, grease and other lubricants, boils at a temperature between 572 to 700 degrees. After this chemical processes are used to remove impurities. A system of pipes is used to link all the different processes so that refining continues unstopped.

Saudi Aramco is the largest oil corporation in the world and is involved in all stages of oil production. It manages over 100 oil and gas fields in Saudi Arabia. In 2006 its revenue was $199.8 billion.

Source: science.howstuffworks.com/oil-refining4.htm

(a) Using this case as an example, explain what is meant by flow production. **(2 marks)**

(b) What method of production would be used to build a new oil refinery for Saudi Aramco? Explain your answer. **(2 marks)**

(c) How do businesses choose an appropriate method of production? **(6 marks)**

(d) What are the advantages and disadvantages to Saudi Aramco of flow production? **(10 marks)**

▲ **Figure 35.4** An oil refinery

Chapter 36

The scale of production

Getting started...

Setting up a business and surviving is very challenging. However, once a business is established the owners often want it to grow. They want to increase the **scale** of the business. This means that they want to increase its size. One of the benefits of increasing the scale of operations is that certain costs start to fall. Look at the example below.

CaterGroup

CaterGroup is a large catering company based near Sydney. It supplies sandwiches to supermarkets in New South Wales. It sells about 1,000,000 units a week. CaterGroup employs 210 workers and buys ingredients direct from farmers and manufacturers. For example, it buys thousands of loaves of bread from a Sydney baker for $1.10 each. It buys tomatoes from a local farm for $1.50 a kilo and cheese for $5.00 a kilo. It sells sandwiches at an average price of $1.40 per round. CaterGroup pays 7.5% interest on a $1,000,000 loan.

▲ **Figure 36.1**
Sandwiches for sale at The Snack Box

The Snack Box

The Snack Box sells sandwiches and other snacks from a Kiosk by Sydney Harbour. It serves office workers, shoppers and some tourists. The Snack Box is run by two sisters and they sell about 900 sandwiches a week. They buy their ingredients from supermarkets and wholesalers. For example, the business buys about 20 loaves of bread per day at a cost of $1.80 each. Tomatoes cost $2.50 a kilo and cheese is $7 a kilo. Most of their sandwiches sell for $2.00 a round. The business has a $5,000 loan which was taken out to help set up the business. An interest rate of 8.9% is paid on the loan.

(a) (i) Which of the two businesses is the largest?
(ii) Which business has the lowest costs?

(b) Which business is likely to be the most efficient?

(c) How might CaterGroup benefit from its cost advantage?

Economies of scale

Big firms can usually produce goods more cheaply than small firms. The size of a firm has an important affect on the *average costs* (see Chapter 38) of production. As a firm increases its size, average costs start to fall. This is because of **economies of scale** and is shown in Figure 36.2. When the business is producing 20,000 units of output, the average cost is $25. If it raises output to 40,000 units, average costs fall to $15. The firm could carry on expanding and lower its average costs until it is large enough to produce 70,000 units. At this level of output average costs are minimised at $10 per unit. It is the ideal size because average costs are at an absolute minimum. If the firm grows beyond 70,000 units, average costs will start to rise. For example, if the firm increases its size and produces 90,000 units, average costs will now rise to $12.50 per unit. This is because of **diseconomies of scale** that arise because of inefficiency.

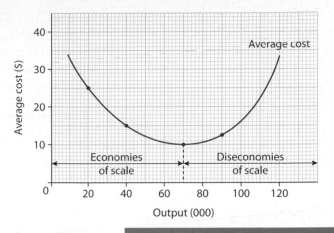

Figure 36.2
Economies and diseconomies of scale

Internal economies of scale

Internal economies of scale are the cost benefits that an individual firm can enjoy when it expands. The reasons why costs fall are summarised in Figure 36.3.

- **Purchasing economics**: Big firms that buy lots of resources get cheaper rates. Suppliers offer discounts to firms that buy raw materials and components in bulk. This is similar to consumers buying multi-packs in supermarkets. They are better value for money. Bulk buying is a purchasing economy. In the example above, CaterGroup was able to buy bread for $1.10 a loaf. However, The Snack Box was having to pay $1.80 because it was buying smaller quantities.

Figure 36.3
Sources of internal economies of scale

- **Marketing economies**: A number of marketing economies exist. For example, it may be cost-effective for a large firm to run its own delivery vehicles. For a large firm with lots of deliveries to make this would be cheaper than paying a distributor. Marketing economies can also occur because some marketing costs, such as producing a television advert, are fixed. These costs can be spread over more units of output for a larger firm. Therefore the average cost of the advert is lower for a large firm.

- **Technical economies**: Technical economies arise because larger plants are often more efficient than smaller ones. There can be more specialisation and more investment in machinery. One example of a technical economy is the way a big firm will make better use of an essential resource than a smaller firm. For example, a small engineering company may buy some computer-aided design (CAD) software for $1,000. It is needed by the business but is only used one day a week. A much larger engineering company may buy the same software but use it every day of the week. Clearly, the larger company is making better use of the software and therefore its average cost will fall.

- **Financial economies**: Large firms can get cheaper money. They also have a wider variety of sources to choose from. For example, a large limited company can raise money by selling shares. This option is not available to a sole trader. Large firms can put pressure on banks when negotiating the price of loans. Banks are often happier lending large amounts to large companies at lower interest rates. In the example above, CaterGroup was paying 7.5% to borrow $1,000,000. In contrast, The Snack Box was paying 8.9% to borrow just $5,000.

- **Risk bearing economies**: Larger firms are more likely to have wider product ranges and sell into a wider variety of markets. This reduces the risk in business. For example, many supermarkets have extended their product ranges to include household goods, consumer durables, books, a café, financial services, garden furniture and pharmaceuticals.

- **Managerial economies**: As firms expand they can afford specialist managers. A small business may employ a general manager responsible for finance, human resources, marketing and production. The manager may find this role demanding and may be weak in some fields. A large firm can employ specialists. As a result efficiency is likely to improve and average costs fall.

 QUESTION 1

In 2008 the world's biggest printing plant was opened by News International, publisher of *The Times*, *Sunday Times* and the *Sun*. The plant contains 12 modern printing presses, which cover an area the size of 23 football pitches. The presses are quieter and much faster than those they replaced. The plant can print 70,000 papers an hour compared to 30,000 at the previous plant. Also, the new presses require fewer staff – 200 instead of 600. This could give the newspaper industry a new lease of life in the digital media world.

Source: adapted from bbc.co.uk/news

(a) What is likely to happen to average costs at News International as a result of opening the new plant?

(b) Use this case as an example to explain what is meant by technical economies of scale.

External economies of scale

Sometimes all firms in an industry can enjoy falling average costs as the whole industry grows. This is called **external economies of scale**. External economies are more likely to arise if an industry is concentrated in a particular region.

Skilled labour If an industry is concentrated in an area, there may be a build-up of labour with the skills and work experience required by that industry. As a result, training costs will be lower when workers are recruited.

Infrastructure If a particular industry dominates a region, the roads, railways, ports, buildings and other facilities will be shaped to suit that industry's needs. For example, a specialised industrial estate may be developed to help a local IT industry.

Ancillary and commercial services An established industry in a region will encourage suppliers in that industry to set up close by. Specialist marketing, cleaning, banking, waste disposal, distribution, maintenance and components suppliers are likely to be attracted to the area. All firms in the industry will benefit from their services.

Cooperation When firms in the same industry are located close to each other they are likely to cooperate with each other so that they can all gain. For example, they might join forces to share the cost and benefits of a research and development centre.

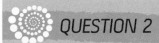

QUESTION 2

Silicon Valley is the southern part of the San Francisco Bay Area in the US. Originally it was home to a large number of silicon chip manufacturers. However, it gained a reputation as the major US high-tech businesses centre. Despite the development of other high-tech economic centres in the US, Silicon Valley is still the leading high-tech area. This is because of its large number of computer experts, engineers and venture capitalists.

Even in the 1970s there were many semiconductor companies in the area. There were also computer firms using their devices and programming and service companies serving both. Industrial space was plentiful and housing was inexpensive. The growth of Silicon Valley was also aided by the development of the venture capital industry, which specialised in providing funds for high-tech companies.

(a) What is meant by external economies of scale?

(b) What examples of external economies exist in this case?

Diseconomies of scale

Figure 36.2 shows that if a firm continues to expand, average costs eventually rise. This is because the firm suffers from diseconomies of scale. Average costs start to rise because aspects of production become inefficient. Why might this happen?

Bureaucracy If a business becomes too bureaucratic it means that too many resources are used in administration. Too much time may be spent filling in forms or writing reports. Also, decision making may be too slow and communication channels too long. If resources are wasted in administration and communication, average costs will start to rise.

Labour relations If a firm becomes too big, relations between workers and managers may worsen. There may be a lack of empathy for workers and they may become demotivated. As a result, conflicts may arise and resources may be wasted resolving them.

Control and coordination A very large business may be difficult to control and coordinate. Thousands of employees, billions of dollars and dozens of plants all over the world can make running a large organisation demanding. There may be a need for more supervision, which will raise costs, for example.

Key terms

Diseconomies of scale – rising average costs when a firm becomes too big.
Economies of scale – falling average costs as a result of expansion.
External economies of scale – the cost benefits that all firms in the industry can enjoy when the industry expands.
Internal economies of scale – the cost benefits that an individual firm can enjoy when it expands.
Scale – the size of a business.

Chapter review – Sensations

Sensations is a Canadian clothes chain. It sells high-quality garments, shoes and fashion accessories. It has an excellent reputation for good customer service and now has 96 shops in Canada and 52 in the northern states of the US. In 2002 Sensations employed a specialist marketing manager. The new manager raised the profile of the Sensations brand right across Canada. As a result, the company grew quickly and became very profitable. Sensations buys most of its garments and shoes from China.

In 2006 Sensations bought a clothes chain in the Middle East. It was thought that the company could further exploit economies of scale and make even more profit. However, there were some problems. Communications became difficult because of language and cultural difficulties. There was also a lack of employee empathy. Many of the staff did not seem to care whether the company succeeded or not. Some of the store managers also complained that the company was becoming too bureaucratic.

(a) What is meant by the term 'scale' in business?
(2 marks)

(b) Explain the effect that economies and diseconomies of scale are likely to have on Sensations' average cost.
(4 marks)

(c) Why is employing a specialist marketing manager an economy of scale?
(4 marks)

(d) Do you think that Sensations benefited from purchasing economies of scale? Explain your answer.
(4 marks)

(e) Do you think that Sensations might be experiencing diseconomies of scale?
(6 marks)

▲ **Figure 36.4** A clothes store

Chapter 37

Lean production

Getting started...

Businesses are under increasing pressure to improve efficiency. If they cannot cut costs, they will find it hard to compete. In recent years a number of Japanese production techniques have been introduced. This has helped businesses to reduce the amount of resources used up in production. It has also improved the quality of products. Look at the example below.

Thara Engineering

Thara Engineering is an Indian company that makes fasteners, studs, bolts and cap nuts. It has two plants and employs 34 people. To improve performance Thara introduced some Japanese production methods:

- It standardised some procedures and changed the factory layout.
  This led to a 17% gain in production space.
- It recognised that improvements required staff involvement. Therefore more training was organised.
- It improved cleaning practices and stock storage and handling.

As a result of these measures turnover increased by 50% and production set-up time was reduced by 74%. Also, machine down-time was cut by 73%, delivery targets were increased by 21% and product rejection fell by 50%. Investment in staff training also improved staff motivation.

Source: adapted from www.1000ventures.com

(a) How important was staff involvement at Thara when trying to make improvements?

(b) How did Thara benefit from introducing Japanese production methods?

What is lean production?

Lean production is an approach to production developed by Toyota, the Japanese car manufacturer. Its aim is to use fewer resources in production. Lean producers use less of everything. This includes factory space, materials, stocks, suppliers, labour, capital and time. As a result, lean production:

- raises productivity;
- reduces costs and cuts lead times;
- reduces the number of defective products;
- improves reliability and speeds up product design.

Lean production involves using a range of practices designed to reduce waste and improve productivity and quality. Some of these are discussed in this unit.

Kaizen

There is a strong link between lean production and **Kaizen**. Kaizen is a Japanese word that means *continuous improvement*. There is a belief in Japan that everything can be improved. Even at work the Japanese believe it is possible to make small improvements continuously. This means that workers are always coming up with ideas to improve quality, reduce waste or increase efficiency. The improvements may be very small but over a long period of time they have a huge impact. In Japan workers come up with ideas naturally. It is part of their culture. However, when Kaizen is adopted in other countries workers have to be trained.

The elimination of waste in business is an important part of Kaizen. This is why Kaizen has a strong link with lean production. Examples of waste may be:

- time wasted while staff wait around before starting tasks, such as waiting for materials to arrive;
- time wasted when workers move unnecessarily in the workplace, such as walking to a central point in the factory to get tools.

Just-in-time production

If a business holds stocks, money is tied up and therefore wasted. For example, if a business has $1 million of stocks in a warehouse, that $1 million cannot be used for anything else. The money is unproductive. To overcome this problem many businesses have adopted **just-in-time** (JIT) production.

- This means that a business does not hold any stocks at all. Suppliers have to deliver resources straight to the production line at regular intervals. This might be several times a day.
- JIT also means that goods are not produced unless they have been ordered. This avoids the need to hold stocks of finished goods. The advantages and disadvantages of JIT are shown in Figure 37.2.

Advantages

Cash flow is improved
No waste, obsolete or damaged stock
Space is released
No stock holding costs
Stronger links with suppliers
Fewer suppliers

Disadvantages

Higher ordering and administration costs
Huge reliance on suppliers' reliability
Advantages of bulk-buying may be lost
Hard to cope with fluctuations in demand
Vulnerable to a break in supply

▲ **Figure 37.2**
Advantages and disadvantages of JIT

 QUESTION 1

Harley Davidson, the famous motorcycle manufacturer, nearly collapsed in 1985. To survive it had to improve efficiency. Therefore the company introduced lean production. One method used was JIT manufacturing. Previously, Harley had used a complex, computerised stock control system. This involved keeping stock levels high so the assembly line would not be halted if problems arose. This was inefficient because it assumed that problems would occur. It was like sweeping dirt under the carpet. After JIT was introduced there were some impressive improvements at Harley:

- stock turnover up from 5% to 20% and stock levels down 75%;
- percentage of motorcycles coming off the line completed up from 76% to 99%;
- scrap and rework reduced by 68%;
- productivity up by 50% and space requirements down by 25%.

(a) What is meant by just-in-time (JIT) manufacturing?

(b) Discuss the benefits to Harley Davidson of JIT manufacturing.

Cell production

Flow production involves mass producing a standard product on a production line. In contrast, **cell production** involves dividing the workplace into 'cells'. Each cell produces a 'product family'. This is a group of products that use similar production methods. For example, a metal product might need cutting, punching, folding, welding and dispatch. This could all be carried out in one cell. Inside a cell, machines are grouped together and a team of workers sees the production from start to finish. The cell may also be responsible for tasks such as designing, planning, maintenance and problem solving.

The are several advantages of cell production:

- Floor space is released because cells use less space than a production line.
- Product flexibility is improved and lead times are cut.
- Movement of resources and handling time is reduced.
- Teamworking is encouraged.
- There may be a safer working environment and more efficient maintenance.

Workers

Most lean production techniques rely heavily on the workforce. Workers are expected to play a more decisive role in the business.

Teamworking This involves dividing the workforce into small groups. Each team will focus on a particular area of production and team members will have the same common aims. Both the business and employees might benefit from teamwork:

- Workers should develop a 'team spirit'. This may improve motivation and productivity.
- Flexibility might improve. For example, team members might be more willing to cover for an absent colleague.
- Teams might plan their own work schedules, share out tasks and solve their own problems. This should lead to quicker decision making and more ideas.
- Communication and labour relations might also improve.

However, there may be conflict between team members and managers who may resent the responsibility delegated to teams.

Multi-skilling If workers are trained in a variety of skills they are said to be **multi-skilled**. Multi-skilled workers are more useful to a business because they provide more flexibility. For example, workers can cover for absent colleagues in different work areas more easily. Workers might also be better motivated if they are allowed to do a range of different jobs. It might help to make their work more interesting.

Suggestion schemes These encourage workers to suggest ideas for improving production or reducing costs. A simple scheme involves workers writing their ideas down and putting them into a suggestion box. If a worker's idea is adopted he/she will be rewarded – with cash or a prize perhaps. Suggestion schemes are often a feature of Kaizen.

Key terms

Cell production – involves producing a 'family of products' in a small self-contained unit (a cell) within a factory.

Just-in-time manufacturing – a production technique that is highly responsive to customer orders and uses very little stock holding.

Kaizen – a Japanese term that means continuous improvement.

Lean production – an approach to production aimed at reducing the quantity of resources used.

Multi-skilling – where workers are trained in more than one skill, which enables them to do a range of jobs.

Chapter review – Delhi Metal Products

Delhi Metal Products is an Indian company and employs over 200 staff. It produces metal components for domestic appliances and exports 25% of its output. The company wanted to become a lean producer and improve performance. To achieve this it took several measures:

- Introduced Kaizen.

- Training was organised that focused on the standardisation of procedures and processes in the factory. As a result about 50% of the production processes were standardised.

- Workers were trained in additional skills, which increased labour flexibility. This meant that 57% of the workforce became multi-skilled.

- Foremen were told to set aside at least half an hour every week as Kaizen time – time to do nothing but think about improvement in the factory. Factories are advised not to hold meetings during this 30-minute period, and foremen should not even answer the telephone.

(a) Delhi Metal Products wanted to become a 'lean producer'. What does this mean? **(2 marks)**

(b) Explain why a multi-skilled workforce improves flexibility. **(4 marks)**

(c) Outline the benefits to Delhi Metal Products of suggestion schemes. **(2 marks)**

(d) (i) What evidence is there that Delhi Metal Products is committed to Kaizen? **(2 marks)**

   (ii) How will Kaizen improve performance? **(4 marks)**

(e) Do you think that Delhi Metal Products has improved its performance since becoming a 'lean producer'? **(6 marks)**

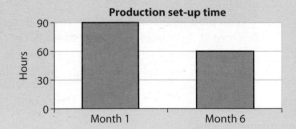

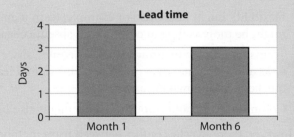

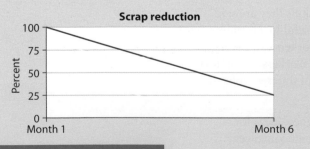

Benefits within first 6 months:
- 25% lead time reduction
- 45% production space increase
- 75% scrap reduction
- 60% machine down-time reduction
- 42% response time reduction

Source: adapted from www.1000ventures.com

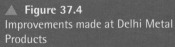
Figure 37.4
Improvements made at Delhi Metal Products

Chapter 38

Costs and cost classification

Getting started...

Businesses have to pay for the resources they use. These expenses might include wages, raw materials, components, energy and machinery. They are called **costs**. However, there are different types of business costs. Some costs stay the same when a business produces more output, but others increase. Look at the examples below.

Agustina's Zapatos

Agustina Mendes runs a shoe shop in Buenos Aires, Argentina. Two of the main costs are rent of 2,500 pesos and interest of 1,500 pesos on a bank loan. These are paid monthly. Other large costs include stocks of shoes and wages to sales assistants.

Figure 38.1 A shoe shop

Costantini Design

Costantini Design produces a line of home furnishings, lighting and art. The company uses a variety of hardwoods, leathers, and fine fabrics in production. Costantini Design serves both residential and commercial customers. It manufactures in Buenos Aires and has a showroom in Los Angeles. The company employs 50 skilled craftsmen and the products are hand made using tools. In 2009 the company invested in an exhibition to show some of their newest models in Milan, Italy.

Source: adapted from www.costantinidesign.com

(a) Which of the costs described in the above cases will increase when output increases?

(b) Which of the costs described in the above cases will remain unchanged when output increases?

Why does production generate costs?

The production of goods and services uses up resources. For example, tyre production uses resources such as rubber, synthetic fabrics, steel bands, machinery, a factory, labour and energy. These resources represent some of the costs generated during tyre production. Other costs will also be incurred. In this example the selling of tyres will incur marketing, distribution and administration costs. Also, if the business has borrowed any money, there will be interest to pay. All these costs, and many others, can be classified. Two methods of classification are outlined below.

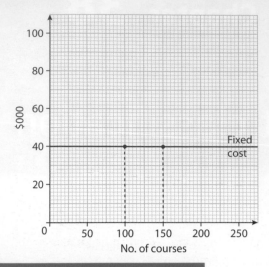

Figure 38.2
Fixed costs for Millhouse Training

Fixed costs

Costs can be classified according to how they behave when output changes. Some production costs remain exactly the same whatever the level of output. These are called **fixed costs**. Examples of fixed costs include rent, business rates, advertising, insurance premiums, interest payments, and research and development costs. These costs will not increase even if a firm produces more output. However, fixed costs will still have to be met if the firm produces nothing. Fixed costs are sometimes called *overheads*.

Fixed costs can be shown on a graph. Figure 38.2 shows the fixed cost for Millhouse Training. This business provides training courses for heavy goods vehicle (HGV) drivers. The business incurs fixed costs of $40,000 per annum (pa). The graph shows that fixed costs stay the same at all levels of output. If the business provides 100 training places, fixed costs are $40,000. If the number of places rises to 150, fixed costs are still $40,000.

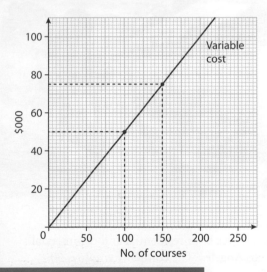

Figure 38.3
Variable costs for Millhouse Training

Variable costs

Production costs that do vary with output are called **variable costs**. If a firm produces more output, variable costs will increase. Similarly, if output levels are cut, variable costs will fall. Examples of variable costs include raw materials, packaging, fuel and labour. If a firm produces nothing, variable costs will be zero.

Figure 38.3 shows variable costs for Millhouse Training. The business has variable costs of $500 per course. If 100 courses are provided, variable costs will be $50,000 (100 × $500). If 50 extra courses are provided, variable costs rise to $75,000 (150 × $500). The graph shows that variable costs change whenever output changes.

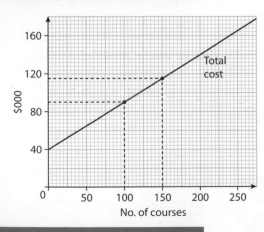

Figure 38.4
Total costs for Millhouse Training

Total costs

The cost to a firm of producing all output over a period of time is called **total cost**. Total cost (TC) can be calculated by adding fixed costs (FC) and variable costs (VC) together.

$$TC = FC + VC$$

If Millhouse Training provides places for 100 training courses, total costs will be:

$$TC = \$40,000 + (100 \times \$500)$$
$$= \$40,000 + \$50,000$$
$$= \$90,000$$

The total cost graph in Figure 38.4 shows that total cost increases from $90,000 to $115,000 when the number of courses provided rises from 100 to 150.

QUESTION 1

BatCraft Pty manufactures high-quality cricket bats. The company, which is based in Canberra, Australia, employs six skilled craftsmen. The table in Figure 38.5 shows some cost information for the company.

(a) Using examples from the case, explain what is meant by a fixed cost.

(b) In 2008 BatCraft produced 4,800 bats. Calculate the total cost of production.

(c) What would happen to total costs in 2009 if the rent increased to $60,000 and 6,000 bats were produced?

Rent	$50,000 pa
Business rates	$5,000 pa
Other fixed costs	$25,000 pa
Wood	$30 per bat
Other raw materials	$10 per bat
Labour	$50 per bat
Other variable costs	$10 per bat

▲ **Figure 38.5** Cost information for BatCraft Pty

Average costs

The **average cost** of production is the cost of producing a single unit of output. The formula for calculating average cost is given by:

$$\text{Average cost} = \frac{\text{Total cost}}{\text{Quantity produced}}$$

So, for example, the average cost of a training course provided by Millhouse Training, if 100 places were provided, would be:

$$AC = \frac{TC}{Q} = \frac{\$90,000}{100} = \$900$$

This means that each course provided to trainee HGV drivers costs Millhouse Training $900.

Direct and indirect costs

The costs discussed above are classified according to how they behave when output changes. Another way of classifying costs is to distinguish between direct and indirect costs. **Direct costs** are costs that can be identified with a particular product or process. Examples of direct costs are raw materials, packaging, and direct labour. **Indirect costs** or **overheads** result from the whole business. It is not possible to link these costs directly with particular products or processes. Examples are rent, insurance, the salaries of office staff and accountancy fees. Indirect costs are usually fixed costs and direct costs variable costs, although in theory both direct and indirect costs can be fixed or variable.

Total revenue and profit

Total revenue The amount of money a firm receives from selling its output is called **total revenue**. Total revenue can be calculated by multiplying the price of each unit by the number of units sold:

Total revenue = Price × Quantity

If Millhouse Training, in the above example, charged $1,500 for its HGV training courses, the total revenue from the sale of 100 courses is given by:

Total revenue = $1,500 × 100 = $150,000

Key terms

Average cost – the cost of producing a single unit of output.

Costs – expenses that must be met when setting up and running a business.

Direct cost – a cost that can be clearly identified with a particular unit of output.

Fixed costs – costs that do not vary with the level of output.

Indirect cost or overhead – a cost that cannot be identified with a particular unit of output. It is incurred by the whole organisation or department.

Total costs – fixed cost and variable cost added together.

Total revenue – the money generated from the sale of output. It is price × quantity.

Variable costs – costs that rise as output levels are increased.

This means that Millhouse Training generated £150,000 of revenue from providing 100 places on their HGV driving course.

Profit One of the main reasons why firms calculate their costs and revenue is to work out *profit* or *loss*. Profit is the difference between total revenue and total costs.

$$\text{Profit} = \text{Total revenue} - \text{Total costs}$$

The profit made by Millhouse Training from providing 100 places is given by:

$$\text{Profit} = \$150,000 \times 100 - (\$40,000 + \$50,000)$$
$$= \$150,000 - \$90,000$$
$$= \$60,000$$

It is possible to calculate the profit for a firm at any level of output using this method.

QUESTION 2

Jenkins Ltd manufactures electronic control systems that open and shut swing gates. Its most popular product is the underground system, which sells for $250. The systems are assembled in a factory using components supplied by nearby firms. In 2008 Jenkins sold 4,500 systems. Total fixed costs for the year were $160,000 and variable costs were $120 per system.

(a) Calculate the total cost of producing 4,500 control systems.

(b) Calculate the total revenue from the sale of 4,500 control systems.

(c) Calculate the profit from the sale of 4,500 control systems.

(d) In 2009 fixed costs and the price charged remained the same. However, variable costs rose to $140 per system. Calculate the profit made in 2009 if 5,200 systems were sold.

Chapter review – Glenn Alderman

Glenn Alderman owns a fishing cruiser. In 2008 he decided to operate daily fishing trips at Lakes Entrance, Victoria, Australia. The venture went very well and during the peak season he was very busy. He charged $500 per day for a fishing trip and could take fishing parties of up to six people. He provided all tackle, which he hired from a tackle shop, bait, fishing lessons and a picnic hamper for the day. Figure 38.6 shows costs for January and February 2008.

Costs	January	February
Tackle hire	$560	$440
Insurance	$50	$50
Interest payment	$3,000	$3,000
Picnic hampers	$2,800	$2,200
Fuel	$1,400	$1,100
Advertising	$100	$100
Other fixed costs	$300	$300
Number of trips	**January**	**February**
	28	22

Figure 38.6 ▶
Costs for Glenn's Fishing Trips

(a) Using examples from the case, explain the difference between direct costs and indirect costs. **(2 marks)**

(b) (i) What is fixed cost per month? **(1 mark)**
    (ii) What is variable cost per trip? **(1 mark)**
    (iii) Plot fixed cost and variable cost on a graph. (Use a range of output of 0 to 30 trips.) **(4 marks)**

(c) Calculate Glenn's total costs in January. **(2 marks)**

(d) Calculate the profit made by Glenn in January. **(4 marks)**

(e) Calculate the average cost of a trip in January. **(2 marks)**

(f) In January 2009, Glenn plans to raise the price of the trips to $600. If all costs remain the same and he manages to sell 28 trips again, how much profit will he make? **(4 marks)**

Chapter 39

Break-even analysis

Getting started...

In business it is helpful to know how much output needs to be sold to cover costs. If costs are not covered by revenue, the business will make a loss. If revenue is greater than costs, the business will make a profit. If costs are exactly the same as revenue, the business will **break even**. Look at the examples below.

ANEK Lines

ANEK Lines is a Greek shipping company. It owns 11 vessels and provides passenger services across the Adriatic and Aegean Seas. In 2008, the company's total revenue was €278.9 million. Its total costs before tax were €285.3 million.

Source: adapted from www.anek.gr/english/company/history.html

Chellappan Ltd

Chellappan Ltd assembles satellite dishes for a major television broadcaster in India. Its fixed costs were Rs 20 million in 2008. Variable costs were Rs 2,000 per dish and in 2008 100,000 dishes were made and sold. So its total variable costs were Rs 20 million (Rs 2,000 × 10,000). The total revenue resulting from the sale of 10,000 satellite dishes was Rs 40 million.

(a) Show whether the firms in the above examples are making a profit, loss or breaking even.

Figure 39.1 Satellite dishes ▶

The break-even point

A business will break even if its total cost (TC) and total revenue (TR) are exactly the same. This is called the break-even point. At this point the business does not make a profit or a loss. For example, if a business produces 40,000 units and sells them for $5 each, total revenue will be $200,000 ($5 × 40,000). If fixed costs are $100,000 and variable costs are $2.50 per unit, total costs will also be $200,000 ($100,000 + $2.50 × 40,000). Here the business is breaking even and 40,000 units is the break-even point.

Calculating the break-even point

To calculate the break-even point, the following information is needed:

- fixed cost;
- variable cost per unit;
- selling price per unit.

The following formula can be used to calculate the break-even point:

$$\text{Break-even point} = \frac{\text{Fixed cost}}{\text{Selling price} - \text{variable cost per unit}}$$

For example, Ed Winchester Ltd has a contract with a local authority to install fire alarms in housing owned by the local council. Ed charges $25 for each installation. Fixed costs are $20,000 pa and variable costs are $5 per installation. How many alarms have to be installed before the business breaks even?

$$\text{Break-even point} = \frac{\text{Fixed cost}}{\text{Selling price} - \text{variable cost per unit}}$$

$$= \frac{\$20,000}{\$25 - \$5}$$

$$= \frac{\$20,000}{\$20}$$

$$= 1,000 \text{ units}$$

So, Ed has to fit 1,000 fire alarms to break even.

✸ QUESTION 1

Galle Ice Cream Ltd makes ice cream that is sold to retailers and caterers in Sri Lanka. Its standard ice cream product sells for Rs100 per kilo. The fixed costs in standard ice cream production are Rs100,000. Variable costs of production are Rs50 per kilo.

(a) How many kilos of ice cream must the business sell to break even?

(b) What is total cost and total revenue at the break-even point?

(c) What would happen to the break-even point if fixed costs were reduced to Rs80,000?

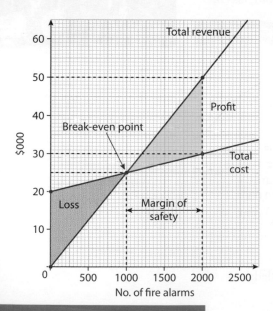

▲ **Figure 39.2**
Break-even chart for Ed Winchester

Break-even chart

The break-even point can be shown graphically. The **break-even chart** in Figure 39.2 shows total cost and total revenue for Ed Winchester's business in the above example. Output is measured on the horizontal axis and revenue, costs and profit are measured on the vertical axis. What does the break-even chart show?

• The break-even point is where total cost and total revenue intersect. In this example, the business breaks even when 1,000 fire alarms are fitted. At this point total cost and total revenue are both $25,000.

• At any level of output below the break-even point the business makes a loss.

• At any level of output above the break-even point the business makes a profit. For example, if Ed Winchester fits 2,000 fire alarms, the business will make a profit of $20,000. (Total costs are $30,000 and total revenue is $50,000.)

- If Ed Winchester fits 2,000 alarms the **margin of safety** is 1,000 units. This is the range of output over which the business can make a profit (the difference between current output and the break-even level of output).
- Some break-even charts show fixed cost. In this example, fixed cost would be shown by a horizontal line at $20,000.

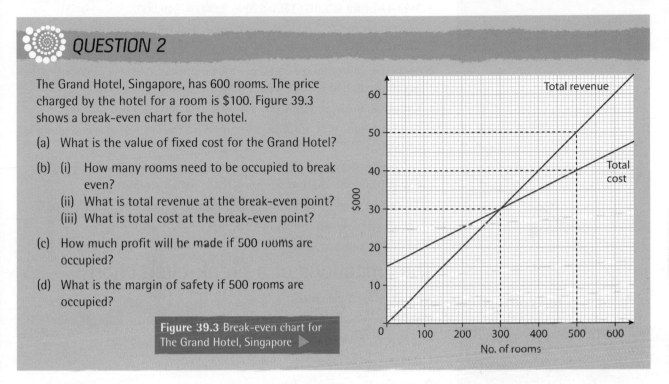

QUESTION 2

The Grand Hotel, Singapore, has 600 rooms. The price charged by the hotel for a room is $100. Figure 39.3 shows a break-even chart for the hotel.

(a)   What is the value of fixed cost for the Grand Hotel?

(b) (i)   How many rooms need to be occupied to break even?
    (ii) What is total revenue at the break-even point?
    (iii) What is total cost at the break-even point?

(c)   How much profit will be made if 500 rooms are occupied?

(d)   What is the margin of safety if 500 rooms are occupied?

Figure 39.3 Break-even chart for The Grand Hotel, Singapore ▶

Constructing a break-even chart

A break-even chart can be drawn by following the steps shown in the example below.

Example: Nanjing Holdings

Nanjing Holdings assembles circuit boards. Fixed costs are $10,000, variable costs are $10 per circuit board and the assembled boards are sold for $20 each.

Step 1 Calculate the break-even point using the formula above. It is useful to know the break-even point before constructing the chart. In this example the break-even point is 1,000 units ($10,000 ÷ $20 − $10).

Step 2 Since both total cost and total revenue are straight lines, two sets of coordinates are needed to construct the lines. It is necessary to choose two levels of output and work out the total cost and total revenue at each level.

- Choosing 0 as one level makes the calculations easier. If output is 0, TC will be $10,000 (remember that fixed costs are still incurred when nothing is produced).
- When output is 0, TR will also be 0 (there are no sales if nothing is produced).

Output	TC	TR
0	$10,000	0
2,000	$30,000	$40,000

▲ **Figure 39.4**
TC and TR at two different levels of output for Nanjing Holdings

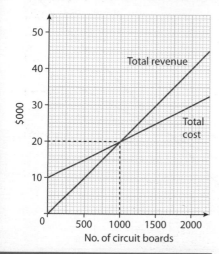

▲ **Figure 39.5**
Break-even chart for Nanjing Holdings

Key terms

Break even – the level of output where total costs and total revenue are exactly the same. Neither a profit nor a loss is made.
Break-even chart – a graph that shows total cost and total revenue. The break-even point is where total cost and total revenue intersect.
Margin of safety – the amount of output sold above the break-even point where the business makes a profit.

- When choosing the second level of output choose a value that is double the break-even point. This means the break-even point will appear right in the middle of the chart. Therefore, the second level of output will be 2,000 (2 × 1000).
- When output is 2,000 TC = $10,000 + ($10 × 2,000) = $30,000.
- When output is 2,000 TR = $20 × 2,000 = $40,000.
- The values for TC and TR at each level of output are summarised in Figure 39.4.

Step 3 The values shown in Figure 39.4 represent two sets of coordinates that can be used to plot TC and TR for the break-even chart.

- Output is measured on the horizontal axis and goes up to 2,000.
- Costs, revenue and profit are measured on the vertical axis and go up to $40,000.
- TC can be drawn by plotting the coordinates (0, $20,000) and (2,000, $30,000) on the chart and joining them with a straight line.
- TR can be drawn by plotting the coordinates (0,0) and (2,000, $40,000).
- The chart is shown in Figure 39.5.

The limitations of a break-even chart

A break-even chart shows:

- how much output a business has to produce in order to break even;
- the costs, revenue and profit at different levels of output;
- the margin of safety.

However, the chart does have some limitations:

- The TC and TR are shown as straight lines. In practice, they may not be straight lines. For example, a business may have to offer discounts on large orders, so total revenues fall at high outputs. In this case the total revenue line would rise and then fall. A business can lower costs by buying in bulk. So costs may fall at high outputs and total cost will be curved.
- It is assumed that all output is sold and no stocks are held. Many businesses hold stocks of finished goods to cope with changes in demand. There are also times when firms cannot sell what they produce and choose to stockpile their output to avoid laying off staff.
- The accuracy of the break-even chart depends on the quality and accuracy of the data used to construct total cost and total revenue. If the data is poor and inaccurate, the conclusions drawn on the basis of the data will be wrong.

Chapter review – Style Travel

Style Travel is owned by Mohammed Abass. He operates a limousine taxi service between hotels in Dubai and the airport. He charges $100 per trip. His main costs are fixed costs, which include leasing the limousine, insurance and other fixed motor expenses. Total fixed costs for the year are $40,000. The main variable costs are fuel, labour and other running costs. Total variable costs per trip are $20.

(a) Construct a break-even chart for Style Travel.
(8 marks)

(b) (i) What is the break-even point for Style Travel? (1 mark)
(ii) What is the total cost and total revenue at the break-even point? (2 marks)

(c) How much profit will be made if Mohammed makes 800 trips during the year? (2 marks)

(d) (i) Explain what is meant by the margin of safety? (2 marks)
(ii) What is the margin of safety for Style Travel if 800 trips are made? (1 mark)

(e) Outline the limitations of break-even analysis to Style Travel. (4 marks)

▲ **Figure 39.8**
A limousine taxi service at an airport

Chapter 40

Quality control

Getting started...

Businesses must produce good quality products. This means products have to be well designed, perform the function for which they were intended, look good and be safe to use. Businesses that fail to produce quality products are likely to lose out to competitors. For most businesses quality really matters. Look at the example below.

Quality at Casio

Casio is a Japanese multinational. It employs over 11,000 people and makes watches, cameras, calculators, musical instruments and other mobile technologies. Casio aims to impress customers. It creates products that are reliable, durable, safe and serviceable. Casio also considers the environment and complies with legislation in designs. In 1996, Casio started its 'Delight Our Customers' programme. This was to ensure that employees became familiar with Casio's philosophy about products and services. The key aspects of Casio's quality policies are outlined below (see Figure 40.1):

- Casio aims to create a good corporate image by offering products and services that please and impress customers.

- Casio responds to customer feedback with sincerity and speed. Customer comments are reflected in their products and services.

- Casio uses a numerical approach to monitoring quality. Data is analysed and then used to make continuous improvements.

(a) How important do you think quality is to Casio?

(b) What was the purpose of Casio's 'Delight Our Customers' programme?

(c) State two possible advantages to Casio of producing good quality products.

▲ **Figure 40.1**
Quality as viewed by Casio

What is quality?

When consumers are shopping they may consider **quality** when choosing products. Quality could be described as those features of a product or service that allow it to satisfy customers' wants. For example, a family buying a new car may consider some of the following features:

- Physical appearance – they may want a certain style and colour.

- Reliability and durability – will it last for 10 years?

- Special features – does it have a satellite navigation system?
- Suitability – can it seat six people comfortably?
- Repairs – how much does it cost to maintain the car?
- After sales service – how prompt is delivery?

Traditional quality control

Traditionally, production departments were responsible for ensuring quality. Their objectives might have been to make sure that products:

- satisfy consumers' needs;
- operate in the way they should;
- can be produced cost-effectively;
- can be repaired easily;
- conform to safety standards set down by legislation and independent bodies.

Quality control in the past often involved *quality controllers* or *quality inspectors* checking other people's work and the product itself after production had taken place. By today's standards this is not quality control. This is a method of finding a poor quality product before it is sold.

Quality assurance

Today inspection is carried out during the production process. This means that poor quality products can be prevented before production is complete. Such a preventative approach has been used by Japanese businesses and is known as **total quality management (TQM)**. It involves all employees being responsible for ensuring quality at all stages in the production process. Today many firms use TQM.

Quality assurance is a commitment by a business to maintain quality throughout the organisation. The aim is to stop problems before they occur rather than finding them after they occur. Quality assurance also takes into account customers' views in the production process.

QUESTION 1

VisitScotland.com is a business that provides a bookings and information service for visitors to Scotland. One of its roles is to assess the standard of accommodation and places to eat in Scotland. VisitScotland uses a 5-star grading scheme to assess quality. The scheme is quick and clear and helps to reassure visitors. VisitScotland's quality assurance schemes also assess visitor attractions such as castles and museums, tours and leisure centres. The schemes look at the standard of the welcome, hospitality, cleanliness, accommodation, comfort and service they provide, they are based on the grades below.

(a) How does VisitScotland assess quality?

(b) What are the benefits of the system to visitors?

Acceptable:	1 star
Good:	2 stars
Very good:	3 stars
Excellent:	4 stars
Exceptional:	5 stars

Source: adapted from www.visitscotland.com

Total quality management

TQM is designed to prevent errors, such as poor quality products, from ever happening. What are the features of TQM?

- **Quality chains**: Every worker in a business is like a link in a chain and every worker is both a customer and a supplier. This is because a worker on a production line will only receive (as a customer) and pass on (as a supplier) semi-finished work if it has reached specified quality standards. This avoids faulty products ever being made. The chain also includes customers and suppliers outside the business.

- **Everyone is involved**: Every department, activity and individual is organised to take into account quality at all times. TQM must start from the top with the chairperson and spread throughout the business to every employee.

- **Quality audits**: Statistical data is used to monitor quality standards. These checks or audits aim to reduce variability, which is the cause of most quality problems. Variations in products, delivery times, materials and staff performance often occur. Such variations can be detected easily if statistical data is used.

- **Teamwork**: TQM stresses that teamwork is the most effective way of solving problems. This is because teams have more skills, knowledge and experience than a single person.

- **Customer focused**: Firms using TQM are committed to their customers. They respond to changes in people's needs and expectations.

- **Zero defects**: Many quality systems have a zero defect policy. This aims to ensure that every product that is manufactured is free from defects.

Advantages

The focus is on customer needs
Quality is improved in all aspects of business
Waste and inefficiencies are removed
Helps develop ways of measuring performance
Improves communication and problem solving

Disadvantages

High training and implementation costs
Will only work if everyone is committed
May be bureaucratic (lots of documents)
The focus is on processes not the product

▲ **Figure 40.3**
Advantages and disadvantages of TQM

Why does quality matter to a business?

- Quality is more important than ever. Consumers are more aware. They get information through the media and the Internet. As a result, they have higher expectations than ever before.

- Increased competition has forced firms to improve quality. Consumers do not need to buy products from businesses that fail to deliver quality.

- Government legislation designed to protect consumers has forced firms to improve quality. For example, the production of food products has to be carried out in a hygienic environment and comply with health and safety legislation.

- Faulty products are costly for a business. Machinery that breaks down or constantly needs to be repaired will also be expensive. Late delivery and productivity that results from poor quality in production can harm a business's reputation.

Quality matters to a business because sales will be higher if it can deliver quality products. Poor quality is likely to result in lost customers.

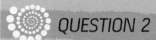

QUESTION 2

Boots is a member of Alliance Boots, an international pharmacy-led health and beauty group. In September 2009, the notice in Figure 40.4 appeared in the press.

PRODUCT RECALL

Boots 100% Pure Cotton Buds (80 in a pack)

Item code: 42-90-550

Batch numbers: 01092103 and 01092093

As part of our ongoing quality-monitoring programme we've discovered a problem with the above product. We've found that the material used to make the cotton buds is contaminated. This could lead to an infection, especially if used in the eyes, nose or mouth. The safety and well-being of all our customers is very important to us. Therefore, we're asking that if your cotton buds are from the above batch numbers, that you stop using the buds immediately. Return them to your nearest Boots store where you'll receive an alternative or refund. We're sorry for any inconvenience this may cause you.

Figure 40.4
Boots product recall notice

(a)   Use this case to explain what is meant by a product recall.

(b)   Why is quality so important for products like the one in this case?

(c)   How might Boots be affected by this product recall?

Quality standards

Businesses can earn a reputation for quality by following a *code of practice* or gaining quality awards. Recognition for quality in business may be awarded by a number of organisations. One important example is The British Standards Institution (BSI). This is an independent organisation that sets quality standards in industry. One **internationally** recognised standard is ISO 9000. Firms that achieve and maintain a certain standard can carry the BSI *kitemark*. The kitemark tells the customer that BSI quality standards are consistently achieved by the business. The benefits to a business of ISO 9000 certification are summarised overleaf.

Key terms

Quality – features of a product that allow it to satisfy customers' needs.

Quality assurance – a method of working for businesses that takes into account customers' wants when standardising quality. It often involves guaranteeing that quality standards are met.

Quality control – making sure that the quality of a product meets specified quality standards.

Total quality management – a managerial approach that focuses on quality and aims to improve the effectiveness, flexibility and competitiveness of the business.

The benefits to businesses of ISO 9000 certification

- Examines and improves systems, methods and procedures to lower costs
- Motivates staff and encourages them to get things right first time
- Defines key roles, responsibilities and authorities in a business
- Ensures orders are consistently delivered on time
- Highlights product or design problems and develops improvements
- Records and investigates all quality failure and customer complaints
- Shows customers that they are taking measures to improve quality
- Helps to identify staff training needs

Chapter review – Bangalore Business Software (BBS Ltd)

BBS Ltd produces data management software for businesses. One of its products, DataCare, helps businesses to manage large customer databases. BBS Ltd is committed to quality assurance and has been awarded ISO 9001, the internationally recognised standard for the quality management of businesses. Some of the basic requirements of certification include:

- a set of procedures that cover all key processes in the business;
- monitoring processes to ensure they are producing quality products;
- keeping records;
- checking for defects, with corrective action where necessary;
- regularly reviewing the quality system itself;
- ensuring continual improvement.

Regular monitoring ensures that these standards are upheld and that BBS Ltd remains worthy of its title as an accredited ISO 9001 provider.

(a) How does BBS Ltd ensure quality in its business?
(2 marks)

(b) What role does the BSI play in BBS Ltd quality assurance? (4 marks)

(c) Why does quality matter to businesses such as BBS Ltd? (4 marks)

(d) What benefits might BBS Ltd enjoy as a result of ISO 9001 certification? (4 marks)

(e) BBS Ltd is considering the introduction of TQM. Discuss the possible advantages of this to the company. (6 marks)

Chapter 41

Location decisions

Getting started...

Businesses have to decide where to operate from. Should they choose a site in the town centre, on an industrial estate, close to a major road, by a port or in the countryside? Businesses may be located in a wide range of different places. Look at the examples below.

Prawn farming

Thailand has around 20,000 prawn farms. Its tropical climate and abundance of suitable coastal locations have made prawn farming one of its biggest industries. Prawn farms need plenty of clean water that can be introduced into the ponds throughout the rearing period. Hatchery sites should not be located near to cities, harbours and industrial centres, or other activities that may pollute the water supply. There must also be enough soil available for pond construction, and it is best to site the farm where the soil is fertile.

Wadi Musa Supermarket

Wadi Musa is a large village near Petra, Jordan. At the busy centre of the village, located by the roundabout, is a small supermarket. It serves local residents and tourists.

(a) Outline two factors that must be taken into account when locating a prawn farm.

(b) Why do you think the site of the small supermarket in Wadi Musa is a suitable location?

▲ **Figure 41.1**
A prawn farm

Location factors affecting manufacturers

Historically, the location of many businesses was linked to power and raw materials. Heavy industries such as steel and chemicals were located close to power sources such as coal, and raw materials such as water and iron ore. This is why the steel industry flourished in the Ruhr and Rhine valleys in Germany. Today, manufacturers are rarely tied to power sources because electricity and gas can be supplied to most locations. Manufacturers are now more likely to be influenced by the factors below.

The cost of premises or land Manufacturers often require large areas of land to locate factories, staff car parks and other production facilities. As a result, they look to minimise land and property costs. For example, they may set up in areas where:

- premises are cheap – perhaps in a business park or on an industrial estate. These are often located away from expensive residential areas;

- *business rates* (a tax paid by businesses to the local authorities) are low;

- land has been earmarked for business development such as **brownfield sites** or **greenfield sites**.

Transport Some manufacturers locate close to effective transport networks. This makes it easier for distributors and suppliers. For example, a manufacturer that exports goods to the EU may locate close to the Channel Tunnel. Manufacturers selling in national markets may locate their premises next to a major road.

Labour costs and skills Manufacturers needing large numbers of workers have to consider wage costs and labour skills. Wage rates may vary in different regions, and large companies may also consider locating in countries where labour is very cheap.

Also labour skills are not evenly distributed throughout a country. If a firm needs a particular type of skilled labour, a certain location might be suitable.

Proximity to customers Some manufacturers locate their factories close to customers. For example, manufacturers that make bulky or heavy products may locate close to customers to keep transport costs down. Also, the manufacturers of components often locate close to their customers.

Government assistance Governments may try to influence location decisions. They do this to:

- avoid congestion where there is already enough or too much development;

- encourage firms to locate where unemployment is high;

- attract foreign businesses into the country.

Some governments use **regional policy** to help develop 'run-down' areas. They use incentives such as quick planning permission, investment grants, tax breaks, employment subsidies and rent-free factory space to attract businesses.

DID YOU KNOW?

In India, Bangalore has a reputation for IT. Firms in Bangalore employ about 35% of India's one million IT professionals. Many multinationals have operations in Bangalore for this reason.

DID YOU KNOW?

In the car industry, firms making components such as braking systems, light fittings and car seats may locate close to a car assembly plant. The use of JIT production (see Chapter 37) has encouraged this trend. It is easier for suppliers to make several deliveries per day, for example, if they are located 'next door' to their main customer.

QUESTION 1

Guangxi Yuchai Machinery Company Ltd (GYMCL) makes diesel engines for trucks, construction equipment, buses, and cars in China. In 2009 it completed phase one of its new diesel engine assembly factory. The factory is located in the Xiamen Automobile Industry City in Guannan Industrial Park, near to Xiamen Port. This is a major auto-parts, bus and construction equipment area. This will allow the business to increase its scale of operations, shorten its supply chain and lower production costs. Xiamen is a popular and growing business development area. Locating a factory there will help to improve the firm's competitiveness and strengthen its customer relations.

Source: adapted from news.prnewswire.com

(a) Discuss the possible reasons why GYMCL located its new factory in the heart of the Xiamen Automobile Industry City in Guannan Industrial Park.

Location factors affecting service providers

Some of the factors that affect the location of service providers are the same as those that influence manufacturers. For example, like manufacturers, service providers have to consider the cost of premises, labour costs and skills, and government help. However, there are some differences outlined below.

Proximity to market Many service providers have to locate their premises close to their markets. This is because many services are sold direct to consumers. For example, restaurants, cafes, shops, hair salons, opticians, taxis and dry cleaners have to be located in towns and cities. This is where customers live and shop. However, many people are switching from stores to the Internet when shopping. This means that retailers, for example, can serve national markets and operate in premises away from their customers. For example, an online clothes retailer could operate from a warehouse near a motorway and serve a national market. Figure 41.2 shows the growth in online sales in Germany between 2003 and 2008. Sales have more than doubled over the time period.

Home-based businesses Many small service providers can operate from home. Examples include mobile hairdressers, mobile mechanics, freelance writers and editors, consultants, designers, accountants, tutors, wedding planners, child carers and translators. Home-based businesses have some advantages. For example, the cost of running a business from home can be lower. Also, travelling time may be reduced and it may be easier to combine business commitments and family life.

2003	€5.8 bn
2004	€7.6 bn
2005	€9.0 bn
2006	€10.2 bn
2007	€11.4 bn
2008	€13.6 bn

Figure 41.2
Online sales in Germany 2003–2008 (€bn)

Many corporations locate their head office in high-profile cities such as London. However, recently some businesses have moved their head offices away from central London. AstraZeneca, Rio Tinto and Statoil have all moved away to cut costs.

AstraZeneca is moving from Mayfair to Paddington. It wanted to stay close to the City and Heathrow airport but made it clear that cost was the main issue.

A survey by Savills, the property company, found that rent is now the number one priority when choosing a new business location. In 2007 Savills estimated that rent was the third most important factor. The top priority was a building's ability to attract or retain staff, but that has slipped to fifth place. Paddington is a popular new choice for location. Marks & Spencer is already there and Vodafone is moving there. The cost of office space in Paddington is about half the cost of Mayfair or St James's.

Source: adapted from business.timesonline.co.uk

(a) State two possible reasons why corporations prefer to locate their head offices in high-profile cities such as London.

(b) Explain why some companies are relocating their head offices away from central London.

(c) According to this article, what is the most important location factor?

International location

Multinationals have business operations all over the world. When locating a new operation a multinational will take into account many of the factors discussed above. However, there are some additional factors to consider, outlined below.

Avoiding trade barriers Some countries put up trade barriers, such as tariffs and quotas. This is to protect domestic businesses from foreign competition. One way a multinational business can get round such trade barriers is to locate within the country.

Financial incentives Businesses may be attracted to a particular country if financial incentives are offered. Some of the regional aid available in parts of Europe may have influenced the location of Asian multinationals in the 1990s. Governments may offer cash, sometimes called 'sweetners', to businesses if they locate in their country.

Cost of labour A number of multinationals have located plants in cheap labour countries such as India or China. Cheap labour gives them a competitive advantage. Labour is so cheap in certain Asian countries that production methods tend to be labour intensive rather than capital intensive. This can help to reduce costs.

Proximity to markets or suppliers Transport costs can be much greater over longer distances. Therefore, multinationals locate near their markets or their suppliers to remain competitive. A car component manufacturer, for example, may have to set up a factory in the Far East to be near a car manufacturer.

KEY FACT

Japanese car producers set up car plants in Europe and the US in the 1980s and 1990s partly to avoid trade barriers designed to keep Japanese cars out of their markets.

Exchange rate fluctuations Exchange rate (see Chapter 61) fluctuations may affect location decisions. Businesses trading internationally can experience large movements in exchange rates. Sometimes these movements benefit a business but they can also have a negative impact. For example, a UK business may import components from Germany. If the value of the pound falls against the euro, imports become dearer. One way of getting around this risk is to locate operations in Germany.

Political stability Some countries, such as African states, are unpopular with multinationals because of political instability. Also, some countries are avoided by multinationals because of their poor human rights record. To locate in these countries could result in consumer boycotts or shareholder disapproval.

Language barriers Language can be an important factor in location decisions. One reason why the UK is favoured as a location by US companies is because the UK and the US are both English-speaking countries. Much of the foreign investment over the past 10 years in China has been by companies owned by Chinese people living outside of China.

New markets A multinational may decide to locate in a particular country because it wants to sell goods into a new market. This is a reason why many companies are trying to locate in China. China has the largest population in the world.

Key terms

Assisted areas – areas that are designated as having problems by the UK or EU and are eligible for support in a variety of forms.
Brownfield site – areas of land that were once used for urban development.
Greenfield sites – areas of land, usually on the outskirts of towns and cities, where businesses develop for the first time.
Regional policy – measures used by the government to attract businesses to 'depressed' areas.

Chapter review – CompComp

German-based CompComp makes computer components. It plans to build a new factory in south-east Asia. It has a growing number of customers in China, South Korea, Japan and India. CompComp has found two sites where a new factory could be located. Details about the locations in Shanghai, China and Busan, South Korea are summarised in Figure 41.3.

	Shanghai	Busan
Rent per month	$20,000	$17,500
Unemployment	6.5%	9%
Hourly wage rate	$4.20	$3.60
Government support	None	$500,000

▲ **Figure 41.3**
Information about Shanghai and Busan

Shanghai Shanghai is the largest centre of commerce and finance in China. It has been described as the 'showpiece' of the world's fastest-growing major economy. It is a high-profile business centre and has excellent communication links. However, with a population of over 20 million the city is becoming congested and suffers from serious pollution problems.

Busan Busan is the fifth busiest seaport in the world, with transportation and shipping an important part of the local economy. Busan can handle up to 13.2 million shipping containers per year. It is also well served by rail links and has an airport. The factory site proposed is on a purpose-built brownfield site with excellent amenities. However, there could be a problem finding suitable suppliers in the area.

(a) Why does the German company CompComp want to locate a factory in south-east Asia? **(2 marks)**

(b) State two reasons why governments may try to influence business location. **(2 marks)**

(c) What is meant by a brownfield site? **(2 marks)**

(d) Explain two factors that must be taken into account when locating operations overseas. **(4 marks)**

(e) Which site do you think CompComp should choose for its new factory? Explain your answer. **(10 marks)**

Chapter 42

Making production more efficient

Getting started...

The performance of businesses will improve if productivity increases. Productivity is the amount of output that can be produced with a given quantity of resources. Firms can increase productivity by making better use of their resources. As a result, they become more efficient, their costs fall and profit rises. Look at the examples below.

AMZ Tyres

AMZ Tyres is a tyre manufacturer in Malaysia. The company employs 50 staff and in 2007 produced 450,000 tyres in the company's factory in Shah Alam, Selangor. In 2008, the firm retrained the entire workforce. The training was designed to improve worker flexibility. As a result in 2008, tyre production rose to 520,000.

Figure 42.1 Tyres as produced by AMZ Tyres ▶

PepsiCo

In 2008, PepsiCo, installed a new $2.35 million heat and power system in its bottling plant in New York City. To cut its electric consumption Pepsi installed four natural gas power generators. These produce 80% of the power needed to run the filling, packaging and processing machines. These generators give off heat, which is converted into steam. This is used to warm bottles and clean machines. It has reduced Pepsi's boiler use by 70% and is four times more efficient than the previous system.

Source: adapted from www.nytimes.com

(a) (i) Calculate the improvement in labour productivity at AMZ Tyres.
(ii) How were the improvements in labour productivity generated?

(b) What measures were taken to improve productivity at PepsiCo?

(c) How might the two businesses benefit from the improvements in productivity?

Increasing labour productivity

Businesses try to increase productivity because they will lower costs and make more profit. Productivity may be increased by firms in a number of ways. One approach is to increase labour productivity.

Education and training The state can help improve the quality of labour by investing in the education system. Providing more equipment for schools and improving the quality of teaching and the management of schools might help. To equip young people with the skills needed in the workplace a government might invest more in vocational education.

Firms can also improve the productivity of their workers by providing training. Most workers receive some training when starting a new job. Further training may be provided if there are changes in the way people are expected to work.

Improve the motivation of workers If people are motivated at work, they will be more productive. One approach might be to use financial incentives. See Figure 42.2.

Some workers are not motivated by money but may respond to non-financial incentives:

- **Job rotation** involves an employee changing jobs from time to time. If people are trained to do different jobs, their time at work may be more interesting. They may be less bored and therefore better motivated.

- **Team working** involves organising workers into small groups. People often work better in teams because they can support and encourage each other. Motivation is more likely to be improved if a 'team spirit' can be developed.

Improve working practices The way labour is organised and managed can affect productivity. Working practices are the methods and systems that staff use in their workplace. Some examples are outlined below.

- **Changing factory layout**: It may be possible to change the factory layout by repositioning work stations or reorganising the flow of production. Such changes can improve labour productivity because workers may not have to move around as much, for example.

- **Increasing labour flexibility**: Labour can be more flexible if workers are trained to do different jobs and can switch at short notice. Some firms use flexitime where workers can choose their hours of work (within limits). For example, a call centre could be kept open from 7.00 am to 8.00 pm if individual workers choose to work at different times of the day. Shift work can be used to keep factories running for 24 hours a day.

- **Adopting lean production**: Lean production involves reducing waste in production. Workers may learn a variety of new working practices when this system is adopted. This is discussed in Chapter 37.

KEY FACT

Some examples of financial incentives include:
Piece rates where workers are paid according to the output they produce.
Performance related pay (PRP) where workers receive extra pay if targets are met. This might be a lump sum or a percentage of their salary.
Profit sharing where workers receive a share of the profit made by the business in addition to their normal pay.

 QUESTION 1

Millions of Asian rice farmers use urea (nitrogen-based) fertiliser to increase yields. Many farmers spread urea into floodwaters to fertilise rice. However, this is inefficient because two-thirds is lost. Urea deep placement (UDP) is a more efficient and environmentally friendly method of fertilisation. It was introduced in Bangladesh in the 1980s. It involves placing urea briquettes into soil near the rice plants. This improves efficiency because most of the fertiliser stays in the soil where it is absorbed more effectively. As a result, crop yields rise while pollution is reduced. Rice yields are up by more than 20% while using 40% less urea. In Bangladesh production is up by 268,000 tonnes annually and UDP farmers earn an extra $188/hectare. UDP use has also reduced Bangladesh's urea imports, saving $22 million. UDP has generated an additional 9.5 days of labour per hectare – almost 4.6 million additional days of labour. More importantly, the additional rice has made 1.5 million more Bangladeshis food-secure.   **Source: adapted from www.farmingfirst.org**

(a) Explain how efficiency has been improved by new technology in this case.

(b) What benefits have been enjoyed as a result of improvements in efficiency in this case?

Automation and new technology

Productivity usually rises when new technology is introduced. This is because new technology is more efficient. Productivity is also likely to increase if production becomes more capital intensive. Advances in technology have helped improve productivity in all three sectors of the economy. The impact of technology on productivity is discussed in Chapter 8.

Benchmarking

Benchmarking is used by some businesses to help improve productivity and quality. It involves identifying other firms who have a reputation for being the 'best' and then copying their methods. Businesses can benchmark different methods, systems, procedures or techniques. Examples of benchmarks that are important to customers are consistency of product, correct invoices, shorter delivery times, shorter lead times and improved after sales service.

One of the problems with benchmarking is choosing a suitable business to set the benchmark against. Clearly a competitor is not going to tell a business why it is so efficient. It might be necessary to go overseas or find a business that is not a competitor.

Other methods of improving productivity

Downsizing Some firms have tried to improve efficiency by **downsizing**. This involves reducing capacity, that is, laying off workers and closing unprofitable divisions. The advantages of downsizing may be:

- cost savings and increased profit;
- a leaner, more competitive operation.

Work study This involves looking at a particular job very carefully and working out the most efficient way it can be done. A **work study** may be carried out by a specialist engineer. Once the best way has been established workers will adopt the new approach and efficiency will improve.

Relocation Businesses often relocate their operations to improve efficiency. By relocating firms can take advantage of cheaper resources such as lower rent, lower wages or lower transport costs. A number of multinationals have located call centres in India to take advantage of cheap and skilled labour. Also, a number of firms have located factories in China for similar reasons.

Outsourcing It may be possible to improve efficiency by **outsourcing** specific business activities. This means that work currently done by a business is given to specialists that can do the same work at a lower cost. For example, a manufacturer may decide to outsource its distribution operation. This might be done by a transport company at a cheaper rate.

 DID YOU KNOW?

In the car industry the making of most components is now outsourced. The big car makers are often just giant assemblers.

Key terms

Benchmarking – adopting the methods of an established leader in quality.

Downsizing – the process of reducing capacity, usually by laying off staff.

Outsourcing – the contracting out of work to other businesses that might otherwise have been performed within the organisation.

Work study – a process that identifies the best possible way to carry out a task by looking closely at the way a job is done.

QUESTION 2

Airbus is a European aircraft manufacturer. A number of countries contribute to production. In 2007 Airbus announced 1,600 job cuts in the UK. This was part of a general downsizing operation involving 10,000 staff cuts in total. It also involved the closure of three plants in France and Germany and plans for outsourcing. Some production is likely to go to China where costs are lower. Louis Gallois has been appointed Chief Executive of Airbus to stabilise the company following production delays and the impact of a falling dollar.

Most of the 1,600 UK job losses will be in Bristol, where parts for wings, fuel systems and landing gear are produced. Airbus said that most jobs would go through natural wastage. Three other sites, one in France and two in Germany will either be sold or closed. Mr Gallois, who has a reputation for bold and decisive moves said: 'We have no choice ... we have to reduce our costs.'

Source: adapted from the *Guardian*, 28 February 2007

(a) Using this case as an example, explain what is meant by downsizing.

(b) Why has Airbus decided to downsize its operations?

(c) Airbus plans to outsource some production to China. What does this mean?

Chapter review – Glen Morgan Mail Order

New Zealand-based Glen Morgan Mail Order (GMMO) sells a variety of electrical goods such as kettles, irons, blenders, microwave ovens, TVs, music systems and computers. It advertises heavily on TV and relies on low prices to generate sales. In 2008 the company directors decided to improve efficiency and develop online selling. Two key changes were made:

- **Improve labour flexibility:** GMMO introduced some new flexible working practices. For example, staff could choose 60% of the hours they worked in return for being on call at certain times. One problem that GMMO had was a surge in demand straight after a TV advert. This often meant that staff were overworked and mistakes were made with order picking and dispatch. Staff would also be trained to do a variety of different jobs so that they could be moved around when necessary.

- **Introduced new technology:** A sophisticated IT system was installed that could deal with both telephone orders and online orders and process them automatically. This included:

  ○ a voice recognition system to take telephone orders;

  ○ an order reading facility that could read orders printed on a standard form available online.

Customers could also track their orders online. As a result of this new technology, staffing in the order processing department was cut from 120 to 32. The table in Figure 42.2 shows a comparison of performance indicators before and after the efficiency drive.

	2006	2009
Lead time	10 days	3 days
Order picking errors	7,445	2,187
Absenteeism	10.10%	6.90%
Customer complaints	1,343	312
Sales revenue	$34 million	$47 million
Wage bill	$5.3 million	$4.1 million

▲ **Figure 42.2**
Key performance indicators at GMMO 2006 and 2009

(a) What measures have GMMO taken to become a more flexible business? **(4 marks)**

(b) What evidence is there to suggest that worker motivation has improved? **(2 marks)**

(c) Outline two problems that GMMO may have encountered when introducing new technology. **(4 marks)**

(d) Do you think the efficiency drive has worked at GMMO? **(8 marks)**

Chapter 43

Cash and cash flow forecasts

Getting started...

The flow of money into and out of a business is called **cash flow**. Cash flows out of a business when payments are made for resources. Cash flows into a business when customers pay for goods and services. Cash also flows in when other income, such as interest, is received. Look at the cash flows in the examples below.

NK's Galle Bus Service

Nadeeka Karunaratne runs a bus service along the busy Galle Road transporting passengers between Colombo, the capital of Sri Lanka, and the coastal town of Galle. During May 2009 Nadeeka paid out Rs 3,200 for diesel, Rs 3,500 for repairs to a bus, Rs 2,000 in wages and Rs 500 in other running costs. During the month Nadeeka's bus service collected a total of Rs 9,300 in bus fares.

Northbridge Engineering

Northbridge Engineering makes concrete products such as chimney copings, concrete slabs, lintels, sills and door thresholds for the building industry in Western Australia. In June 2009 the business paid AUD45,600 to its workers, AUD145,000 for raw materials, AUD31,890 in bills for rent, utilities and other expenses and AUD12,300 to the tax authorities. During the same month the company received payments of AUD311,800 from customers, AUD1,400 interest and AUD50,000 from a bank loan to help pay for some new machinery.

▲ **Figure 43.1**
The road approaching Galle

(a) Identify ways in which cash is flowing into and out of the above businesses.

(b) (i) Calculate the net cash flow (cash inflows – cash outflows) for NK's Galle Bus service.
(ii) What does the answer in (i) show?

The importance of cash

Cash is the most **liquid** of all business assets. Cash is the notes and coins a business keeps on the premises and any money it has in the bank. Without cash a business cannot trade. It is reckoned that about 20% of business failures are because of poor cash flow. Even when trading conditions are good, businesses can fail. If a business does not have enough cash to pay its immediate bills, it cannot trade.

Controlling cash flow

It is important that a business continually monitors and controls its cash flow. It must ensure that it has enough cash to pay staff wages and bills when they are due. A business will have better control over its cash flow if it:

- keeps up-to-date business records;
- always plans ahead by producing accurate cash flow forecasts, for example;
- operates an efficient credit control system that prevents slow or late payment.

Cash inflows and outflows

Cash inflows The money coming into a business is called a **cash inflow**. Cash flows into a business when income is received. Examples of cash inflows are sales revenue, loans, fresh capital from the owners, interest and the sale of assets. The expected cash inflows for Kamal Motor Services (Cairo) in June 2009 are shown in Figure 43.2.

Cash outflows The money going out of a business is called a **cash outflow**. Cash flows out of a business when payments are made. This might include wages, materials, utilities, machinery, rent and tax. Expected cash payments for Kamal Motor Services in June 2009 are shown in Figure 43.2.

Net cash flow The difference between cash inflows and cash outflows is called the **net cash flow**. A business will hope that for most of the time the net cash flow is positive. This means that more cash flows in than flows out. However, there will be times when the net cash flow is negative. This means that a business may have to borrow some money. The net cash flow for Kamal Motor services in June 2009 is E£1,450 (E£8,950 – E£7,500)

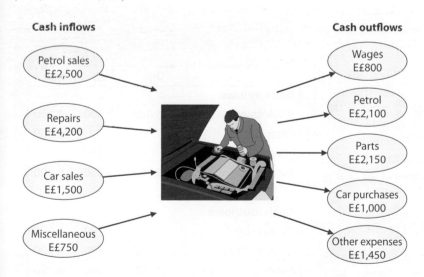

Cash inflows

Petrol sales E£2,500

Repairs E£4,200

Car sales E£1,500

Miscellaneous E£750

Cash outflows

Wages E£800

Petrol E£2,100

Parts E£2,150

Car purchases E£1,000

Other expenses E£1,450

Figure 43.2
Expected cash inflows and outflows for Kamal Motor Services – June 2009

Cash flow forecasts

Most businesses produce a regular **cash flow forecast**. This is a financial document and shows the expected *cash inflows* and *cash outflows* over a future period of time. All the figures in the forecast are estimated because they are in the future. The forecast shows the planned cash flow of the business month by month. A cash flow forecast is shown for Kamal Motor Services in Figure 43.3. It is a three-month forecast.

▼ Figure 43.3
Cash flow forecast for Kamal Motor Services

The forecast shows that the cash position is expected to improve over the three months. At the end of June the business expects to have a closing cash balance of E£1,900. By the end of August the cash balance is expected to be E£3,150. However, there is a negative net cash flow in August. This is because of the extra money the business plans to spend buying cars for resale.

Total cash inflow
This is the total amount of cash Kamal Motor Services expects to generate during the month, i.e. E£8,950 during June

Total cash outflow
This is the total amount of cash Kamal Motor Services expects to pay out during the month, i.e. E£7,500 during June

Closing balance
This is the opening balance plus the net cash flow for the month. For June it is E£1,900 (E£450 + E£1,450). The closing balance for June is also the opening balance for July

Net cash flow
This the difference between the total cash inflow and the total cash outflow. For June it is E£1,450 (E£8,950 − E£7,500)

Opening balance
The amount of cash the business has at the beginning of the month, i.e. E£450 at the beginning of June

	June	July	August
Cash inflows			
Petrol sales	2,500	2,600	2,700
Repairs	4,200	4,000	4,500
Car sales	1,500	2,000	1,500
Miscellaneous sales	750	750	800
Total cash inflows	8,950	9,350	9,500
Cash outflows			
Wages	800	800	800
Petrol	2,100	2,100	2,300
Parts	2,150	2,200	2,400
Car purchases	1,000	1,000	3,000
Other expenses	1,450	1,500	1,500
Total cash outflows	7,500	7,600	10,000
Net cash flow	1,450	1,750	−500
Opening balance	450	1,900	3,650
Closing balance	1,900	3,650	3,150

QUESTION 1

Yosuke Makino owns a book shop near the University of Osaka, Japan. He sells educational books to students but also has a large stock of fiction books. Unfortunately the business has been struggling in recent months. He thinks that many students are sharing books and therefore his sales are suffering. Figure 43.4 shows a cash flow forecast for the book shop at the beginning of 2009. It is incomplete.

(a) Using examples from this case, explain the difference between cash inflows and cash outflows.

(b) Complete the cash flow forecast for Yosuke Makino's book shop to show:
   (i) the total cash outflows for each month;
   (ii) the closing balance for each month;
   (iii) the opening balance for February and March.

(c) What evidence is there in the forecast to support the view that the business is struggling?

Figure 43.4 Cash flow forecast for Yosuke Makino's book shop ▷

	Jan	Feb	Mar
Cash inflows			
Book sales	3,000	3,500	3,100
Fresh capital			2,000
Interest		150	
Total cash inflows	3,000	3,650	5,100
Cash outflows			
Stock	1,700	1,790	1,900
Casual labour	500	500	500
Rent	1,000	1,000	1,000
Other expenses	230	240	230
Total cash outflows	?	?	?
Net cash flow	?	?	?
Opening balance	230	?	?
Closing balance	?	?	?

Why are cash flow forecasts important?

Businesses draw up cash flow forecasts to help control and monitor cash flow. What are the advantages?

Identifying cash shortages A forecast can help to identify in advance when a business might need to borrow cash. The forecast clearly shows how much cash is left at the end of each month. This will help to identify when a bank overdraft will be needed.

Supporting applications for funding When trying to raise finance, lenders often insist that businesses support their applications with a cash flow forecast. This will help to show the future outlook for the business.

Help when planning the business Careful planning in business is important. It helps to clarify aims and improve performance. Producing a cash flow forecast is a key part of the planning process.

Monitoring cash flow A business should compare the predicted figures in the cash flow forecast with those that actually occur. By doing this it can find out where problems have arisen. It could then try to find out why differences have occurred.

Key terms

Cash flow – the flow of money into and out of a business.
Cash flow forecast – the prediction of all expected receipts and expenses of a business over a future time period that shows the expected cash balance at the end of each month.
Cash inflow – the flow of money into a business.
Cash outflow – the flow of money out of a business.
Liquid asset – an asset that is easily changed into cash.
Net cash flow – the difference between the cash flowing in and the cash flowing out of a business in a given time period.

Chapter review – Evans Garden Maintenance

Jill Evans set up her own garden maintenance business in 2007. She put in some of her own capital and persuaded a bank to lend her more. By February 2007 Jill had found several customers who promised her regular work. Figure 43.5 shows the predicted revenue for the first nine months of trading. The following financial information was also gathered:

• A bank loan of $3,000 would be needed in April.
• Jill would contribute $2,000 of her own savings as capital in April.
• A van for $2,000 would be purchased in April.
• Tools and equipment for $3,400 would be purchased in April.
• A laptop computer with specialist design software for $600 would be purchased in April.
• A business directory listing would cost $100 in May.
• General overheads would be $400 per month.

• Advertising would be $100 in alternate months starting in May.
• Jill would take out $800 per month starting in June.
• Loan repayments would be $200 per month.

(a) Explain the meaning of the term 'cash flow forecast'. **(2 marks)**

(b) Draw up a 9-month cash flow forecast for Evans Garden Maintenance. (Use a spreadsheet if possible.) **(12 marks)**
(i) Comment on the cash position of the business during the 9-month period. **(2 marks)**
(ii) What would you expect to happen to the cash position of the business in early 2008? Explain your answer. **(4 marks)**

	APR	MAY	JUN	JUL	AUG	SEP	OCT	NOV	DEC
Predicted revenue (£)	2,000	2,100	2,000	2,500	2,500	2,000	1,000	500	0

▲ **Figure 43.5** Predicted revenue for Evans Garden Maintenance (first 9 months)

Chapter 44

Profit and the profit and loss account

Getting started...

Most business owners want to make a profit. It is the main reason why they went into business. At the end of the financial year businesses produce a **profit and loss account**. This shows all the income and the costs for a business and is used to calculate the profit. It might also be used to help make decisions such as how much the business should invest in the future. Look at the example below.

Profit and loss account for Golf Discount Store

The Golf Discount Store is run by Hank Donavan, a sole trader. He buys golf clubs, accessories and golf wear from suppliers and rents a shop in Jacksonville, Florida. A profit and loss account for the business is shown in Figure 44.1.

(a) Using Figure 44.1, state the (i) turnover; (ii) total expenses; and (iii) profit made by the Golf Discount Store.

(b) How might Hank Donavan use the profit and loss account?

Golf Discount Store Profit and Loss Account Year ended 31 December 2008		
	$	$
Sales		256,400
Cost of sales		137,100
Gross profit		**119,300**
Less expenses:		
Wages	24,100	
Rent	36,000	
Business rates	2,300	
Interest	600	
Motor expenses	3,900	
	11,600	
Other expenses		
		78,500
Net profit		**40,800**

▲ **Figure 44.1**
2008 profit and loss account for the Golf Discount Store

Why does profit matter?

Without **profit** businesses would not exist in the private sector. Profit has two important functions:

- **Incentive:** Profit is the driving force behind most businesses. It motivates people to set up in business. Without profit there would be little incentive for people to commit their time and money to a business venture. Profit is also the *reward for risk taking* in business. Entrepreneurs are prepared to risk their own money because they think they can make a profit.

- **Measure of performance**: The amount of profit made by a business is an indicator of its performance. It is possible to compare the performance of businesses by comparing the size of profits. Larger profits generally mean that businesses have performed well. However, other factors may affect performance such as the amount of competition in a market.

Measuring profit

Businesses usually calculate their profit at the end of the *financial year*. This is a 12-month trading period and can vary. For example, it might be from 1 June 2008 to 31 May 2009. A business normally calculates its profit using two steps. First it calculates **gross profit**. This is the profit made before expenses or overheads are subtracted. It is found by using:

   Gross profit = turnover – cost of sales

Then it calculates **net profit**. This is profit after expenses and is found by:

   Net profit = gross profit – expenses

Sometimes a business receives other income such as interest. Net profit is then:

   Gross profit + income – expenses

Figure 44.2 summarises this.

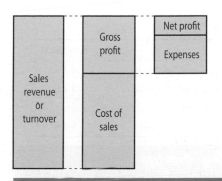

▲ **Figure 44.2**
Calculating gross and net profit

Retained and distributed profit

Some of the net profit made by a business is used to pay taxes. Sole traders and business partners may pay *income tax* whereas limited companies may pay *corporation tax*. The profit after tax can be **distributed** or **retained**. Some of the profit is likely to be distributed to the owners of the business. For example, limited companies may return some of the profit to shareholders. They are paid a **dividend**. Any undistributed profit is retained by the business. This may be 'ploughed back' into the business. This means it may be used to help fund investment projects. It may also be kept as a reserve in case trading conditions become difficult in the future.

 ## QUESTION 1

French Ltd produces packaging for the food industry. In 2009, its turnover was $12.56m. Its cost of sales was $7.6m and expenses were $2.56m.

(a) Calculate: (i) gross profit; (ii) net profit.

(b) (i) If $0.8m is distributed to shareholders, how much profit is retained?
     (ii) What happens to retained profit?

The profit and loss account

The **profit and loss account**, or the **income statement**, as it is now called, shows the income and expenses of a business during the financial year. It is used to calculate the gross profit and net profit. The layout of the account is important. Information must be presented in a standard way. For example it is divided into three sections: the **trading account**; the **profit and loss account**; and the **profit and loss appropriation account**.

The trading account This is the first section of the account and is used to calculate gross profit. The trading account for Xu Hong Ltd, a large cloth and fabric merchant, is shown in Figure 44.3. What does the trading account show?

	$ million
Sale turnover	23.7
Cost of sales	13.2
Gross profit	10.5

▲ **Figure 44.3**
Trading account for Xu Hong Ltd – 2008

- It shows the turnover of the business. In this case it is the money generated from the sale of cloth and fabric to retailers: $23.7 million.

- The second figure is the **cost of sales**. This is the direct costs of a business. In this case it represents the cost of the fabric and cloth bought from suppliers. For a manufacturer it would be direct production costs such as direct labour and raw materials. In this case the cost of sales is $13.2 million.

- Gross profit is calculated by subtracting cost of sales from turnover. In this case the gross profit is $10.5 million. It is the profit made before expenses are deducted.

The profit and loss account The second section is called the profit and loss account. It shows how net profit is calculated. The profit and loss account for Xu Hong Ltd is shown in Figure 44.4. What details does it contain?

	$ million
Gross profit	10.5
Expenses	6.0
Operating profit	4.5
Non-operating income	0.4
	4.9
Interest paid	0.6
Net profit	4.3

▲ **Figure 44.4**
Profit and loss account for Xu Hong – 2008

- The account starts with gross profit. This was calculated in the trading account.

- The total expenses or overheads are $6 million.

- Operating profit is the gross profit minus total expenses. In this case it is $4.5 million.

- Non-operating income includes any income which does not come from sales. It may be dividends, or perhaps rent from the lease of property belonging to the business. It must be shown separately in company accounts and in this case is $0.4 million. This is added to operating profit.

- Interest paid also has to be shown separately in company accounts. In 2008 Xu Hong Ltd paid $0.6 million interest. This is subtracted from operating profit.

- Net profit is the profit before tax and is $4.3 million for Xu Hong Ltd.

The profit and loss appropriation account This third section shows how the net profit is distributed. Figure 44.5 shows the profit and loss appropriation account for Xu Hong Ltd.

- It starts with net profit. This was calculated in the profit and loss account.
- Taxation of $0.9 million is deducted to get net profit after tax. This is $3.4 million.
- An amount of $1.2 million has been distributed to shareholders in dividends.
- A total $2.2 million has been retained in the business.

	$ million
Net profit	4.3
Taxation	0.9
Profit after taxation	3.4
Dividends	1.2
Retained profit for the period	2.2

▲ Figure 44.5
Profit and loss appropriation account for Xu Hong Ltd – 2008

In practice, the profit and loss account is not split into three sections. It is shown as one account like that in Figure 44.5. There are also differences between the accounts of sole traders, such as the one shown in Figure 44.1, and those of companies, such as Xu Hong Ltd. For example, a more detailed breakdown of expenses is usually given in sole trader accounts. Finally, accounts usually show the figures for two years. This allows comparisons to be made.

QUESTION 2

SoftHart plc produce software for computer games. It employs 230 staff and operates from Bermuda. Figure 44.7 shows an incomplete profit and loss account for 2009.

(a) Complete the profit and loss account for SoftHart plc by calculating the operating profit and retained profit for 2009, and the cost of sales and profit after tax for 2008.

(b) Comment on the performance of the business over the two years.

Figure 44.6 ▶
Profit and loss account for SoftHart plc (incomplete)

SoftHart plc Profit and loss account Year ending 31 December 2009		
	$m	$m
	2009	2008
Sales turnover	26.9	29.2
Cost of sales	17.4	?
Gross profit	9.5	11.1
Expenses	4.6	4.8
Operating profit	?	6.3
Interest paid	1.8	1.5
Net profit	3.3	4.7
Taxation	1.1	1.6
Profit after taxation	2.2	?
Dividends	0	1
Retained profit for the period	?	2.1

The difference between cash and profit

It is important to recognise that cash and profit are different. At the end of a trading year the value of profit will not be the same as the cash balance. Some of the reasons for this are outlined below:

- Some goods are sold on credit. So, at the end of the year, some customers will still owe money. Therefore, profit is greater than cash. Similarly, a business may receive cash at the beginning of the trading year from credit sales made in the previous year. This would increase the cash balance, but not affect profit.

Key terms

Distributed profit – profit that is returned to the owners of a business.

Dividend – money paid to shareholders when profit is distributed.

Gross profit – sales revenue minus cost of sales.

Net profit – gross profit minus expenses.

Profit – the money left over after all costs have been subtracted from revenue.

Profit and loss account or income statement – a financial document showing a firm's income and expenditure in a particular time period.

Profit and loss account – shows how net profit is calculated by subtracting expenses from gross profit.

Profit and loss appropriation account – shows how the profit after tax is distributed between owners and the business.

Retained profit – profit that is kept by the business and may be used in the future.

Trading account – shows how gross profit is calculated by subtracting cost of sales from turnover.

- Sometimes owners might put more cash into the business. This will increase the cash balance, but have no effect on the profit made. The effect will be the same if a business borrows money from a bank.

- Purchases of fixed assets will reduce cash balances, but have no effect on the profit a company makes. This is because the purchase of assets is not included as a cost in the profit and loss account.

- The amount of cash at the end of the year will be different from profit because at the beginning of the year the cash balance is unlikely to be zero.

It is possible for a business to trade for several years without making a profit. Provided it has enough cash it can carry on trading. However, if a business runs out of cash it will collapse.

Chapter review – Spring Valley Farm Ltd

Spring Valley Farm Ltd is located in Kenya. It produces flowers and specialises in rose growing. Most of its output is exported to Europe. The farm is a Gold member of the Kenya Flower Council. This has an internationally respected code of practice. Membership helps to sell flowers in Europe. Some financial information is shown in Figure 44.7.

	$	$
	2009	2008
Sales turnover	560,400	470,600
Dividends	20,000	10,000
Interest paid	20,000	20,000
Cost of sales	302,100	270,500
Distribution expenses	89,600	81,900
Administration expenses	24,100	21,300
Taxation	40,000	25,000

▲ **Figure 44.7**
Financial information for Spring Valley Farm Ltd (year ending 31 December 2009)

(a) Use this case as an example to explain what a profit and loss account shows. **(2 marks)**

(b) Explain two reasons why profit matters. **(4 marks)**

(c) Draw up a profit and loss account for Spring Valley Farm Ltd. **(6 marks)**

(d) Comment on the performance of the business over the two years. **(4 marks)**

(e) At the end of the financial year the cash balance for Spring Valley Farm Ltd was $136,700. Explain two reasons why it is different from the profit made in 2009. **(4 marks)**

Chapter 45

Balance sheets

Getting started...

Businesses keep a record of all the resources they own such as land, property, machinery, tools, stock and cash. They also keep a record of all the money they owe to banks, suppliers, the owners and other businesses. At the end of the financial year, a business produces a summary of these financial details called a **balance sheet**. Look at the example below.

Benazir Patel

In 2008, Benazir Patel set up an interior design business. She bought a car, a computer, some design software and rented a small office in Bengaluru, India. She used $10,000 of her family's money and a five-year bank loan of $3,000 to start the business. By the end of the first trading year Benazir had made a profit of $16,200. She was owed $2,400 by customers, had $4,500 cash in the bank and owed $1,200 to suppliers. During the year she took $11,000 from the business for personal use. Figure 45.1 shows a balance sheet for Benazir Patel's business at the end of the first trading year.

(a) What is the value of all the assets owned by the business?

(b) How much money does the business owe to:
(i) the owner; (ii) all other creditors?

(c) What do you notice about the value of assets and the total amount owed by the business?

Figure 45.1
Balance sheet for Benazir Patel as at 31 August 2009

Benazir Patel
Balance sheet as at 31 August 2009

	$	$
Fixed assets		
Car		9,000
Computer equipment		3,500
		12,500
Current assets		
Debtors	2,400	
Cash	4,500	
	6,900	
Current liabilities		
Trade creditors	1,200	
Working capital		5,700
Long-term liabilities		
5-year bank loan		(3,000)
Net assets		15,200
Capital		
Opening capital	10,000	
Add profit	16,200	
	26,200	
Less drawings	11,000	
Closing capital		15,200

What is a balance sheet?

In addition to a profit and loss account, most businesses produce a balance sheet at the end of the financial year. A balance sheet is like a photograph of a firm's financial position at a particular point in time. It provides a summary of a firm's **assets**, **liabilities** and **capital**.

KEY FACT

In all balance sheets the value of assets (what a business uses or owns) will equal the value of liabilities and capital (what the business owes). This is because all resources purchased by a business have to be financed from either capital or liabilities. Therefore:

Assets = capital + liabilities

So, if a business has capital of $5 million and liabilities of $2.6 million, the value of assets must be $7.6 million ($5 million + $2.6 million).

- **Assets** are the resources owned by a business. Examples include buildings, machinery, equipment, vehicles, stock and cash. Businesses use assets to make products or provide services.

- **Liabilities** are the debts of the business, that is, what it owes to others. Liabilities are a *source of funds* for a business. They might be short-term, such as an overdraft, or long-term, such as a mortgage.

- **Capital** is the money put into the business by the owners. It is used to buy assets.

QUESTION 1

Anwa Gawli runs a garage and petrol station. The value of his business's assets is $145,600. Anwa has $105,600 of his own money invested in the business and a 25-year mortgage. Anwa sells petrol and motor accessories and carries out minor repairs in a workshop at the back of the petrol station.

(a) Using this case as an example, explain the difference between assets and liabilities.

(b) Calculate the value of the mortgage for this business. (There are no other liabilities.)

The structure of a balance sheet

The balance sheet for Li Shangbin, a refrigeration engineer, is shown in Figure 45.2. Li Shangbin is a sole trader and provides a refrigeration maintenance service for businesses in Hong Kong. The presentation of balance sheets may vary between different businesses. For example, the balance sheets of limited companies are slightly different from those of sole traders. The details likely to be found in a balance sheet are outlined below.

Fixed assets

Details of a firm's **fixed assets** are given at the top of the balance sheet. Fixed assets are those that last for more than one year. They are the most productive resources of a business. Li Shangbin's business has two fixed assets: a van, and tools and equipment. The total value of these fixed assets at 31 December 2008 was $18,000.

Current assets

Current assets are assets that will be changed into cash within one year. They are *liquid* assets. The liquidity of an asset is how easily it can be changed into cash.

Examples might include:

- **Stocks** of raw materials, semi-finished goods and finished goods. Li Shangbin's business holds stocks of spare parts for refrigerators. These are valued at $2,300.
- **Debtors** – customers that owe money to the firm. In this case Li Shangbin is owed $2,400.
- **Cash** 'in hand' or in the bank. The balance sheet in Figure 45.2 shows that Li Shangbin has $4,300 in cash.

Current liabilities

Current liabilities are business debts that must be repaid within 12 months. They might include:

- **Trade creditors**, which is money owed to suppliers. Li Shangbin's business owes $3,700. This money might be owed to suppliers of spare parts, utility providers or any other business supplying commercial services.
- **Leases and hire purchase**, which are other forms of borrowing.
- **Short-term loans and overdrafts**, which is money owed to banks repayable within 12 months.

Li Shangbin's business does not have any lease, hire purchase, short-term loans or overdrafts.

Working capital or net current assets

Figure 45.2 shows that Li Shangbin's business has $5,300 of **working capital**. Working capital is also known as **net current assets**. It is calculated by subtracting current liabilities from current assets (in this case $9,000 – $3,700). This is an important figure in the balance sheet. It shows the amount of liquid resources a business has available. Working capital is used to meet the running costs of a business. If a business is short of working capital it could have cash flow problems. Working capital is discussed in more detail in Chapter 47.

Long-term liabilities

Any money owed for more than one year is called a **long-term liability**. Examples might include the following:

- **A mortgage** is a long-term secured loan usually taken out to buy property. It is secured against the value of property so that if the borrower cannot repay the loan the lender can repossess the property.
- **A long-term loan** is any loan taken out for more than one year. Li Shangbin's business has a five-year loan for $5,000. Note that this is shown in brackets in the balance sheet. This means that it is subtracted when calculating net assets;
- **Long-term leases and hire purchase** if the money has been borrowed for more than a year.

Li Shangbin's business does not have any mortgages, long-term leases or hire purchase.

Li Shangbin Balance sheet as at 31 December 2008		
	$	$
Fixed assets		
Van		9,500
Tools and equipment		8,500
		18,000
Current assets		
Stocks of spare parts	2,300	
Debtors	2,400	
Cash	4,300	
	9,000	
Current liabilities		
Trade creditors	3,700	
Working capital		5,300
Long-term liabilities		
5-year bank loan		(5,000)
Net assets		18,300
Capital		
Opening capital	12,500	
Add profit	26,800	
	39,300	
Less drawings	21,000	
Closing capital		18,300

▲ **Figure 45.2**
Balance sheet for Li Shangbin – 31 December 2008

Net assets

Net assets is the total at the bottom of the first part of the balance sheet. It is the value of all assets minus the value of all liabilities. It can be calculated by adding working capital to fixed assets and subtracting long-term liabilities. The value of net assets for Li Shangbin's business is $18,300.

Capital

The bottom of the balance sheet shows the capital of the business. Closing capital is found by adding profit to the opening capital and then subtracting drawings. Drawings is the money taken from the business by the owners for personal use. The opening capital is the closing balance from the previous year. In 2008 Li Shangbin made a profit of $26,800 and withdrew $21,000 for personal use. The closing capital is therefore $18,300. This is what the business owes Li Shangbin and is also equal to the net assets.

QUESTION 2

Tariq Khan runs a small construction company. He specialises in the construction of conservatories, property extensions and loft conversions. He employs six other people and has enjoyed a profitable run since setting up in business in 2002. Figure 45.3 shows an incomplete balance sheet for his business at 31 July 2009.

(a) What is the value of (i) stocks; (ii) overdraft; (iii) net assets?

(b) Using examples from the case, explain the difference between fixed assets and current assets.

Tariq Khan
Balance sheet as at 31 July 2009

	$	$
Fixed assets		
Vans		18,000
Tools and equipment		25,000
		43,000
Current assets		
Stocks of raw materials	?	
Debtors	30,000	
	33,400	
Current liabilities		
Lease	5,000	
Trade creditors	7,800	
Overdraft	?	
	20,400	
Working capital		13,000
Long-term liabilities		
Mortgage		(25,000)
Net assets		?
Capital		
Opening capital		23,000
Add profit		53,200
		76,200
Less drawings		45,200
Closing capital		31,000

Figure 45.3 ▶
Tariq Khan as at 31 July 2009 (incomplete)

Limited company balance sheets

The balance sheet for a limited company is set out slightly differently to that of a sole trader. An example is shown in Figure 45.4.

Note that figures for two years are shown so that comparisons can be made.

How might the balance sheet be used?

A balance sheet shows the financial position of a business and can be used to evaluate its performance and potential:

- It shows the value of all business assets, capital and liabilities.
- It shows the asset structure of a business. It can show how the money raised by the business has been spent on different types of asset.
- It shows the capital structure of a business. A business can raise funds from many different sources, such as shareholders' capital, retained profit and long-term and short-term sources.
- The value of working capital shows whether a firm is able to pay its everyday expenses or is likely to have problems. It shows the money left over after all current liabilities have been paid. This can be used to settle the day-to-day debts of the business.
- A balance sheet may provide a guide to a firm's value. Generally, the value of the business is represented by the value of net assets.

Mecasystems Ltd Balance sheet as at 31 May 2009		
	2009 $m	2008 $m
Fixed assets		
Factory	34.65	36.44
Plant and equipment	9.12	7.34
	43.77	43.78
Current assets		
Stocks	4.56	4.33
Debtors	6.99	4.34
Cash	2.11	4.19
	13.66	12.86
Current liabilities		
Trade creditors	6.77	6.21
Taxation	2.50	3.00
	9.27	9.21
Net current assets	4.39	3.65
Long term liabilities		
Mortgage	(5.00)	(5.00)
Net assets	48.04	47.99
Capital and reserves		
Share capital	10.00	10.00
Retained profit	34.14	32.78
Other reserves	3.90	5.21
Capital employed	48.04	47.99

▲ **Figure 45.4**
Balance sheet for Mecasystems Ltd as at 31 May 2009

Key terms

Assets – resources used or owned by the business in production.
Balance sheet – a summary at a point in time of business assets, liabilities and capital.
Capital – a source of funds provided by the owners of the business that is used to buy assets.
Current assets – assets likely to be changed into cash within a year.
Current liabilities – debts that have to be repaid within a year.
Fixed assets – assets with a life span of more than one year.
Liabilities – the debts of the business that provide a source of funds.
Long-term liabilities – debts that are payable after 12 months.
Net current assets – current assets minus current liabilities. Also known as working capital.

Chapter review – The Golden Inn Ltd

The Golden Inn is a small hotel located in Plettenberg Bay, South Africa. It employs eight staff and has a good reputation for high-quality accommodation. In 2009, a £60,000 mortgage was taken out to build an indoor swimming pool. Some financial information for the hotel is shown in Figure 45.5.

	$000		$000
Property	440	Trade creditors	112
Fixtures and fittings	100	Taxation	12
Stocks	120	Share capital	100
Debtors	108	Retained profit	395
Cash	56	Other reserves	45
Mortgage	60		

▲ **Figure 45.5**
Financial information for The Golden Inn Ltd

(a) State two ways in which a balance sheet might be used? (2 marks)

(b) Explain how The Golden Inn Ltd is funding its business activities. (4 marks)

(c) Prepare a balance sheet for The Golden Inn Ltd. (10 marks)

(d) What is the value of The Golden Inn Ltd? (2 marks)

(e) Do you think the business has enough working capital? (2 marks)

Chapter 46

Ratio analysis

Getting started...

The balance sheet can show the financial position of a business and the profit and loss account can show how well it has performed. For example, the profit and loss account shows how much profit a business has made and the balance sheet shows whether a business can pay its bills. Look at the example below.

LemCo Ltd

Bangkok-based LemCo Ltd makes soft drinks for the Thai market. At the end of 2008, a competitor entered the market, which had an impact on the performance of LemCo. In 2009, LemCo Ltd announced that it would lay off 12 of its 32 staff in 2010.

LemCo Ltd
Profit and loss account year ending 31 August 2009

	$	$
	2009	2008
Sales turnover	890,600	1,231,500
Cost of sales	302,100	334,100
Gross profit	588,500	897,400
Distribution expenses	254,700	298,700
Administration expenses	276,400	325,600
Operating profit	57,400	273,100
Interest paid	59,800	34,000
Net profit	(2,400)	239,100
Taxation	0	80,500
Profit after taxation	(2,400)	158,600
Dividends	0	50,000
Retained profit for the period	(2,400)	108,600

Figure 46.1 ▶
Profit and loss account for LemCo Ltd

▼ **Figure 46.2**
An extract from the balance sheet for LemCo Ltd as at 31 August 2009

	2009	2008
Current assets		
Stocks	129,600	111,400
Debtors	412,400	445,200
Cash	12,000	128,900
	554,000	685,500
Current liabilities		
Creditors	539,700	446,200
Working capital	14,300	239,300

(a) Look at Figures 46.1 and 46.2. What evidence is there to support the view that LemCo Ltd has been adversely affected by the arrival of new competition in the market for soft drinks?

(b) How might the staff lay-offs improve financial performance at LemCo?

What is ratio analysis?

It is possible to look at a balance sheet and profit and loss account and draw some conclusions about the financial position of a business. However, a more precise way is to use **ratio analysis**. This involves taking key figures from the accounts and calculating financial ratios. There are different types of financial ratios:

- **Profitability ratios**: These measure the performance of the business and focus on profit, turnover and the amount invested in the business.

- **Liquidity ratios**: These assess how easily a business can pay its debts.

- **Gearing ratios**: These look at the capital structure of a business and compare the amount of share capital a business has in relation to its loan capital.

- **Shareholders' ratios**: These assess the returns to shareholders on their investment in the business.

	2008	2007
	$000	$000
Turnover	23,500	18,400
Cost of sales	12,500	10,100
Gross profit	11,000	8,300
Net profit	4,600	3,200
Current assets	13,600	11,900
Stocks	4,900	5,000
Current liabilities	8,700	7,800
Capital employed	20,000	18,000

▲ **Figure 46.3**
Financial information from the accounts of Ecohomes plc

KEY FACT

To increase the gross profit margin turnover must be increased or cost of sales reduced. The gross profit margin will be different for different industries. For example, firms that sell stock quickly, such as supermarkets, can operate with lower gross margins.

Gross profit margin

Figure 46.3 shows some financial information that has been taken from the accounts of Ecohomes plc, a supplier of environmentally friendly homes in Sweden. The information will be used in this unit to calculate a number of useful ratios. The **gross profit margin** is also known as the mark-up. This shows the gross profit made on sales turnover. It is calculated using the formula:

$$\text{Gross profit margin} = \frac{\text{Gross profit}}{\text{Turnover}} \times 100$$

For Ecohomes in 2008 gross profit was $11,000,000 and turnover was $23,500,000.

$$\text{For 2008 gross profit margin} = \frac{\$11,000,000}{\$23,500,000} \times 100 = 46.8\%$$

$$\text{For 2007 gross profit margin} = \frac{\$8,300,000}{\$18,400,000} \times 100 = 45.1\%$$

Higher gross margins are better than lower ones. The gross margin for Ecohomes plc has improved slightly over the two years from 45.1% to 46.8%.

Net profit margin

The **net profit margin** helps to measure how well a business controls its overheads and cost of sales. If the difference between the gross margin and the net margin is small, this suggests that overheads are low. The net profit margin can be calculated by:

$$\text{Net profit margin} = \frac{\text{Net profit}}{\text{Turnover}} \times 100$$

For Ecohomes in 2008 net profit was $4,600,000 and turnover was $23,500,000.

$$\text{For 2008 net profit margin} = \frac{\$4,600,000}{\$23,500,000} \times 100 = 19.5\%$$

$$\text{For 2007 net profit margin} = \frac{\$3,200,000}{\$18,400,000} \times 100 = 17.4\%$$

KEY FACT

Higher margins are better than lower ones. Net margins over 10% would be regarded as good.

The net profit margin for Ecohomes has improved over the two years. This suggests that the business kept control of overheads more effectively in 2008 than in 2007.

QUESTION 1

The Guangzhou Metal Company (GMC) makes metal components for the construction industry. In 2006 and 2007 the company received a flood of orders to supply components to companies completing building work for the Beijing Olympics. Some financial information for GMC is shown in Figure 46.4.

	2003	2004	2005	2006	2007
Sales turnover	12.4	13.8	14.9	19.8	24.1
Gross profit	4.9	5.6	6.1	9.8	12.3
Overheads	3.9	4.4	4.8	7.7	9.7
Net profit	1	1.2	1.3	2.1	2.6

▲ Figure 46.4
Guangzhou Metal Company profit and loss account – five-year summary ($ million)

(a) Just looking at the sales figures in Figure 46.4, do you think GMC performed well between 2003 and 2007?

(b) What impact has the flood of orders had on GMC?

(c) Calculate: (i) gross profit margin; and (ii) net profit margin.

(d) Discuss possible reasons for the changes in (c) over the time period.

Current ratio

The **current ratio** is a liquidity ratio and focuses on current assets and current liabilities. It is calculated using the formula:

$$\text{Current ratio} = \frac{\text{Current assets}}{\text{Current liabilities}}$$

KEY FACT

It is suggested that a business will have enough liquid resources if the current ratio is between 1.5 and 2. If the ratio is below 1.5, it might be argued that a business does not have enough working capital. This might mean that it is running short of liquid assets. Operating above 2 may suggest that too much money is tied up unproductively.

KEY FACT

If the acid test ratio is less than 1, it means that current assets minus stocks do not cover current liabilities. This might be a problem. However, as with the current ratio, the acid test ratios of businesses in different industries tend to vary.

For Ecohomes current assets were £13,600,000 in 2008 and current liabilities were £8,700,000.

$$\text{For 2008 Current ratio} = \frac{\$13,600,000}{\$8,700,000} = 1.56$$

$$\text{For 2007 Current ratio} = \frac{\$11,900,000}{\$7,800,000} = 1.53$$

The current ratio for Ecohomes rose very slightly from 1.53 to 1.56.

Acid test ratio

The **acid test ratio** is a more severe test of liquidity. This is because stocks are not treated as liquid resources. Stocks are not guaranteed to be sold. Therefore, they are excluded from current assets when calculating this ratio.

$$\text{Acid test ratio} = \frac{\text{Current assets} - \text{stocks}}{\text{Current liabilities}}$$

$$\text{For 2008 Acid test ratio} = \frac{\$13,600,000 - \$4,900,000}{\$8,700,000} = 1$$

$$\text{For 2007 Acid test ratio} = \frac{\$11,900,000 - \$5,000,000}{\$7,800,000} = 0.88$$

Over the two years, the acid test ratio for Ecohomes has improved slightly from 0.88 to 1.

 QUESTION 2

HR Owen operates vehicle franchises in the prestige car market. For example, it sells Rolls-Royces, Maseratis, Ferraris and Lamborghinis. BPI (British Polythene Industries) manufactures over 300,000 tonnes of polythene product a year. Figure 46.5 shows current assets and current liabilities for the two companies.

	HR Owen		BPI	
	2008	2007	2008	2007
	£000	£000	£000	£000
Stocks	42,481	81,559	59,500	55,300
Other current assets	20,074	49,615	60,500	64,100
Total current assets	62,555	131,174	120,000	119,400
Current liabilities	53,757	136,531	68,300	75,500

Figure 46.5
Current assets and current liabilities for HR Owen and BPI

Source: adapted from HR Owen and BPI Annual Reports and Accounts

(a) Calculate the: (i) current ratios; (ii) acid test ratios for both companies in 2008 and 2007.

(b) (i) Which is the more liquid of the two companies? (ii) Suggest and explain one reason for your answer in (i).

Return on capital employed

One of the most important profitability ratios is the **return on capital employed (ROCE)**. It compares the profit (return), made by the business with the amount of money invested (its capital). The advantage of this ratio is that it relates profit to the size of the business. ROCE can be calculated using the formula:

$$ROCE = \frac{\text{Net profit}}{\text{Long-term capital employed}} \times 100$$

Net profit for Ecohomes in 2008 was \$4,600,000. Long-term capital employed was \$20,000,000. Long-term capital employed is capital and reserves plus any long-term loans.

$$\text{For 2008 ROCE} = \frac{\$4,600,000}{\$20,000,000} \times 100 = 23.0\%$$

$$\text{For 2007 ROCE} = \frac{\$3,200,000}{\$18,000,000} \times 100 = 17.7\%$$

The return on capital employed will vary between industries. Over the two years Ecohomes has seen its ROCE increase from 17.7% to 23.0%. These are good returns on capital if compared with the rate of interest at this time. Rates were around 3% or 4% on bank deposits in 2008. However, it must be remembered that investing money in business is risky compared with leaving it in a bank.

Key terms

Acid test ratio – similar to the current ratio but excludes stocks from current assets. Sometimes called the quick ratio.
Current ratio – assesses the firm's liquidity by dividing current liabilities into current assets.
Gross profit margin – gross profit expressed as a percentage of turnover.
Net profit margin – net profit expressed as a percentage of turnover.
Ratio analysis – a numerical approach to investigating accounts by comparing two related figures.
Return on capital employed (ROCE) – the profit of a business as a percentage of the total amount of money used to generate it.

Chapter review – Muscat Shippng Co

Muscat Shipping Co is owned by the Al-Dhabit family in Oman. Its main business is the transportation of oil. In 2008, the company was hit by the world recession and the owners injected £2 million to help it survive. Some financial information for the company is shown in Figure 46.6.

(a) What evidence is there in Figure 46.6 to suggest that Muscat Shipping Co was affected by the world recession? (2 marks)

(b) The ROCE is a performance ratio. What does this mean? (2 marks)

(c) Calculate: (i) net profit margin; (ii) current ratio; (iii) ROCE for Muscat Shipping Co in each of the three years. (9 marks)

(d) How do you think the business has performed over the three-year period? (7 marks)

	2007	2008	2009
Turnover	12.5	9.6	11.9
Net profit	1.13	0.34	1.17
Current assets	3.21	2.59	3.99
Current liabilities	2.16	2.55	2.43
Capital employed	10	12	12

▲ Figure 46.6
Extracts from the accounts of Muscat Shipping Co (\$ million)

Chapter 47

Working capital

Getting started...

Businesses need money to meet the costs of day-to-day trading. For example, an airliner will need money to pay for aviation fuel, airline meals, airport services, wages, and so on. If it does not have enough money to meet these costs, it will not be able to trade. Look at the example below.

ELCO

On 23 July 2009 Felipe Passarella, the managing director (MD) of ELCO, was a worried man. The electrical engineering company was running out of cash. He had just heard that a customer had gone bankrupt owing the company $24,000. This money was needed to help buy some materials for a new $200,000 order. Staff wages of $12,700 were also due to be paid on 30 July 2009 and ELCO was $12,300 overdrawn at the bank. The overdraft limit was $20,000. The profit on the $200,000 order would be $48,000, but this would not be received until the order had been completed and delivered.

(a) How much money does ELCO need to pay the wages on 30 July 2009 (assume no other income or expenses)?

(b) How might Felipe Passarella deal with the problem?

(c) What might happen to the business if Felipe cannot get enough cash to pay the wages on 30 July 2009?

What is working capital?

Working capital is the amount of money needed to pay for day-to-day trading. It is used to buy resources and pay bills such as wages, insurance and advertising. Working capital is the difference between the liquid assets of a business such as cash and stocks, and the money owed by a business that must be repaid within a year. Working capital is shown in the balance sheet and is calculated by subtracting current liabilities from current assets:

Working capital = current assets − current liabilities

So, if a business has current assets of $675,600 and current liabilities of $435,200, the value of working capital is $240,400. This means that the business has $240,400 to meet its immediate expenses.

The amount of working capital a business has is important. It can show how well a business is performing.

 DID YOU KNOW?

A business that is struggling is likely to have less working capital. Consequently, if a balance sheet shows a low level of working capital, this suggests that the business may be in trouble.

The working capital cycle

The **working capital cycle** in Figure 47.1 shows the movement of cash and other liquid resources into and out of a business. It helps to illustrate the time intervals between payments made by a business and the receipt of cash.

What does the working capital cycle show?

- Businesses often purchase resources on credit. This means that a business can obtain resources without having to pay for them immediately.

- A second interval exists while resources are made into goods or services. Other costs such as wages are incurred during this time.

- When production is complete goods may be stored before they are sold. This enables a business to cope with unexpected increases in demand. When goods are distributed there will be transport and handling costs.

- A final interval occurs when goods have been sold. If trade credit is given to customers it might be 30–90 days before payment is received. Once cash has been collected much of it is used to keep the process going – buying more materials and paying wages, for example.

- A business may get injections of cash from loans, asset sales and fresh capital. However, there will also be cash drains. Cash will leak from the cycle to pay dividends, tax, repay loans or buy new fixed assets.

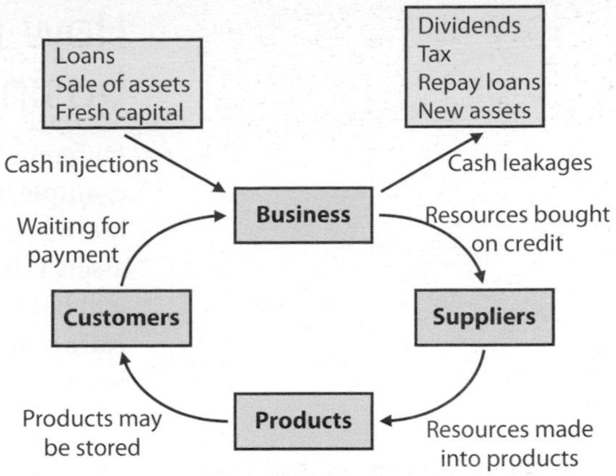

▲ **Figure 47.1**
The working capital cycle

Managing working capital

The time intervals outlined above are important when managing working capital. Businesses can improve their working capital by:

- delaying payments to suppliers;

- reducing the time goods are stored before they are delivered to customers;

- reducing the time it takes for customers to settle their bills.

⊛ QUESTION 1

The Angula family run a gift shop in Windhoek, Namibia. The shop is busy during the tourist season but can struggle during the low season. Figure 47.2 shows the current assets and current liabilities for the business at the end of the busy season in 2009.

(a) Why do businesses such as the Angula family's gift shop need working capital?

(b) How much working capital does the gift shop have?

(c) What is likely to happen to working capital during the low season? Explain your answer.

Figure 47.2 Current assets and current liabilities for the Angula family's gift shop ▶

	2009
Current assets	(NAD)
Stocks	4,500
Debtors	230
Cash	6,700
Current liabilities	
Trade creditors	1,200
Leasing charges	500
Other creditors	2,100

How much working capital does a business need?

Different businesses may need different amounts of working capital. For example, firms that sell goods for cash, such as retailers, can operate with less working capital. However, it is often said that if the value of current assets is between 1.5 or 2 times bigger than current liabilities, a business will have enough working capital. The **current ratio** and the **acid test ratio** can be used to monitor the size of working capital. This is discussed in Chapter 46.

Working capital problems

A business may run short of working capital for many reasons. Here are some examples:

- **Buying too many fixed assets:** When a business first starts trading money is short. Buying expensive assets such as equipment and vehicles uses up cash. It may be better to lease some of these to save working capital.

- **Unexpected expenditure:** Businesses may have to meet some unforeseen expenditure. Equipment breakdowns, tax demands and strikes are common examples.

- **Unexpected fall in demand:** Working capital may dwindle if sales start to fall as a result of an unexpected fall in demand. This might be caused by a sudden change in fashion, a new competitor entering the market or a decline in trading conditions.

- **Seasonal factors:** Sometimes trade fluctuates for seasonal reasons. For example, farmers have a large cash inflow when their harvest is sold. For much of the year, though, they have to pay expenses without any cash flowing in.

Methods of improving working capital

Cash flow problems might be avoided by controlling working capital. The use of budgets and cash flow forecasts will improve the financial management of the business. However, firms may still run short of working capital. The following measures might be used to help:

- **Get an overdraft or a short-term loan:** One way to boost working capital is to borrow some money. Most businesses can use overdrafts (see Chapter 22) when cash is short. It may also be possible to get a short-term loan if working capital is low.

- **Get some fresh capital:** Owners may be able to put some new capital into the business. For example, small business owners may be able to use savings or take out loans. They may use personal possessions as security. Limited companies may be able to sell shares to raise fresh capital.

- **Sell goods for cash:** Some businesses can boost working capital by offering discounts for cash sales. Customers may be keen to pay cash if discounts are attractive.

- **Delaying payments:** A business may be able to delay payments to suppliers. This will help to save cash for a while.

QUESTION 2

Urals Energy is a Russian oil company. In January 2009, it managed to borrow some money to keep production going, and meet some other debts. The company, which is heavily in debt, also said it was selling two important assets. The money raised will be used to pay off debt. On 6 January the company said it would get a small loan to maintain liquidity until the asset sale had been finalised. Urals owed money to contractors and suppliers that had to be paid by the end of January. News of the new funding sent Urals shares up 13% to 3.25 cents per share.

Source: adapted from www.reuters.com

(a) What evidence is there to suggest that Urals Energy was short of working capital?

(b) Why do you think Urals Energy's shares rose just after new funding was announced?

Key terms

Working capital – the funds left over to meet day-to-day expenses after current debts have been paid. It is calculated by current assets minus current liabilities.
Working capital cycle – the flow of liquid resources into and out of a business.

Chapter review – Canton Metals

Canton Metals makes metal components for car engines. It has a factory in Guangzhou and employs more than 50 staff. In 2008, the company experienced a 40% fall in demand because of the global recession. This meant that the cash coming into the business fell sharply. Another problem was the 90-day credit terms agreed with customers. This meant that the business had to wait over three months to receive payment from customers. Some customers were also very slow to pay. Canton Metals was about to exceed its $2,500,000 overdraft limit and would run out of cash within two weeks. As a result an emergency board meeting was held and the following measures were agreed.

- Obtain an unsecured loan from the bank (if possible).
- Reduce the trade credit period to 30 days.

(a) What is meant by the term 'working capital'? **(2 marks)**

(b) (i) Calculate the working capital for Canton Metals in 2007 and 2008. **(4 marks)**
  (ii) Do the answers in (i) support the view that Canton Metals has a shortage of working capital? **(2 marks)**

(c) How might Canton Metals encourage customers to pay immediately for their goods? **(2 marks)**

(d) How will the measures agreed by the board improve Canton Metals' working capital position? **(4 marks)**

(e) Discuss whether you think Canton Metals is in danger of going out of business. **(6 marks)**

	2008 $000	2007 $000
Current assets		
Stocks	1,229	1,001
Work-in-progress	3,445	1,765
Debtors	2,189	1,778
Cash at bank	0	1,239
Current liabilities		
Trade creditors	3,112	2,311
Taxation	1,299	1,365
Other creditors	2,100	1,765
Bank overdraft	2,460	0

Figure 47.3
Current assets and current liabilities for Canton Metals

Chapter 48

Financial budgets

Getting started...

To run a successful business it is important to plan ahead. Business planning often involves forecasting future income and expenditure. These forecasts are presented in a **budget** and can help a business achieve its financial aims. Look at the example below.

Gethin Foods

Gethin Foods is a large food processor and makes ready meals for supermarkets (see Figure 48.1). Every four months the production manager prepares a production cost budget. It shows the costs of producing the planned output for the four-month period. This helps to keep production costs under control. It also helps the purchasing department to plan orders for materials and the finance department to plan payments to suppliers. Figure 48.2 shows a production cost budget for Gethin Foods.

▲ **Figure 48.1**
A food processing factory

	Jul	Aug	Sep	Oct	Total
					($m)
Food products	11.5	11.7	11.9	12.1	47.2
Other raw materials	2.6	2.7	2.8	3	11.1
Factory wages	9.5	10	10	10.2	39.7
Factory overheads	4.6	4.6	4.6	4.6	18.4
Total	28.2	29	29.3	29.9	116.4

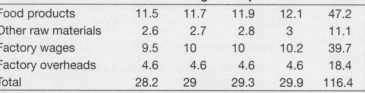

▲ **Figure 48.2** Production cost budget for Gethin Foods

(a) What does the budget in Figure 48.2 show?

(b) How does Gethin Foods use its production cost budget?

What is a budget?

Larger businesses are more difficult to control than smaller ones. A small business can be run informally. The owner is the manager, who will know everyone, be aware of what is going on and will make all decisions. In larger firms work and responsibility are delegated. This makes informal control ineffective. Budgeting will help to improve control.

A budget is a plan. It shows how much money a business, or a department, plans to spend or receive in the future. Budgets are normally presented in a table using a spreadsheet. Each column represents monthly expenditure or income plans. Budgets are usually prepared for a 6- or 12-month period. Figure 48.3 shows a 6-month overheads budget for Harry Enser Ltd, a producer of leather goods.

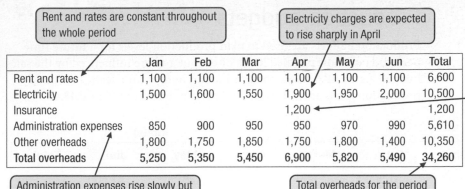

	Jan	Feb	Mar	Apr	May	Jun	Total
Rent and rates	1,100	1,100	1,100	1,100	1,100	1,100	6,600
Electricity	1,500	1,600	1,550	1,900	1,950	2,000	10,500
Insurance				1,200			1,200
Administration expenses	850	900	950	950	970	990	5,610
Other overheads	1,800	1,750	1,850	1,750	1,800	1,400	10,350
Total overheads	5,250	5,350	5,450	6,900	5,820	5,490	34,260

Rent and rates are constant throughout the whole period

Electricity charges are expected to rise sharply in April

A one-off insurance premium has to be paid in April. This will increase overheads sharply in that month

Administration expenses rise slowly but consistently over the time period

Total overheads for the period are €34,260,000

▲ **Figure 48.3**
Overheads budget for Harry Enser Ltd (€000)

Sales budgets

Sales budgets are important because they affect all other budgets in the business. For example, if a business plans to increase sales, it will also have to increase production. A sales budget can show the quantities of output a business plans to sell or the sales revenue. Figure 48.4 shows a sales budget for CleanCo, a producer of cleaning products.

							(units)
	Jan	Feb	Mar	Apr	May	Jun	Total
Floor cleaner	50,000	50,000	51,000	52,000	52,000	53,000	308,000
Bathroom cleaner	34,000	35,000	35,000	36,000	36,000	36,000	212,000
All purpose cleaner	102,000	104,000	105,000	107,000	109,000	110,000	637,000
Window cleaner*	3,000	5,000	7,000	10,000	15,000	20,000	60,000

* Window cleaner is to be launched in January 2009

◀ **Figure 48.4**
Sales budget for CleanCo 2009

QUESTION 1

Pablo is a department store located in the centre of Malaga, Spain. It attracts a lot of English shoppers because its layout and product range is similar to some UK department stores. Figure 48.5 shows the 6-month sales budget for the store. It is used by the manager to help forecast the sales revenue for the 6-month period.

							(€)
	Jan	Feb	Mar	Apr	May	Jun	Total
Foodhall	24,500	25,800	26,500	26,500	27,000	27,500	157,800
Ladieswear	45,000	46,000	46,000	47,000	50,000	52,000	286,000
Menswear	31,000	31,500	31,500	32,000	34,000	34,500	194,500
Childrenswear	36,000	36,000	37,000	38,000	38,000	39,000	224,000
Total	136,500	139,300	141,000	143,500	149,000	153,000	862,300

◀ **Figure 48.5**
Sales budget for Pablo department store

(a) Why is a sales budget so important?

(b) What is the planned sales revenue for the 6-month period at Pablo?

(c) What is expected to happen to monthly revenue at Pablo over the time period?

Production budgets

Production budgets are used to plan production levels for a future time period. They show planned levels of output and are influenced by the sales budget. Figure 48.6 shows the production budget for CleanCo. Monthly production levels are influenced by the sales budget in Figure 48.4.

	Jan	Feb	Mar	Apr	May	Jun	Total
							(units)
Floor cleaner	51,500	51,500	51,500	51,500	51,500	51,500	309,000
Bathroom cleaner	35,000	35,000	35,000	35,000	35,000	35,000	210,000
All purpose cleaner	107,000	107,000	107,000	107,000	107,000	107,000	642,000
Window cleaner*	10,000	10,000	10,000	10,000	10,000	10,000	60,000

▲ **Figure 48.6**
Production budget for Clean Co – 2009

Marketing budgets

A marketing budget is often used to help control costs in the marketing department. It may show how the money allocated to the marketing department is spent. The marketing budget in Figure 48.7 shows how the marketing department for a business plans to spend money on staff, advertising, the company website and other marketing expenses. The budget shows:

- The business plans to increase expenditure on Internet advertising at the expense of newspaper advertising.

- A big expense is to be incurred in March where other marketing expenses rise from the usual $2,000 to $9,000. This might be a one-off PR or exhibition expense.

- The marketing department plans to spend a total of $109,000 in the time period.

▼ **Figure 48.7**
An example of a marketing budget

	Jan	Feb	Mar	Apr	May	Jun	Total
							($)
Wages	5,000	5,000	5,000	5,000	5,000	5,000	30,000
Internet advertising	3,000	4,000	5,000	6,000	7,000	8,000	33,000
Newspaper advertising	4,000	4,000	3,500	3,500	3,000	3,000	21,000
Website	1,000	1,000	1,000	1,000	1,000	1,000	6,000
Other marketing expenses	2,000	2,000	9,000	2,000	2,000	2,000	19,000
Total expenses	15,000	16,000	23,500	17,500	18,000	19,000	109,000

The advantages of budgets

Some of the key advantages of budgets are outlined below.

Control and monitoring Managers can keep control of a business by setting objectives and targets. These can be represented by budgets. Success in achieving those targets can be found by comparing the actual results with the budget. If there are big differences between the two, a business will need to find out why and take action.

Reduce fraud Budgets can help to reduce fraud in a business. All spending in a business has to be authorised by budget holders. This means that no one else can spend money without the budget holder's permission. It stops staff from spending money fraudulently, such as buying things for themselves.

Planning Budgeting forces management to think ahead. Without budgeting, too many managers would work on a day-to-day basis, only dealing with opportunities and problems as they arise. Budgets help to anticipate problems and develop solutions in advance.

Efficiency One of the main reasons why budgets are used is to keep costs down. Budgets often mean that budget holders have to justify expenditure. If they can't do this money will not be granted. This means that money is not wasted and efficiency improves.

Motivation Budgeting should act as a motivator to the workforce. It provides workers with targets and standards. Improving on the budget position is an indication of success. Fear of failing to reach budgeted targets may make staff work harder.

Key terms

Budget – a plan that shows how much money a business expects to spend or receive during a set period of time.

Chapter review – Kosovo Mining Corporation

Kosovo Mining Corporation operates several coal mines in Kosovo. In the last 6 months of 2008, the company was confident that its coal would sell for €60 a tonne. Based on this price a sales revenue budget was drawn up for this time period. It is shown in Figure 48.8. A production cost budget for the mining company is shown in Figure 48.9.

(a) Calculate the planned sales revenue for Kosovo Mining Corporation for the whole 6-month period. **(2 marks)**

(b) Calculate the monthly and total production costs for the 6-month period. **(4 marks)**

(c) Why do you think production costs rose in the last 3 months? **(2 marks)**

(d) Describe the possible advantages to Kosovo Mining Corporation of preparing budgets. **(12 marks)**

	Jul	Aug	Sep	Oct	Nov	Dec
Output (tonnes)	100,000	110,000	110,000	130,000	140,000	150,000
Revenue (€000)	6,000	6,600	6,600	7,800	8,400	9,000

Figure 48.8
Sales budget for Kosovo Mining Corporation – 2008

						(€000)
	Jul	Aug	Sep	Oct	Nov	Dec
Wages	1,100	1,200	1,200	1,400	1,600	1,700
Electricity	270	280	280	290	300	310
Transport	900	990	990	1,100	1,200	1,400
Production overheads	2,300	2,300	2,400	2,500	2,500	2,600

Figure 48.9
Production cost budget for Kosovo Mining Corporation

Chapter 49

Users of accounts

Getting started...

Accounts are produced by businesses because they provide useful information for stakeholders. However, different stakeholders may look at the accounts for different reasons. For example, a bank may look at accounts when deciding whether or not lend a business some money. Employees may look at accounts to see whether a business can afford a pay rise. Look at the examples below.

Zheng Peng

Zheng Peng has been farming for 41 years. He supplies restaurants and retailers with chicken meat. However, increasing competition means that profit has fallen recently. He has decided that if the farm does not make a profit of $25,000 in 2009 he will retire from farming. Figure 49.1 shows the profit and loss account for his business in 2009.

The Birmingham Brick Company

The Birmingham Brick Company produces building materials for the construction industry. In 2009, the company began looking for a new supplier of calcium silicate, a key raw material. A suitable supplier was found but would not supply goods on credit until it had looked at the company's accounts. The supplier was particularly interested in the amount of working capital the Birmingham Brick Company had.

	2006	2007	2008	(£) 2009
Current assets				
Stock	128,500	132,900	123,700	121,200
Debtors	78,500	86,400	78,500	65,800
Cash	12,800	13,900	4,800	300
Total	219,800	233,200	207,000	187,300
Current liabilities				
Trade creditors	132,100	134,300	143,100	165,400
Other creditors	22,100	14,300	25,200	27,600
Total	154,200	148,600	168,300	193,000

Figure 49.2 Current assets and current liabilities for The Birmingham Brick Company

Zheng Peng
Profit and loss account year ending 30 June 2009

	$	$
Sales		145,600
Cost of sales		102,000
Gross profit		43,600
Less expenses:		
Wages	10,000	
Business rates	700	
Interest	500	
Motor expenses	3,200	
Other expenses	9,500	
		23,900
Net profit		**19,700**

Figure 49.1 Profit and loss account for Zheng Peng, year ending 30 June 2009

(a) How will Zheng Peng use the profit and loss account in this case?

(b) Which stakeholder is interested in the accounting information in Figure 49.2?

(c) What conclusion might the stakeholder in (b) draw from the information shown in Figure 49.2? Explain your answer.

Stakeholders

A wide range of stakeholders may be interested in the accounts of businesses.

Managers Managers need up-to-date financial information to run the business.

- **Control**: Managers need financial information such as budgets, details of current assets and creditors to help keep control of the money flowing in and out of the business. This becomes more important as the firm grows.

- **Analysis and evaluation**: Managers will want to assess the performance of the company. They might make comparisons with competitors and keep a record of the firm's progress over a period of time.

- **Decision making**: Managers use financial information to help make business decisions. Financial information is numerical, which is very useful when making decisions.

Employees Employees might need financial information during wage negotiations. Information about profit and the prospects of the business could be used to decide whether the business can afford to raise wages. Employees may also look at accounting information to see whether their jobs are secure.

Owners Owners of small businesses will obviously be interested in the performance and the financial position of the business. For example, a sole trader might look at the profit to see if targets have been met for the year.

Shareholders In limited companies, shareholders will also be interested in the performance of the business. They may look at the size of dividends. They may use ratio analysis to see how their investment is performing and make comparisons with other companies.

DID YOU KNOW?

Managers might use cost information in profit and loss accounts to help identify targets for cost cutting.

QUESTION 1

Arnolds Insurance plc provides boat insurance in the US serving clients in Florida. The shareholders expect a 10% return on capital employed. They use the accounts each year to check whether this target has been achieved. Figure 49.3 shows some financial information for Arnolds Insurance that has been extracted from the accounts.

	2006	2007	2008	2009
Sales turnover ($m)	45.66	47.85	49.41	47.11
Net profit ($m)	3.98	4.12	4.1	3.16
Return on capital employed	11.10%	11.40%	10.90%	8.30%

◄ Figure 49.3
Financial information for Arnolds Insurance plc

(a) What do you think is the main reason why owners use accounts?

(b) Has the business reached the targets set by the owners in this case?

Bankers Banks need up-to-date financial information when deciding whether to lend money to a business. Banks will look at the accounts to see whether a business can repay the loan with interest. Banks often want to look at accounts from several years of trading.

Suppliers Many businesses buy resources using trade credit. However, a supplier is likely to carry out a credit search before granting trade credit. Accounts can be used by suppliers to see whether new customers are creditworthy and likely to pay their invoices.

Investors and financial analysts The accounts of plcs help to inform shareholders about the progress and performance of the company. They are also used by potential investors and **financial analysts** to help make decisions when buying shares.

Other users

Government Many governments gather business and financial information. This is made available to the public. Some of the data is taken from accounts. The government uses the information to monitor the progress of the economy and help evaluate the success of its economic policies. It might also be used by people when doing research.

Competitors Limited company accounts are available to the public. Therefore competitors can analyse them to make comparisons. Also, if a competitor is thinking about a takeover, it can use the information to help make a decision.

The media Newspapers, TV and radio often produce reports on business and commerce. There are specialists that focus on business information. For example, in the US *The Financial Times* is a business and financial newspaper.

Tax authorities The tax authorities may require details of income when working out how much tax businesses and their owners must pay. Accounts can be used to provide details of income. They may require access to business accounts when calculating VAT and excise duties owed by businesses.

DID YOU KNOW?

Some of the big shareholders such as pension funds and insurance companies, employ financial analysts to manage the money collected from pension contributions and insurance premiums. A lot of this money is invested in shares and financial analysts will use accounts to help them decide which companies to invest in.

QUESTION 2

Alan Wong is a financial analyst who works for a large investment bank in Hong Kong. He is currently looking at four supermarkets. He has $200 million to invest on behalf of the bank. He has drawn up a short list of four. Financial information for each of them is shown in Figure 49.4.

(a) What information from the accounts will be required to calculate the current ratio?

(b) What is the role of a financial analyst?

(c) Which supermarket might provide Alan with the best investment?

	A	B	C	D
Net profit margin	3.40%	5.20%	2.70%	5.10%
Return on capital employed	9%	11.90%	10.15%	8.30%
Current ratio	1.1	1.2	1.4	1.3

▲ **Figure 49.4** Financial information for four supermarkets

Auditors Every year the accounts of limited companies have to be checked by an independent firm of accountants and registered auditors. The process of checking the authenticity of accounts is called **auditing**.

Registrar of Companies In many countries, limited companies have to register with the Registrar of Companies. One of the conditions of registration is that they submit a copy of their final accounts every year. These accounts are available to the general public.

Key terms

Auditing – an accounting procedure which checks thoroughly the authenticity of a company's accounts.
Financial analyst – someone who manages the money paid into pension and insurance funds.

Chapter review – Goldenport Holdings

Goldenport Holdings provides shipping services. It transports containers and bulk loads such as iron ore, coal and grain. Goldenport is committed to updating its fleet with the acquisition of younger vessels. Some information from the accounts is shown in Figures 49.5 and 49.6.

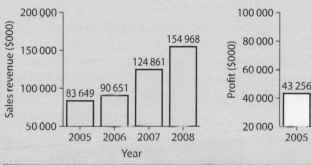

Figure 49.5 Bar charts showing financial information for Goldenport Holdings

Source: adapted from Goldenport Holdings Annual report and Accounts 2008

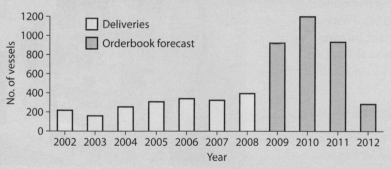

Figure 49.6
A bar graph showing trading information for Goldenport Holdings

(a) State two possible reasons why employees at Goldenport Holdings might be interested in the information shown. **(2 marks)**

(b) One of the objectives of Goldenport Holdings is growth. What evidence is there to suggest that this objective has been achieved? **(2 marks)**

(c) How might managers use the information shown in this case? **(2 marks)**

(d) Explain why: (i) the media; (ii) competitors might wish to look at the accounts of Goldenport Holdings. **(4 marks)**

(e) Why do auditors need to see company accounts? **(2 marks)**

(f) How well has Goldenport Holdings performed over the time period? **(8 marks)**

Role of work in satisfying human needs

Getting started...

People can satisfy some important human needs by going to work. For example, most people go to work to earn a living. This means they get jobs to pay for food, accommodation, clothes, transport and leisure activities. However, work can also satisfy other human needs. Look at the examples below.

Jevaughn Hines

Jevaughn Hines sells house insurance and works in a sales team with five other staff. The team is responsible for organising its own work. It is given a lot of freedom and flexibility in the way it operates. However, the team is set challenging sales targets which must be met. Jevaughn enjoys his job. He says: 'I don't mind going to work. It's what you have to do. Here though I have made some great friends. They are supportive and we help each other out. We meet up after work and go out at weekends. We have respect for each other and also have a good laugh.'

Jessica De Groot

Jessica De Groot is a marketing manager for a South African media company. She has been employed for 12 years. She says: 'This company looks after its workers. You feel valued and that's really important to me. I work hard but I have been given lots of opportunities. I have been sent on some good training courses and developed lots of new skills. Two years ago the company paid £6,000 for me to go on a four day management training course in London.'

(a) Describe the needs that work meets in these two examples.

(b) Do you think all people have the same needs? Explain your answer.

▲ Figure 50.1
Women working in an office

Why do people work?

What would you do all day if you did not work? You could stay in bed, listen to music, watch television, go to the movies, go shopping, visit friends, go out for meals and play sport. This sounds great but you would need money to be able to do some of those things. Relaxing and doing what you please is great for a holiday. However, after a while the pleasure can wear off. You may feel aimless, bored, dissatisfied, unfulfilled and isolated – especially if all your friends are at work! Work can meet a wide range of human needs. Some of these are shown in Figure 50.2.

◀ Figure 50.2
Human needs met by work

Physiological needs

Humans have some very basic needs. These are called **physiological needs**. They include food, drink, shelter, warmth and rest. Humans also need protection from physical and physiological threats. If these needs are not met, humans cannot survive. Work provides the means to satisfy these needs. By going to work people can earn money to buy food, clothes and safe accommodation. Hopefully some money will be left over to spend on recreational activities and entertainment. But these are wants rather than needs.

Social needs

People are social animals. This means that they have **social needs**. People like to communicate and make friends. People also want to be liked and to be part of a group. Work can satisfy social needs. This is because people often work with others. This provides opportunities for people to meet and develop friendships and relationships.

Other needs

In addition to physiological and social needs people also have higher needs:

- Most people want to be respected and recognised. At work people can earn respect by being good at their job, supporting work colleagues or showing leadership skills.

- Most people want to respect themselves. At work they may do this by earning praise from line managers, achieving work targets, getting promotion or taking on more responsibility.

- A lot of people want to develop skills and also develop as a person. At work people are trained to help them develop skills. Also, by getting promoted, learning how to deal with different situations and people, and solving problems, someone can develop as a person at work.

 DID YOU KNOW?

More and more businesses organise their workers into teams. This is because teams of workers are more productive. It also helps to satisfy social needs. This is because people are given the chance to form closer ties with people who have a common aim. Belonging to a team gives people a sense of identity and they may feel more secure.

Key terms

Physiological needs – the basic needs of humans for their survival.

Social needs – the need of humans to communicate, develop friendships and belong to groups.

• Many people want to reach their full potential. For example, they may want to create something or excel in some way. At work people, may get the opportunity to reach their full potential. For example, an employee might start work on the shop floor and rise to be a managing director.

Maslow's Hierarchy of Needs

In 1954, Abraham Maslow classified the needs discussed above. He developed a theory that classified the needs of humans in order of importance. He also suggested how people at work could be motivated by meeting these needs. This is discussed in Chapter 53.

Chapter review – Marriott International

Marriott International is a leading hospitality company. It has nearly 2,800 properties in 70 countries around the world and employs 11,000 people.

At Marriott there is a culture of respect and recognition. There is also training specifically on teamwork, a quality prized by the company. Staff say that senior managers help them fulfil their potential and motivate them. They say they are excellent role models and regularly show appreciation.

Marriott, where the average length of service for managers is 17 years, likes to promote from within the company. Each staff member has a development plan that helps to identify their training needs. On-the-job training is important and staff can gain qualifications.

Marriott values its staff. There are rewards for outstanding contribution and long service, plus an annual staff appreciation week. In 2008 the firm spent about $530,000 on fun events for employees. Staff can use the hotel leisure clubs and have access to a confidential helpline to discuss personal worries.

Benefits include between 20 and 25 days' basic holiday, two weeks' paternity leave on 90% of pay, childcare vouchers, dental insurance, critical illness cover, life assurance and a company pension. Employees say Marriott is run on strong principles by an inspirational boss. They are proud to work for the company.

(a) Why do people need to work? (2 marks)

(b) Explain the difference between physiological needs and social needs. (4 marks)

(c) How does Marriott satisfy the social needs of its employees? (4 marks)

(d) How does Marriott encourage the personal development of its staff? (4 marks)

(e) What evidence is there to suggest that Marriott values its staff? (6 marks)

Chapter 51

Financial rewards

Getting started...

Most people go to work to earn money. However, businesses may use different payment systems to reward their staff. For example, workers might be paid an hourly rate, which means they get paid so much per hour for every hour they work. Each system has advantages and disadvantages. Look at the examples below.

GVS Life Assurance

Nasir Gul works for GVS Life Assurance. He sells life assurance policies. He earns a basic salary of $400 per month. However, for every policy he sells he gets another $200. Nasir is well motivated and hard working. He is happy with the payment method and can earn up to $3,500 a month. Some of his colleagues are less happy. They lack Nasir's charm and skills and are often under a great deal of stress trying to earn a living.

Gazzetta di Brescia

Edmundo Canonica is a reporter for the *Gazzetta di Brescia*, a newspaper published in Brescia, Italy. He is paid €24,000 per annum. His work involves digging out local stories and editing the reports of junior staff. Edmundo's working hours vary a lot. If he is chasing a big story he might work more than 12 hours a day – even at weekends. However, when it is quiet he may only work 6 hours a day. Most of the staff working for the newspaper are paid annual salaries.

Figure 51.1 A newspaper reporter ▶

(a) (i) How much would Nasir earn if he sold 11 insurance policies during a month?
    (ii) State one advantage and one disadvantage of the payment system used by GVS Life Assurance.

(b) (i) What system of payment is used for most of the employees at *Gazzetta di Brescia*?
    (ii) What might be a disadvantage of this method for the employer?

Time rates

Many workers are paid according to the amount of time they spend at work. This payment system is called a **time rate**. It is a common system and involves paying workers so much per hour or week. Therefore, someone who earns $8.50 an hour and works 37 hours a week will receive $314.50 ($8.50 × 37). This is **gross pay**, that is, pay before deductions. A worker's **net pay** is what they take home. It is gross pay minus deductions such as:

- income tax;
- national insurance contributions;
- pension contributions;
- contributions to an employer savings scheme;
- trade union membership fees.

Workers may be paid **overtime**. This means they get a higher hourly rate for working extra hours. For example, workers might get time and a half for working after the normal working day, at weekends or during public holidays. Therefore, if the hourly rate is $8.50 an hour, the overtime rate at time and a half would be $12.75 ($8.50 × 1.5).

Some employees are paid a **salary** that is expressed in annual terms and paid monthly. Salaries are usually paid to *non-manual* workers as in the above example. Edmundo Canonica's salary was €24,000 per annum. His monthly gross pay would have been €2,000 (€24,000 ÷ 12). Salaried workers are not always paid overtime. For example, teachers receive a salary and are expected to work as long as it takes to do their jobs.

Time rates are a suitable method of payment when it is difficult to measure the output of workers. They are also appropriate if work involves a high degree of skill, care or precision. Rushing such work may be dangerous or result in costly errors. However, one problem with time rates is that productivity is not rewarded. With time rates people are paid for their attendance at work. Conscientious and productive workers get the same as those who try to avoid work.

Piece rates

Some workers are paid according to how much they produce. This system is called **piece rates**. An example would be a labourer picking grapes in a vineyard being paid 50 cents a kilo. The main benefit of this system for businesses is that it rewards productive workers. Workers who are lazy or slow will not earn as much as those who are conscientious and productive. This system helps to motivate workers and businesses are likely to 'get more' out of their employees. However, piece rates do have problems:

- Piece rates cannot be used if work cannot be measured. For example, it is very difficult to measure the output of a hotel receptionist or a research scientist.
- The quality of output may suffer if people work too fast. They may take short cuts and make mistakes. In the vineyard example above, a labourer picking grapes may damage some of the fruit when picking too quickly.
- Workers might use dangerous practices trying to work too fast. For example, machinists may remove protective guards to speed up production and therefore risk injury.

QUESTION 1

West Park Motor Services carries out maintenance, servicing and repair work on motor cars. The company employs one manager, nine mechanics, one labourer and a receptionist. The mechanics are paid $9 per hour and time and a half for every hour they work over 38 hours during a week. The manager is paid a salary of $32,000 per annum with no overtime payments.

(a) One of the mechanics worked 53 hours during a busy week in September. Calculate the gross pay earned by this mechanic.

(b) Explain the difference between gross and net pay.

(c) (i) What is meant by a salary?
    (ii) How many hours do you think the West Park Motor Services manager works during a week?

Bonus payments

Some firms make **bonus payments** to workers. Bonuses are paid in addition to the basic wage or salary. They are usually paid if targets are met. For example, machinists may be paid a bonus if they reach a weekly production target. Bonuses can also be paid to groups of workers. For example, a sales team may get a bonus if the whole team meets a sales target. The main advantage to businesses of bonus payments is that they are only paid if targets are met. This means that money is only paid if it has been earned. Bonus payments may help to motivate workers as they strive to reach a target to earn their bonus.

Performance related pay

Performance related pay (PRP) is used to motivate non-manual workers. PRP is designed specifically to reward workers whose output is difficult to measure. It was popular in financial services and the public sector in the 1990s in the UK. PRP works best if businesses use an *appraisal* system to evaluate staff performance. This involves meeting with individual workers every year to:

- discuss progress at work;
- assess whether targets have been met;
- set new targets for the next year.

If targets have been met or exceeded, workers get paid more. Businesses like PRP because it links pay to productivity and only workers who perform well get paid more. However, the system does have problems:

- Some workers feel that it is unfair because appraisers may be inconsistent. For example, pay awards may be given to certain workers out of favouritism. This may demotivate staff and cause conflict.

KEY FACT

Some businesses pay their staff *loyalty bonuses*. These are usually paid annually. Such bonuses are not necessarily linked to productivity. They are designed to reward workers for their loyalty.

Key terms

Bonus systems – a payment in addition to the basic wage for reaching targets or in recognition for service.

Gross pay – pay before deductions.

Net pay – take home pay, that is, pay after deductions such as income tax and pension contributions.

Overtime – a rate of pay above the normal rate to compensate employees for working extra hours.

Performance related pay (PRP) – a payment system designed for non-manual workers where pay increases are given if performance targets are met.

Piece rates – a payment system where workers receive an amount of money for each unit produced.

Profit sharing – where workers are given a share of the profits, usually as part of their pay.

Salary – pay, usually to non-manual workers, expressed as a yearly figure but paid monthly.

Time rates – a payment system based on the amount of time employees spend at work.

• The financial incentives may not be high enough to motivate workers to improve their performance.

• Some workers may feel that the performance targets set are too demanding.

• Some workers may blame other factors if targets are missed. For example, there may have been problems with computer systems that affected performance.

Profit sharing

One way to reward staff is to give them a share of the profit. This is called **profit sharing**. One approach is to give workers a share of the profit as a bonus or an extra payment on top of their basic pay. What are the advantages of this method?

• It should help to motivate workers. This is because if they produce more the business is likely to make more profit. This means their pay will be higher.

• It might help to unite workers and shareholders. They will have the same goal because both stakeholders will benefit from higher profits.

• All employees can be involved whether they are production workers or administrative workers.

• It can be used to show workers that they are appreciated. Giving workers a share of their profit suggests that they are valued by the owners.

The main disadvantage of profit sharing is that profit is determined by many factors. Some of these are beyond the control of individual workers. For example, employees may work very hard during the year only to find that the business has made a loss because a new competitor has joined the market. Also, profit sharing is not likely to motivate workers if the amount received is small.

 QUESTION 2

Benson Industries is a large engineering company. It makes electronic mechanisms, switching gear, computer components and panel instruments. Benson employs 7,560 workers and has operations in Europe, Asia and Australasia. The workers have a wide range of skills and are employed in many different jobs. Two years ago the company introduced a profit sharing scheme. At Christmas employees are paid 15% of the profit made by the business.

(a) Calculate the amount each worker will receive if the business makes a profit of $81.65 million.

(a) Explain three advantages of profit sharing to Benson Industries.

Chapter review – Zeal Mining Co

Zeal Mining Co is a copper mining company based in Zambia. In 2007, it introduced a new payment system for production workers. The old time rate system was considered inappropriate. Productivity in most of the company's mines had been flat for 10 years. The new system was a piece rate system. It involved paying teams of miners according to their weekly output. There was resistance to the new system when it was first introduced. This was because workers were prevented from working when machinery broke down. However, this problem was solved when the company bought new machinery.

Six months after piece rates were introduced labour productivity improved by 18%. However, accidents in the mine rose by 32%. Workers found ways of working faster by neglecting health and safety procedures. Another problem was that admin staff were complaining. They said that because productivity had increased, their workload had risen. However, the new piece rates did not apply to them.

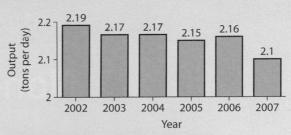

▲ Figure 51.2
Labour productivity at Zeal Mining Co

(a) What evidence is there to suggest that workers at Zeal Mining Co need motivating? **(2 marks)**

(b) How does this case highlight the main disadvantage of time rates as a method of payment? **(2 marks)**

(c) Using this case as an example, analyse the advantages and disadvantages of piece rates as a system of payment. **(8 marks)**

(d) The human resources manager at Zeal Mining Co has suggested using PRP to reward the administration workers. Do you agree with this? **(8 marks)**

▲ Figure 51.3
An open pit in a copper mine

Chapter 52

Non-financial rewards

Getting started...

All businesses pay workers money for their services. However, some businesses also use other ways of rewarding workers. For example, limited companies often give senior employees shares in the company as part of their pay. Alternatively, some businesses find ways of making work more interesting or fulfilling for their staff. Look at the examples below.

Oil & Gas Development Company (Pakistan)

The Pakistan government plans to give employees a 12% stake in the state-owned Oil & Gas Development Company Ltd (OGDCL). The 438 million shares will be given free to the 10,576 employees in lots of 3,000 shares each. Workers will receive between one and 20 lots each, depending on their length of service. However, they will only be entitled to shares if they have been employed for five years. They will get dividends while in employment. It was hoped that the scheme would create a sense of ownership among the workers, and that they would put more effort into their work.

Source: adapted from www.brandsynario.com

Figure 52.1 Workers at OGDCL ▶

Vodafone

Valuing and rewarding staff is important at Vodafone. Staff get exciting opportunities, such as meeting racing driver Lewis Hamilton through its sponsorship of Formula One, or developing their skills working abroad. Managers, who care about worker satisfaction, set workers challenging goals. These include gaining qualifications in finance, marketing, team leadership, customer service and IT. Vodafone matches funds raised by employees for charities. It also encourages them to take up to 24 hours' paid volunteering time each year. Other benefits include a well-being centre with a gym, childcare vouchers and extra holidays.

Source: adapted from business.timesonline.co.uk

(a) (i) How is the Pakistan government allocating shares to the employees of OGDCL?
   (ii) How might the business benefit from employees holding shares?

(b) List three non-financial benefits used to reward staff at Vodafone.

Non-financial rewards

Businesses use non-financial rewards for a number of reasons:
- Some people are not motivated by money.
- Some workers attach more importance to non-financial rewards.
- Financial incentive schemes cannot be used for many workers.
- As more and more people work in teams, individual financial rewards are less appropriate.

Some non-financial rewards can satisfy workers' needs better than money. Examples of non-financial rewards include fringe benefits; interesting work; opportunities to solve problems and make decisions; a sense of achievement; holidays and breaks; recognition and praise and a chance of promotion. Some of these are discussed in detail below.

Fringe benefits

Some employees receive **fringe benefits** in addition to their normal pay. They are often described as the 'perks' of the job and are payment in kind. Examples of fringe benefits are shown in Figure 52.2.

Why might fringe benefits be used?

There are some good reasons for rewarding workers with fringe benefits:

- It may be cheaper to give employees $2,000 of fringe benefits than $2,000 in cash. Employees may also pay less tax if they take fringe benefits instead of cash.

- Productivity may improve because there is less staff absence. Workers may be healthier as a result of private healthcare and using the company gym, sports facilities and counselling services.

- Some benefits help to attract and retain better qualified employees for a business.

- Many benefits provide protection and security for workers and their families. This might help to improve worker satisfaction.

- Some fringe benefits are performance related. This will help to motivate staff. Also, some fringe benefits are only available to senior staff. This might encourage employees to aim for promotion.

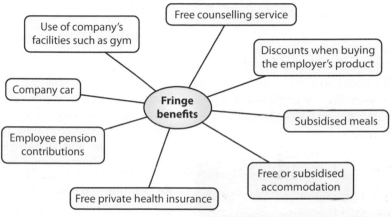

▲ **Figure 52.2**
Examples of fringe benefits

 QUESTION 1

Morgan Stanley is a global financial services provider based in New York, US. Many employees earn over $50,000. Morgan Stanley also provides free private healthcare for the whole family, child care, dental insurance, life assurance, PRP and a share option scheme. An employee assistance programme helps staff outside of work. It includes a legal helpline and one-to-one counselling. Other benefits include a health and well-being programme and a free gym. Staff can also use an onsite medical centre, massage therapist, physiotherapist and acupuncturist.

Source: adapted from business.timesonline.co.uk

(a) Using this case as an example, explain what is meant by fringe benefits.

(b) Outline two possible advantages of fringe benefits to Morgan Stanley.

Other non-financial rewards

Some businesses try to reward employees by making their working life more satisfying and challenging. Here are some of the methods that might be used.

Job enrichment Jobs can be made more challenging and rewarding if tasks require more responsibility and creativity. This is called **job enrichment**. Employees may be given the opportunity to develop unused skills. Developing such skills and taking on more challenging tasks should make work more interesting. It might also help staff to get promoted and they may feel valued.

Job rotation One way to make work more interesting is to allow employees to change jobs from time to time. This will give workers more variety and help to avoid boredom. This is called **job rotation**.

Teamworking This involves dividing the workforce into small groups. Each team will focus on a particular area of production and team members will have the same common aims. This can be rewarding for workers because they can form bonds and develop friendships more easily. Workers may develop a 'team spirit', which can improve motivation and productivity.

Recognition and praise If someone has done a good job it is important to show appreciation and praise them. It costs nothing to say 'thank you and well done'. If said sincerely, this can be uplifting for an employee.

Promotion Many people want to develop a career at work. This means they want to improve their skills, learn new ones and try to get promotion. A business can reward workers if there is a clear route to the top. The chance of promotion at work will help to motivate workers. Therefore businesses must use internal recruitment (see Chapter 54).

DID YOU KNOW?

In a supermarket job rotation might mean that staff switch between shelf-filling, trolley collection, customer services and the checkout. Job rotation should help motivate workers and provide a business with more flexibility.

DID YOU KNOW?

Some businesses reward their employees by giving them awards and prizes as a means of showing recognition. Others offer training, which shows that a business is prepared to invest in workers.

QUESTION 2

Telefonica O2, the communications company, offers its 13,142 staff attractive rewards and benefits. It provides training and career opportunities in a friendly working environment. Managers have regular career conversations with staff to discuss how they can help them learn new skills. Each employee has a personal development plan.

A range of incentive and recognition schemes keeps employees feeling valued. They include the Spirit of O2 awards. This involves giving staff vouchers if they have gone the extra mile during the year. O2 also gives prizes for top performers such as concert tickets or the chance to see London soccer team Arsenal play or an England rugby match. Staff are also set challenges to come up with new business ideas. These help employees' ideas to get recognised. Managers, who care about staff as individuals, show their appreciation when people have done a good job.

Source: adapted from business.timesonline.co.uk

(a) How does Telefonica O2 help staff develop a career?

(b) How does Telefonica O2 show recognition to its workforce?

Drawbacks of non-financial rewards

Some of the drawbacks of non-financial rewards are outlined below:

- Some methods, such as job enrichment and job rotation, may mean changing working practices. Some workers may object to this because they are content with current methods. This change may cause conflict between managers and workers.

- Some methods may be expensive to introduce. Introducing job enrichment and job rotation will need training. There may also be some disruption and loss of output while training takes place.

- Employees may be unhappy if they think managers are using these methods just to get more work out of them for the same pay. Therefore it may be necessary to increase pay.

- For some workers it is not possible to make their jobs more satisfying. These tend to be unskilled jobs such as assembly work where one tedious assembly job is much the same as another.

Key terms

Fringe benefits – payment in kind or 'perks' over and above the normal wage or salary.
Job enrichment – making workers' jobs more challenging by giving them opportunities to be creative and take on responsibility.
Job rotation – allowing workers to change jobs from time to time.

Chapter review – Microsoft

Microsoft wants its people to realise their full potential. Microsoft recruits about 25 graduates every year and immediately they go on a training course. The Microsoft Academy for College Hires is a two-year programme that helps new recruits adapt to the world of work. Over 80% of staff think the job is good for their personal development. A mentoring scheme ensures new graduates are supported by a colleague who has undergone the same induction. A $1,500 bonus also welcomes new graduates when they join Microsoft. Graduates are given training specific to their role and get support if they want to obtain professional qualifications.

Workers are organised into teams, which gives them a buzz. Employees say they also have fun. Regular events at team, department and company level ensure success is celebrated and staff remain engaged. Managers have morale budgets that are used to keep teams happy and motivated. One new building provides a light, open and airy working environment. It has informal areas to encourage creative and relaxed thinking. Other benefits at Microsoft include a share option scheme, a gym, childcare facilities, private health insurance, generous maternity leave and good holidays.

Source: adapted from business.timesonline.co.uk

(a) Using examples from this case, explain what is meant by non-financial rewards. **(2 marks)**

(b) Why do businesses such as Microsoft use non-financial rewards? **(2 marks)**

(c) State two fringe benefits enjoyed by workers at Microsoft. **(2 marks)**

(d) Do you think praise is important at work? Explain your answer. **(2 marks)**

(e) How important do you think training is at Microsoft? **(4 marks)**

(f) How effective do you think team working is at Microsoft? **(4 marks)**

(g) Outline two possible disadvantages of non-financial rewards. **(4 marks)**

Chapter 53

Management styles and motivation

Getting started...

The productivity of labour can vary, which means that some workers produce more than others. There are several reasons for this. Some people are more capable, some are more experienced and others have received more training. However, another reason is that they are better **motivated**. They have drive and are more inclined to work harder. Look at the example below.

Brad Cummings and Alan Shumaker

Brad Cummings and Alan Shumaker both work for Silver City Chemicals, a chemical processing company based in Nevada, US. They are maintenance engineers and have been with the company for eight years. Brad is a highly motivated worker. He is punctual, reliable, supportive of his colleagues, enjoys solving problems and often gives up his own time to help new recruits. He enjoys his job and has recently been promoted. In contrast Alan is poorly motivated. He is unreliable, lacks drive and is often late for work. He also has a reputation for being uncooperative and difficult to work with. He does not like his job and has received a written warning for poor attendance.

(a) State two possible reasons why Alan is poorly motivated.

(b) Explain briefly why you think motivation is important to businesses.

Figure 53.1 A chemical plant ▶

What is meant by motivation?

Motivation is the desire to achieve a goal. Some people are self-motivated. This means they have the drive to achieve goals on their own. They do not need any encouragement. However, others need to be motivated. They need a push, pressure or incentives. For example, some students are self-motivated. They aim to achieve good results. They attend all lessons, meet coursework deadlines and study hard. In contrast, some students lack the drive to achieve goals. This is because people are different. These students will need encouragement such as rewards for good attendance or penalties for missing deadlines.

Why is employee motivation important in business?

Generally, a business with a well-motivated workforce will perform better than one with a poorly motivated workforce. Labour productivity will be higher and therefore profits are likely to be higher. The main benefits are summarised in Figure 53.2.

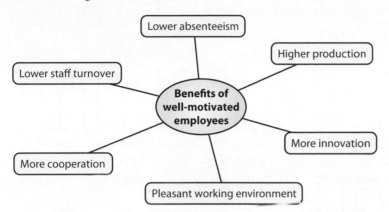

Figure 53.2
The main benefits of having well-motivated employees

Higher production Well-motivated employees will work harder. They are likely to take more pride in their work, complete tasks quickly and feel that their jobs are important. As a result they will produce more.

Lower staff turnover If workers are well motivated, they are less likely to leave their jobs. This means that staff turnover (the rate at which people leave a job) will be lower. This is good for a business because if staff turnover is high, recruitment, selection and training costs will be higher.

Lower absenteeism Poorly motivated staff are more likely to take time off. They may also become depressed, use minor illness as an excuse for missing work or simply take unauthorised time off. This is bad for business because production will be lost.

More cooperation Businesses need workers to cooperate. For example, more and more businesses organise their staff into teams. Therefore, if workers do not cooperate with each other teamwork will be disrupted. At worse, conflict might result if a team member is uncooperative. However, well-motivated employees are likely to be cooperative, so a good team spirit is likely to develop.

More innovation Businesses need to innovate by developing new products, new production processes and new systems to remain competitive. Well-motivated workers are more likely to be innovative than poorly motivated workers. This is because poorly motivated workers 'don't really care'.

Pleasant working environment If workers are well motivated, the working environment and atmosphere is likely to be pleasant. Workers are more likely to be cheerful, courteous, supportive and positive. This is important if workers have to deal with customers. A business may lose customers if the attitudes of poorly motivated workers create a negative impression.

QUESTION 1

Red Star Holdings makes automatic teller machines (ATMs) for the banking industry. Two years ago the company faced a staffing crisis because too many staff were leaving (see Figure 53.3). The production manager had told the board of directors repeatedly that worker morale was low and motivation poor. He thought the main reason for this was because the machinery was out of date and prone to breakdowns. Consequently, earnings were being reduced because of so much 'downtime'. Eventually, in 2007, the board agreed to completely re-equip the factory.

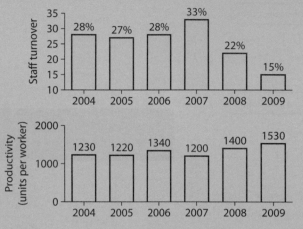

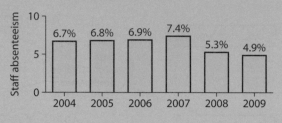

◄ Figure 53.3
Staff information at Red Star Holdings

(a)   What is meant by a well-motivated employee?

(b)   What evidence is there here to suggest that workers were poorly motivated?

(c)   What is likely to be the effect on the working environment if workers are not motivated?

How can businesses influence motivation?

Chapter 50 explained that people go to work to meet a range of needs. A number of experts have developed theories that suggest ways in which workers can be motivated by satisfying their needs. Some of these are outlined below.

Taylor's Scientific Management

Frederick Taylor believed that the main reason why people went to work was to earn money. He said that the best way to motivate workers was to link pay to performance using piece rates or bonus systems. He also said that businesses and employees would benefit from identifying the most efficient way to carry out tasks.

Maslow's Hierarchy of Needs

Chapter 50 identified a range of different human needs. Abraham Maslow recognised these needs but arranged them into a hierarchy showing that some needs are more important than others. **Maslow's Hierarchy of Needs** is usually presented in a pyramid and is shown in Figure 53.4.

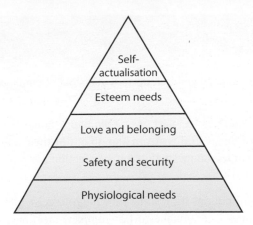

▲ Figure 53.4
Maslow's Hierarchy of Needs

Physiological needs These are at the bottom of the pyramid. They are the basic human needs. They include food, drink, shelter, warmth and rest. If these needs are not met, humans cannot survive.

Safety and security People need protection from any form of danger and physical and psychological threats. They also need routine and familiarity.

Love and belonging These are social needs. People are social animals and need love, affection, trust and acceptance. They also want to belong to a recognised group.

Esteem needs People need to be recognised and respected and their achievements praised. They also want self-respect and self-esteem.

Self-actualisation This means that people need to reach their full potential and feel some fulfilment in what they do. These needs are at the top of the pyramid. Figure 53.5 shows how the needs in the hierarchy can be satisfied at work.

Need	Work can provide
Physiological	Adequate pay – subsidised meals and accommodation
Safety and security	Job security and safe working conditions
Love and belonging	Teamworking, good communication systems and social facilities
Esteem	Praise for doing a good job; awards and rewards for achievement
Self-actualisation	Opportunities to be challenged, creative, solve problems and make decisions

▲ Figure 53.5
How work can satisfy people's needs.

Maslow also said that when businesses try to motivate workers by satisfying their needs, they need to recognise the following:

• Once one set of needs have been satisfied they are no longer a motivator. Workers can only be motivated by achieving the next set of needs in the hierarchy. Therefore if a worker has enough pay and feels secure at work, raising pay levels would not motivate that worker. A business would have to find ways of satisfying higher needs.

• If lower needs are not met, workers cannot be motivated if businesses try to meet higher needs. For example, if pay was inadequate, workers would be demotivated if the business was giving workers the chance to be creative.

• If a business fails to meet a particular need, workers are likely to be demotivated. For example, if a worker is overlooked for promotion, that worker may start to slack or look for another job.

Mothercare is a retailer of products for expectant mothers and children up to 8 years old. It employs 7,221 staff in 428 stores and an online operation.

There's a feelgood factor at Mothercare that makes employees feel part of one big happy family. Employees care a lot about each other. They feel a strong sense of family in their team and go out of their way to help each other. That two-thirds of employees earn £7,500 or less suggests that job satisfaction has more to do with how your colleagues and employer make you feel than money.

Mothercare gives monthly awards for outstanding contributions from staff. They might receive gifts of flowers, dinner or hotel vouchers. Also, senior managers recognise exceptional effort at company meetings, road shows and in personal telephone calls. The firm identifies staff with potential and offers sponsorship for professional qualifications, job swaps, coaching and training courses. Staff say that managers talk honestly and openly with them, are supportive and motivate them to give their best every day.

Source: adapted from business.timesonline.co.uk

(a) Do you think Mothercare satisfies Maslow's love and belonging needs? Explain your answer.

(b) How does Mothercare recognise staff achievements?

Managers and motivation

Managers can play a role in the motivation of workers. This is because they are in control of the means by which workers' needs might be met. It is usually managers who decide things such as pay, working conditions, working practices and promotion. Managers must recognise the achievements of workers, praise individuals, design award schemes and provide workers with opportunities to be creative and reach their full potential.

Key terms

Autocratic leadership – where a manager makes all the decisions without consultation.

Democratic leadership – where managers allow others to participate in decision making.

Job satisfaction – the pleasure and sense of achievement that employees get from their work.

Laissez-faire leadership – where employees are encouraged to make their own decisions, within certain limits.

Maslow's Hierarchy of Needs – the order of people's needs starting with basic human needs.

Motivated – the desire to achieve a goal.

Management styles

Managers are leaders and are responsible for organising, decision making, planning and control. They are accountable to the owners of the company. However, the way managers carry out their duties and responsibilities can vary. A number of leadership styles can be identified:

- **Autocratic:** Some managers like to be in complete control. They set objectives, allocate tasks and insist that workers follow instructions. This is an **autocratic** management style. There is no worker consultation. Workers tend to be poorly motivated and have to be supervised closely. However, in some situations, such as in the armed forces where orders have to be followed instantly, autocratic leadership may be appropriate.

- **Democratic:** Leaders who are **democratic** will share decision making with other workers. They consult subordinates about their views before making a final decision.

- **Laissez-faire:** Some managers allow employees a free rein to carry on with their work without supervision. This is called **laissez-faire** leadership. It creates a relaxed working atmosphere, but some staff lose motivation because there is a lack of guidelines and direction.

Chapter review – Data Connection

Data Connection is a communications technology company. Founded in 1981, Microsoft, Cisco and Juniper are among its clients. The company is progressive in how it treats and trains its personnel. It gives all its 314 employees the chance to take a new direction. Employees say work is an important part of their lives. They feel they can make a valuable contribution to the success of the business and are proud to work for it.

Chief executive John Lazar joined the firm 22 years ago as a software engineer and worked his way up the ranks. This is quite common. A lot of managers have worked their way through the company to the top.

Employees say managers care about them as individuals. They feel supported by them and think they talk openly and honestly with them. New employees are assigned a mentor who, along with managers, sets aside 50 days of their time to train a new starter in their first year. Every employee has an individual development plan that is updated every three months. 'Managing people here is about nurturing and getting the best out of them', says recruitment manager Alison Jackson.

A flexible benefits package includes free private healthcare for employees and their dependents, critical illness cover, life assurance and PRP.

Source adapted from business.timesonline.co.uk

(a) Do you think employees at Data Connection are well motivated? **(2 marks)**

(b) Outline four reasons why staff motivation is important to businesses. **(8 marks)**

(c) Explain the role played by managers in the motivation of employees. **(4 marks)**

(d) What style of leadership do you think is used by managers at Data Connection? **(6 marks)**

Chapter 54

Stages of recruitment and selection

Getting started...

When businesses hire labour they need to attract the best people, those with the right skills and experience. This is called recruitment. There are a number of different stages in the recruitment process. Two of these are outlined in the examples below.

Rossmoor Ltd

Rossmoor Ltd provides sheltered and secure accommodation for the elderly. The company has an apartment block. The job advert in Figure 54.1 was placed in a local newspaper. It aims to attract applicants for a Duty Manager's post.

> **Rossmoor Ltd**
> Require a mature and confident
> ## DUTY MANAGER
> To work 19.6 hours a week on a 5 week rota basis to include some weekends and sleepovers. Excellent working conditions.
> Rate of pay £8.95 per hour plus holiday pay. Sleepover rate £27.35. Relevant N.V.Q. preferred but not essential as training will be provided. This post is subject to an enhanced C.R.B. clearance.
> **Closing date 30th October 2009**
> **Contact manager/Duty manager 00724 111222**

Figure 54.1 Rossmoor Duty Manager advert ▷

Cosmos Electronics

Cosmos Electronics, a Japanese electrical engineering company, recruits a lot of its managers internally. This means it tries to promote people who already work at the company. Suzi Kato, the human resources manager, said: 'We have recruited internally for many years. There are several advantages. For example, promoting from within is safer. We know what these people are like and what their potential is. They are proven workers. It is also cheaper and quicker to recruit in this way.'

▲ **Figure 54.2** An electronics factory

(a) (i) What is the purpose of the advert shown in Figure 54.1?
  (ii) What sort of person is the business trying to attract?

(b) (i) How does Cosmos Electronics recruit many of its managers?
  (ii) State two advantages of recruiting managers in this way.

Recruitment

In a large business, the human resources or personnel department is responsible for recruitment. A business may need new staff because:

- the business is expanding and more labour is needed;
- people are leaving and they need to be replaced;
- positions have become vacant as a result of promotion;
- people are required for a temporary period to cover staff absence because of maternity or paternity leave, for example.

Internal and external recruitment

One way of recruiting staff is to appoint someone who already works for the business. This is called **internal recruitment**. A business might do this by advertising the post internally. The advantages of internal recruitment are that:

- it is cheaper because it saves on advertising;
- internal recruits are familiar with the way the company works;
- staff may be more motivated if they know there is a chance of promotion;
- the ability, personality, attitude and potential of internal recruits is more predictable.

All businesses have to use **external recruitment**. This is where new staff are recruited from outside the business. The advantages of this are that:

- a business will have a much larger pool of potential employees to choose from;
- a new person may be talented and have some have fresh ideas.

A number of different methods might be used to attract applicants from outside the business. Some of the main ones are summarised in Figure 54.3.

KEY FACT

Recruitment is important because if the wrong people are selected it can be expensive. This is because if new recruits leave, all the costs of advertising, interviewing, induction and training will have to be repeated.

Advertising Job adverts are placed in local or national newspapers, specialist publications or online

Word of mouth People apply after finding out that a vacancy exists from friends or other contacts from the business

Jobcentres In the UK, these are run by the government and are used to advertise certain jobs free of charge

Attracting applicants for a job

Employment agencies These are specialists that help recruit staff for businesses; they charge fees for their services

Direct applicants Businesses may keep all speculative applications made by jobseekers

Figure 54.3
Ways in which a business might attract applicants for a job

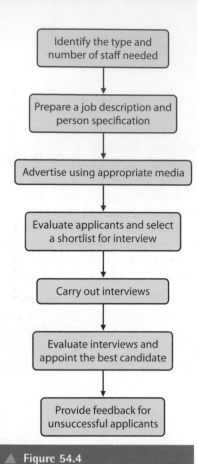

Stages in the recruitment process

The recruitment process may be broken down into the stages shown in Figure 54.4.

- The first stage is to identify the number and type of staff needed. For example, if the business is planning to expand, more applicants will need to be attracted. A business may also need to choose between full-time, part-time, temporary or permanent workers.

- The right people are more likely to be selected if a job description and person specification are drawn up. These are explained below.

- Advertising costs money so job adverts must be placed where they are likely to attract interest from the 'right' sort of applicants. For example, a hospital would not use a national newspaper to advertise jobs for porters. A local newspaper or a jobcentre would be more suitable. In contrast, a senior manager is an important position and a business would want to attract interest from a wide area. Therefore a national newspaper would be suitable.

- Job applications may be made on standard forms. Some applicants might write letters and include a **curriculum vitae (CV)**. This is a document that contains personal details, qualifications, experience, names of referees and reasons why they are suitable for the job. A business must sort through all the applications and draw up a shortlist. This is because it is not usually possible to interview all applicants. Also, some applicants are likely to be unsuitable.

- Short-listed applicants are invited for an interview. This is where interviewers can find out more about the applicants. It also gives candidates the chance to provide detailed information and ask questions. Interviewing is often best done by people who are experienced or have been trained in interviewing. For many jobs interviews are carried out by more than one person. This provides an opportunity for a discussion about the performance of candidates in their interviews.

- After the interviews the interviewers must decide who to appoint. In many cases, interviewees are told the outcome of the interview by post at a later date. This gives the business more time to evaluate the performance of the candidates. A business might also check references before making a final decision.

- The recruitment process ends when a job offer has been made and accepted. It is also courteous to provide feedback to the unsuccessful candidates.

▲ Figure 54.4
Stages in the recruitment process

⚬ QUESTION 1

Mirpur Garments Ltd, based in Dhaka, makes ladieswear for a number of European customers. The company is growing and has been recruiting staff regularly in the last three years. The personnel manager has been instructed to recruit seven new machinists and a purchasing manager – all to start in 10 weeks' time. The machinists will be recruited externally, but the purchasing manager will be recruited from the existing purchasing team. It is expected that three suitable people from the department will apply.

(a) How might the vacancies for the machinists be advertised?

(b) Outline the advantages of recruiting internally for the job of Purchasing Manager.

Job description

A **job description** states the title of a job and outlines the tasks, duties and responsibilities associated with that job. If a new job is created, a new job description may have to be prepared. If a business is replacing someone who is leaving, the job description may be the same. However, when someone leaves it may be updated.

The main purpose of a job description is to show clearly what is expected of an employee. Extracts from it are likely to be used in a job advert. It might also be used during an appraisal to see how well an employee has performed in relation to what was expected of them. Figure 54.5 shows an example of a job description.

Person specification

A **person specification** provides details of the qualifications, experience, skills and any other characteristics that would be expected of a person appointed to do a particular job. It is used to 'screen' applicants when sorting through the applications. Applications that do not match the person specification can be ignored.

It is common to state on the specification whether a particular requirement is 'essential' or 'desirable'. An example of a person specification is shown in Figure 54.6. The style of both job descriptions and person specifications is likely to vary between different businesses according to their specific needs.

Job title
Accounts Clerk

General role
To join the accounting team in the recording of financial transactions and the handling of financial information.

Responsibilities
• Matching, batching and coding invoices.
• Matching invoices to purchase orders.
• Arranging payments through cheques and BACS.
• Allocating items of expenditure to cost centres.
• Dealing with internal expense claims.

Salary
AED60,000–85,000 depending on experience.

Hours and conditions of work
• 40 hours per week (7.30 am–4.30 pm)
• 5 weeks' holiday a year

▲ **Figure 54.5**
A job description for an accounts clerk with Dubai Construction

Key terms

Curriculum vitae (CV) – a document used by a job seeker that lists personal details, qualifications, work experience, referees and other details.
External recruitment – appointing workers from outside the business.
Internal recruitment – appointing workers from inside the business.
Job description – a document that shows clearly the tasks, duties and responsibilities expected of a worker for a particular job.
Person specification – a personal profile of the type of person needed to do a particular job.

▼ **Figure 54.6**
A person specification for a web production manager for Scottish IT company

	Essential	Desirable
Qualifications and Education	3 A Levels GCSE Grade 1 Maths and English Full driving licence Design or web-related qualification	A Level IT A management qualification
Experience	Sound knowledge of HTML Skilled in the use of Adobe Photoshop Proficient in Microsoft Office Knowledge of current legislation	Awareness of dynamic languages
Communication skills	Excellent oral communication skills Report-writing skills Foreign language	Spanish
Other skills	Team player Ability to work flexibly Excellent organisational skills	Ability to negotiate
Personal attributes	Self-motivated Willing to travel abroad	Creative

Nujumba Cement is a large cement manufacturer based in Nagpur, India. The company needs to recruit seven new employees to work in production. The job, called Production Worker, involves heavy manual work and some knowledge of cement manufacturing. The workers will be expected to handle heavy machinery, drive a fork-lift truck, clean machinery and equipment, and work in a team. The job will involve heavy lifting in a harsh working environment. The wage is Rs400 per hour and the working week is 40 hours long. Workers will be entitled to 4 weeks' holiday, free protective clothing and free lunches.

(a) Draw up a job description for the Production Worker jobs at Nujumba Cement.

(b) Outline two reasons why a business draws up a job description.

Job adverts

A perfect job advert would attract a small number of highly suitable candidates. However, it is not always possible to design such a perfect advert. Some of the important information that is likely to be included in a job advert is listed below:

- job title;
- name and address of employer;
- brief details of the job description;
- skills, qualifications and work experience required for the job;
- salary and other benefits;
- method of application;

Chapter review – Internet job advert

The job of Sales and Marketing Director for a travel tour operator was advertised on the internet by fish4jobs, a website that advertises a large number of jobs (see Figure 54.7).

Source: adapted from www.fish4.co.uk

(a) Draw up a simple person specification for the job of Sales and Marketing Director. (You **do not** need to show whether details are essential or desirable.)　**(6 marks)**

(b) How might a business use the person specification?　**(2 marks)**

(c) State four important details that should be included in any job advert.　**(2 marks)**

(d) Applicants for the job shown have to apply with a CV. What is a CV?　**(2 marks)**

(e) Why do businesses draw up short-lists of candidates when interviewing?　**(2 marks)**

(f) Do you think the business was right to recruit externally for this post?　**(6 marks)**

◄ Back to results　✉ Email me jobs like these　✉ Send to a friend　🖨 Print　💾 Save

Sales and Marketing Director UK/Europe
Travel Tour Operator, Bromley Kent
Salary: Up to £60,000 + benefits
Working hours: Full-time
Job type: Permanent
Industry sector: Travel & Leisure, Catering & Hospitality

APPLY NOW

Successful candidates would consider these responsibilities achievable:
Develop and implement a strategic & tactical sales and marketing plan to drive business growth with a focus on creating and developing brand awareness.
Oversee all activities to fulfil strategic objectives to agreed budgets, sales volumes, values, product mix and timescales.
Carry out competitor analysis, market and customer research to analyse market trends to uncover new business and sales opportunities.
Monitor and provide monthly management reports on activities, analysing past performance and proposing future activities and direction.
Arrange and lead business meetings, delivering sales presentation and product launches in a polished, professional manner.
Lead, direct and motivate to build the overall strength and performance of the sales and marketing teams.

Successful candidates will possess:
Degree in appropriate field or equivalent industry qualifications
Min 5 years experience in a similar role either within the travel industry or similar field
Strong presentation & analytical skills
Ability to develop team while maintaining focus and achieving the ultimate goal
Ability to travel regularly and be able to work in the UK

▲ **Figure 54.7** A job advert on fish4jobs

Chapter 55

Training methods

Getting started...

Most businesses have to train their workers. This means they have to be taught how to do their jobs. If workers are trained they will be more productive. However, there are different ways in which workers can be trained. Look at the examples below.

Hemsley Fraser

Hemsley Fraser provides over 250 training courses and trains thousands of people each year. When asked for feedback, 99.8% of trainees say that given the opportunity they would like to attend another Hemsley Fraser course. The company offers courses in:

- management and leadership;
- customer services;
- health and safety, and first aid;
- marketing and PR.
- secretarial and administration;
- sales;
- information technology;

Source: adapted from www.hemsleyfraser.co.uk

Dilip Halappa

▲ Figure 55.1
A motor mechanic servicing a lorry

Dilip Halappa spent five years training as a mechanic in Chennai. He worked for an Indian haulage company and spent one day a week at college. The rest of the time was spent learning how to maintain and service lorries at work. He worked with a senior mechanic who was responsible for his development. Dilip had to pass some exams during the five years and at the end was awarded a recognised qualification as a motor mechanic. He is now a fully qualified motor mechanic and has worked for the same company for nine years. During his apprenticeship Dilip's employer paid all the course fees for his college tuition.

(a) Outline one possible advantage and one possible disadvantage of a large retailer using the services of Hemsley Fraser to train its staff in customer services.

(b) How did Dilip Halappa train to be a motor mechanic?

Training

It is unlikely that an employee would go through their working life without some form of **training**. Training involves increasing the knowledge and skills of workers so they can do their jobs more effectively. Some new recruits need little training because they learnt skills at school, college or another business. However, others may need thorough training because they are young or new to the job. Training can be expensive and in some cases this discourages investment in it. This may result in lower productivity and a loss of competitiveness. It might also be a danger to workers. The need for training is discussed later in this chapter.

Internal and external training

Internal or onsite training means that an employee receives training at work. This type of training is cheaper and trainees can actually see the job that they will be doing. Another advantage is that time is not lost through travelling or staying overnight.

External or offsite training is when employees are trained away from the workplace – at a special training centre perhaps. What are the advantages?

- Training is usually carried out by experts.
- Trainees will not be distracted by their daily work.
- Special training facilities can be used.
- Workers may see the training as a privilege, which may help motivation.

Induction training

When people start a new job they are likely to get some **induction training**. This helps new recruits settle in and become familiar with their new surroundings. If firms fail to provide adequate induction training, staff may feel anxious. This might lead to poor productivity. At worst staff may leave because they have not settled. The nature of induction training will vary between businesses but Figure 55.2 shows what it might involve.

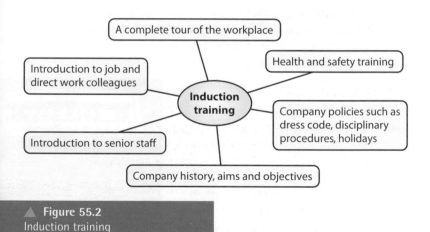

▲ Figure 55.2
Induction training

QUESTION 1

Orange is one of the world's largest mobile communications companies. It recently ran an advertising campaign to tell customers about some new deals. These adverts generated a huge increase in customer calls at Orange's call centres. To cope, Orange recruited 1,000 new customer service workers.

Orange runs a three-week induction programme for new call centre staff. The training covers brand awareness, product and systems training and customer service skills. 'We pride ourselves on our customer service', said Lisa Blewitt, Orange's training manager. 'It is very important that each of our new employees receives a comprehensive induction, so that they can provide excellent service to customers.'

Source: adapted from www.knowledgepool.com/company/case_studies/orange.htm

(a) (i) What is the purpose of induction training?
    (ii) What might new recruits learn during an Orange induction programme?

(b) Why is induction training so important?

On-the-job training

One of the most common methods of training is **on-the-job training**. This means that workers are trained in the workplace while the job is being done. A number of different approaches might be used by a business.

- **Watching another worker**: On-the-job training by an existing member of staff, sometimes called 'sitting next to Nellie', is a common method. It involves a new recruit watching and copying the actions of an experienced and competent employee – 'Nellie'. This method can work well if 'Nellie' is a good and committed teacher. If not, the quality of training might be poor.

- **Mentoring**: This is where a trainee is paired with an experienced member of staff for a period of time. The trainee is put to work without direct supervision but can call on the mentor for advice and guidance. Mentoring is used to help train teachers in the UK.

- **Job rotation**: This may involve a new recruit spending a period of time in different departments at a business. By working in a range of departments they will learn the different skills required and have a broad knowledge of how the business works. This approach will also improve the flexibility of the business.

The advantages and disadvantages of on-the-job training are summarised in Figure 55.3.

Advantages

Output is being produced
Relevant because trainees learn by actually doing the job
Cheaper than other forms of training
Can be easy to organise

Disadvantages

Output may be lost if workers make mistakes
May be stressful for the worker – particularly if working with others
Trainers may get frustrated if they are 'unpaid' trainers
Could be a danger to others, e.g. surgeon or train driver

▲ **Figure 55.3**
Advantages and disadvantages of on-the-job training

Off-the-job training

Some employees receive training away from the normal work area. This is called **off-the-job training**. This may or may not take place at the workplace. For example, it might involve the entire workforce being shown a new health and safety video in the works cafeteria. Alternatively, it might involve a small group of managers going off to learn about a new management techniques overseas. The advantages and disadvantages of off-the-job training are summarised in Figure 55.4.

The need for training

The main reason why training is needed is to provide workers with the skills and knowledge needed to do their jobs effectively. As a result, their productivity will be higher. However, there are several other reasons why workers need training.

Advantages

Output is not affected if mistakes are made
Learning cannot be distracted by work
Training could take place outside work hours if necessary
Customers and others are not put at risk

Disadvantages

No output because employees do not contribute to work
Some off-the-job training is expensive if provided by specialists
Some aspects of work cannot be taught off-the-job
It may take time to organise

▲ **Figure 55.4**
Advantages and disadvantages of off-the-job training

Keeping workers up-to-date Workers will need training if there are changes that might affect their jobs. Some examples might include:

- new health and safety procedures;
- new technology;
- after a takeover;
- new working practices;
- new legislation.

Improving labour flexibility Some businesses train their workers in a range of different jobs so that they are multi-skilled. This provides businesses with added flexibility.

Improving job satisfaction and motivation Workers will feel secure if they have been trained to do their job effectively. Not being able to do a job properly will be a source of frustration and dissatisfaction for workers.

New jobs in the business Sometimes, because of expansion, new products or new technology, new jobs are created. This often means that some staff need retraining.

Training for promotion Training is usually needed when workers are promoted. At each stage of the promotion process staff will need to learn new skills and methods.

QUESTION 2

PricewaterhouseCoopers (PwC) is an international provider of professional services including accountancy, auditing, taxation and business advice. The company provides on- and off-the-job training, particularly for new recruits. PwC provides opportunities for staff to learn and develop new skills. For example, if new recruits opt for a commercial apprenticeship (auditing and accounting), they will spend three years working in different departments to get experience in the different aspects of the business. Employees also attend internal and external training courses to prepare them for final exams. They work in the following areas during their training:

- general operations (marketing, internal services, finance and human capital);
- specialist departments (tax and legal and auditing/assurance).   **Source: adapted from www.pwc.com**

PRICEWATERHOUSECOOPERS 🏢

(a) Explain the difference between: (i) internal and external training; and (ii) off-the-job and on-the-job training.

(b) How might PwC benefit from training their staff in different departments?

The benefits of training

Although it is expensive, a number of stakeholders will benefit from training.

Business owners and managers Business owners will benefit from training if productivity is higher. This is because profit may rise if workers produce more. Managers will benefit because workers may be better motivated and more satisfied. This makes them more cooperative and easier to work with. Workers may also be more flexible, which will help managers in their organisation. Providing training may also improve the image of the business and make it easier to attract and retain high-quality staff.

Employees If workers have been trained, they will be able to do their jobs more effectively. This should reduce anxieties about their work and provide more job satisfaction. Employees may also feel valued if their employer is paying for their training. They may develop a range of skills which they can use in the future – to gain promotion or get a better job.

Customers Customers should benefit from better quality products. They may also get better customer service, such as dealing with complaints, if staff have been trained.

Key terms

Induction training – training given to new employees when they first start a job.

Off-the-job training – training that takes place away from the work area.

On-the-job training – training that takes place while doing the job.

Training – a process which involves increasing the knowledge and skills of a worker to enable them do their job more effectively.

Chapter review – ME plc

ME plc is a growing electrical engineering company. It makes signalling equipment for the rail industry. The company is benefiting from the growth in rail travel and has recently invested in some computerised machinery. However, the introduction of the new technology has not been without problems. The conversation below took place between the production manager and the chief executive of ME plc:

CE: Another $120,000 on training is too much. It is double the annual training budget.

PM: But without the training it will take at least another six months before the new system is up and running.

CE: I know that training is necessary, but it's so expensive. Plus, what happens when the trained workers leave and go and work for someone else?

PM: I appreciate that, but *we* often get workers that have been trained elsewhere.

CE: How many need to be trained?

PM: About 15 – but if we trained all 30 staff we would get more flexibility and won't have to spend on training again for quite a while.

CE: Look – here's the deal. You can have $60,000 for on-the-job training. I don't want workers going off on one of these 'training holidays' for two weeks. We lose too much production and I would rather staff were trained on our system – not some simulator.

(a) Why is training needed at ME plc? (2 marks)

(b) State two other reasons why a business might need to train its staff. (2 marks)

(c) Using examples from this case, explain two reasons why businesses may be reluctant to spend on training. (4 marks)

(d) Explain the advantages and disadvantages of on-the-job training to ME plc. (6 marks)

(e) Describe the benefits of training to employees and customers at ME plc. (6 marks)

Chapter 56

Dismissal and redundancy

Getting started...

Sometimes workers are forced to leave a job. One reason might be because the business no longer needs them. Perhaps a business has automated production and only requires 100 workers instead of 210. Another reason is because they are dismissed. Perhaps they were in breach of their contract. Look at the examples below.

Melvyn Evans

Melvyn Evans was out of work for 14 months after losing his job at a major US investment bank during the financial crisis in 2008. He tried to get a job in another bank, but few were recruiting. Eventually he got a job as a branch manager at mobile phone shop in Chicago. However, after working for seven weeks he was dismissed from the job. It was discovered that some of the information in his CV was false. For example, he claimed that he had some management experience working for a department store in Florida. After a check it was discovered that he had never worked for the store.

▲ **Figure 56.1** A mobile phone shop

Nokia

Nokia has announced job cuts of almost 600 employees in its sales and marketing and R&D departments along with the closure of its Turku site in Finland. About 450 employees will go from the sales and marketing departments. Another 130 in the Nokia Research Center (NRC) will also be lost because the company is going to focus on 'fewer but stronger research areas'. Most of the employees based at Turku will be relocated to other sites in Finland.

Source: adapted from news.icm.ac.uk

(a) Why did Melvyn Evans leave his job at the mobile phone shop?

(b) Why are staff leaving Nokia?

Why do employees leave work?

Figure 56.2 provides a summary of reasons why a worker might leave a job.

Illness Some workers have to leave because they are too ill to work

Dismissal Workers may be forced to leave for misconduct or if they are in breach of their employment contract

Changing jobs or promotion Some workers leave because they have found a better job or because they have been promoted to a new job

Redundancy A business may no longer need the worker – because of a fall in demand perhaps

Reasons for leaving a job

Out of contract Temporary workers often leave when their contract of employment ends

Retirement Workers may leave when they are entitled to a state pension; some retire early and live off private funds

▲ **Figure 56.2** Reasons for leaving a job

Dismissal

A business has the legal right to **dismiss** an employee in certain circumstances.

* **Misconduct**: An employee can be dismissed for misconduct if the terms of employment have been broken. Common reasons include continual absence without a medical certificate, poor discipline, drug or alcohol abuse, theft or dishonesty.

* **Illness**: In some circumstances long-term illness is a reason for dismissal. For example, in some cases the job itself may be causing so much stress that the worker is becoming ill.

* **Inability to do the job**: Workers who can no longer do their job properly may be dismissed. For example, if there is a change in technology and they are unable to cope or if they cannot get on with colleagues, workers can be dismissed.

Sometimes workers are dismissed unfairly. This is discussed in Chapter 58.

Redundancy

Employees can be released if there is no work for them to do. This is called being made **redundant**. Businesses often downsize their organisations to save money. There are several reasons why businesses make their workers redundant.

Recession During a recession a business often faces difficult trading conditions. There may be a sharp fall in demand and the amount of output produced needs to be cut. As a result, the business needs fewer staff.

Automation A common reason for laying people off is because a business switches to more capital-intensive production. When businesses automate production their need for labour often falls.

Merger or takeover Redundancies are very common after a merger or a takeover. This is because when two companies join there is often a duplication of resources. For example, a merged company would not need two head offices so one can be closed.

Factory closure Sometimes businesses close down parts of their operations. A manufacturer may close down a factory or a retailer may close some stores. The reason may be because of reorganisation or because the operations are unprofitable.

Relocation Recently many firms relocated their operations to countries where costs are lower. When this happens jobs are lost at the original location.

KEY FACT

In 2008, Simplot, the US potato processing company, made 30 people redundant when it purchased an automatic packing machine.

KEY FACT

The takeover of Dragonair by Cathay Pacific, the Hong Kong airline, resulted in 191 redundancies. Staff from cargo, engineering, information management and the finance department lost their jobs.

KEY FACT

In 2009 the giant multinational computer company IBM cut thousands of jobs in Western Europe when it switched operations to Eastern Europe, China, India and South America.

Key terms

Dismissal – where workers are 'sacked' from their jobs.
Redundancy – where workers are 'laid off' because they are no longer required.

Chapter review – Garrincha Footwear Ltd

In 2008, Garrincha Footwear Ltd, based in Sao Paulo, Brazil, lowered its prices by 10%. This helped to stem the falling demand caused by the world recession. However, orders were still 15% below 2006 levels. As a result, the directors laid off 120 workers. Redundancies were inevitable, but the production manager was not happy: 'Some of these workers are highly skilled. A lot of money, time and effort has been invested in them. This will all be lost … And then in two years time, when the economy, picks up we will need people again … Not to mention the cost of redundancy pay.'

Another problem that the company might face is a reaction from the whole workforce. They might threaten strike action when they hear about the planned redundancies. In 2007 the whole workforce went on strike when 12 workers were dismissed for poor disciplinary records. The strike only lasted two days because, eventually, the workers admitted they were in the wrong.

(a) State four reasons why people leave their jobs. **(2 marks)**

(b) Using examples from this case, explain the difference between dismissal and redundancy. **(4 marks)**

(c) Explain two other reasons why a business might make workers redundant. **(4 marks)**

(d) Explain why businesses such as Garrincha Footwear Ltd is reluctant to make workers redundant. **(4 marks)**

(e) Look at Figure 56.3. What measures might a business take to avoid making workers redundant? **(6 marks)**

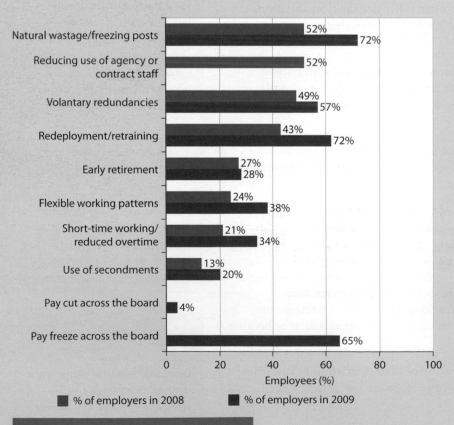

■ % of employers in 2008   ■ % of employers in 2009

▲ **Figure 56.3**
Top 10 steps taken to minimise redundancies

Impact of business decisions on people, the economy and the environment

Getting started...

Business decisions can have an impact on people, the economy and the environment. These can be both positive and negative. For example, the construction of a new housing estate on a greenfield site would create jobs and new accommodation for people. However, wildlife habitat would be destroyed. It is sometimes the responsibility of the government to support or control businesses so that its social and economic objectives are achieved. Look at the examples below.

Car scrappage schemes

During the world recession of 2008–2009 some governments gave support to the car industry. In the UK a £300 million 'scrappage' scheme was introduced to help the industry. In March 2009 new car sales were down 30%. Soon after its introduction the government said one in five new car buyers had taken advantage of the scrappage scheme. In the first week Ford took more than 3,000 orders, while Citroën said demand was up 30%. Other manufacturers also reported increased demand.

Source: adapted from www.guardian.co.uk

Figure 57.1 A car being scrapped ▶

Aldi

In 2009 Aldi the German supermarket chain made a planning application to open a new store in Sheffield, UK. Aldi said the store would provide high-quality products at low prices and would be welcomed by the community. The plan has been met with mixed reception, but objectors are in the majority. They are urging the council to reject the scheme because roads in the area are very congested. Another critic said there were Morrisons and Sainsbury's supermarkets close by and small local shops may not be able to survive the arrival of an Aldi. Another supporter says an Aldi is 'a brilliant idea', creating more choice.

Source: adapted from www.sheffieldtelegraph.co.uk

(a) (i) Why did some governments intervene to help the car industry?
    (ii) To what extent has the car scrappage scheme been a success?

(b) (i) Outline the possible impact of the new Aldi store on the local community.
    (ii) How can the UK government prevent the store from opening if it considers that it is not in the interests of the local community?

(c) How do these two examples show that the government can both support and control businesses?

Why is government intervention required?

Governments are responsible for managing the economy and making sure that social provision is adequate. They have a range of economic and social objectives. For example, they will aim to promote economic growth, keep inflation down and lower unemployment. They will also try to reduce poverty, provide adequate housing, healthcare and education and protect the environment. Sometimes government intervention in business is necessary to help achieve these objectives. This need for intervention is outlined briefly below.

Protect and support people Some groups of people need protection from businesses:

- **Consumers**: If businesses get too powerful they might try to exploit consumers by raising prices or restricting choice. Consumer protection is discussed in detail in Chapter 59.
- **Employees**: Without government intervention some firms might ask employees to work in conditions that are harsh or dangerous. Or they may not pay them a fair wage or treat them fairly. The protection of employees is discussed in Chapter 58.
- **Owners and investors**: The owners of business might also get protection from the government. For example, without stock market regulation shareholders in public limited companies might be exploited. The government might also support businesses by offering help such as advice or tax breaks on investment.

Protect the environment Without government intervention the environment would suffer as a result of business activity. Some businesses have little regard for the environment. For example, businesses might dispose of waste materials irresponsibly. They might release toxic liquids into waterways or discharge dangerous emissions from chimneys. Business development may destroy wildlife habitats. Businesses may also be responsible for resource depletion.

Support the economy Businesses will be more successful if the economy is stable. This means that economic growth should be sustainable with low levels of inflation and unemployment. It is up to government to manage the economy and ensure stability. However, this is often difficult because of external shocks.

How do business decisions impact on others?

Many decisions made by businesses have an impact outside the business. Most recognise this and have become more socially responsible. Many businesses know that if they do not become good corporate citizens their image is likely to suffer. Business decisions can have an impact on the following.

Society Some businesses can have an impact on society. Some of the new products launched by businesses can change lifestyles. For example, the launch of mobile telephones has had a huge impact on communication in societies.

DID YOU KNOW?

Businesses have been blamed for deforestation and the depletion of fish stocks in some of the world's seas and oceans.

DID YOU KNOW?

In 2008–2009 there was a financial crisis and a world recession. Governments all over the world introduced a range of measures, such as lowering interest rates and taxes, to help economic recovery. Without this intervention the world could have suffered a deep depression.

People Every person is potentially affected by business decisions. This is because most people are either consumers, employees or members of a local community.

- Consumers benefit from new products that give them more choice and improved living standards. iPhones, laptop computers, the Internet, budget air travel, and new drugs and medicines are all examples of new products that have contributed to better living standards in many countries. However, some business decisions can have a negative impact. This is likely when consumers are sold products that may harm them, such as cigarettes and alcohol. Consumers can also be exploited by businesses when there is a lack of competition.

- Employees benefit from businesses because they provide jobs. Work can satisfy a wide range of human needs because it provides income and security. It may also help to satisfy social needs and higher-level needs such as providing opportunities to solve problems, make decisions and be creative. However, businesses can have a negative impact on employees. In some countries workers are exploited. For example, some businesses employ child labour or pay very low wages.

- People who live near businesses can be affected by their decisions. For example, some businesses help local communities. They may provide work experience for school children, contribute to local charities or provide employment. However, many people would prefer not to live by a business. This is because they may cause congestion or damage the local environment. This is discussed below.

Environment Business activity can have a serious negative impact on the environment. This is called pollution and some examples are:

- **Water pollution:** This is mainly caused by businesses dumping waste into rivers, streams, canals, lakes and the sea. Examples include warm water or chemicals being leaked into rivers and untreated sewage being dumped into the sea.

- **Air pollution:** This is caused by businesses discharging waste or gases into the air. Examples include emissions from factories and power stations.

- **Noise pollution:** Some business activity can disturb the peace. Noise from factory machinery, loud music from pubs and night clubs and low flying aircraft by airports are examples.

There are also other types of environmental damage:

- **Destruction of wildlife habitats:** When businesses develop on greenfield sites plant and animal life is often destroyed. Also, the sight of new business development can spoil an area of outstanding natural beauty.

- **Traffic congestion:** Extra traffic caused by commercial vehicles or workers travelling to and from work can cause congestion resulting in delays and accidents.

- **Wasted resources:** Some businesses waste resources. For example, many people argue that some of the packaging used by businesses is

DID YOU KNOW?

Vodafone carried out a study into the socio-economic impact of mobile phones in Africa. The study looked at how phones are used in practice. It showed that the impact was very significant. For example, the way that phones are shared between people in communities was a surprise. The growth of phone use in African villages has created thousands of jobs and helped small firms.

DID YOU KNOW?

In Australia, parts of the barrier reef have been destroyed by too much tourist activity, which has been encouraged by businesses.

unnecessary. It is also argued that many businesses do not make enough use of recycled materials. Supermarkets often encourage customers to buy more than they need, which results in food being thrown away.

The impacts that businesses have outside their organisations are often called externalities. They can be both positive and negative and are discussed in Chapter 60.

QUESTION 1

Boots is a health and beauty retailer with over 1,400 stores in the UK employing more than 65,000 people. Many would regard Boots as a socially responsible business with its values of Trust, Respect, Understanding, Simplicity and Together (TRUST). In 2009 Boots reported the following benefits to society:

- helping 500,000 people give up smoking by providing in-store advice;

- helping suppliers to identify environmental savings of over £750,000;

- raising £450,000 for Breast Cancer Care via the sale of product and in-store fundraising, with employees generating some £40,000.

Source: adapted from www.bitc.org.uk

▲ **Figure 57.2** A Boots store

(a) What evidence is there in the case to suggest that Boots has had a positive impact on society?

(b) How might employees benefit from a possible decision by Boots to open 10 new stores?

Methods of government intervention

Governments want to prevent business decisions from having a negative impact on people, the economy and the environment. How can this be done?

Government legislation Pressure has grown on governments in recent years to pass more legislation to protect people and the environment from some business decisions:

- **Consumer legislation**: Legislation exists in many countries to protect consumers from exploitation by businesses. For example, there is anti-competitive legislation, which is designed to promote competition and control monopolies. There is also consumer legislation, which protects consumers against the miss-selling of products. This is discussed in Chapter 59.

- **Employee legislation**: Employees need protection from ruthless employers. In many countries there are laws that protect the rights of workers. They outlaw discrimination, ensure equal opportunities and fair pay, and protect employees from harm. These are discussed in Chapter 58.

- **Environmental legislation**: Much of the pressure for environmental legislation has emerged as a result of the growing concerns about global warming. Under new EU laws power stations, refineries and heavy industry across the EU will be given a limit for how much carbon dioxide they can release into the atmosphere.

- **Company law**: Some legislation exists to protect investors in public limited companies. For example, in some countries legislation provides protection for shareholders in limited companies.

Taxes and subsidies Taxation can be used to reduce pollution. For example, if a tax is imposed on a firm that produces harmful emissions, production costs will increase and the prices charged by the firm will rise. This should reduce demand for the firm's product and therefore result in a reduction in pollution.

Governments can offer grants, tax allowances and other subsidies to firms as an incentive to reduce pollution and encourage 'greener' practices. For example, a firm might receive a subsidy if it builds a plastics recycling plant. This might encourage households and firms to recycle their plastic waste instead of dumping it.

Fines In some countries fines are imposed on those who damage the environment.

Economic policies Governments have a range of economic policy tools that they can use to achieve their economic objectives (see Chapter 7). For example, fiscal and monetary policy measures can be used to both control and encourage business activity. So, if the government wanted to encourage more business development, it could lower taxes and reduce interest rates. The government might also try to influence business location. This is discussed in Chapter 41.

Influence of other agencies

In addition to the government, there are other agencies that can influence business decision making:

- **Trade unions**: Trade unions exist to protect the rights of employees. For example, they may put pressure on businesses to improve working conditions. Trade unions are discussed in more detail in Chapter 58.

- **Pressure groups**: Organisations or groups of people who try to influence business decision making are called **pressure groups**. For example, there are a number of environmental pressure groups, such as Greenpeace, which campaign to prevent business from damaging the environment. Local communities, consumer groups and employee groups may form pressure groups.

Key terms

Pressure groups – groups of people without political power who seek to influence decision makers in politics, society and businesses.

Chapter review – Mining in South Africa

In 2009 a group of South American women flew to the UK to raise awareness about the problems caused by foreign mining companies. In an attempt to save their land and livelihoods, women from Ecuador, Peru and Guatemala lobbied the UK government and European parliament to persuade their governments to refuse mining licences.

- Carmen Mejia, from Guatemala, has been protesting against Montana (owned by Canadian mining company Goldcorp Inc). She said that explosions, dust and the vibrations of heavy trucks to and from the open-pit gold mine have changed the face of her village.

- Gregoria, who cannot give her full name for legal reasons, said: 'As the mine advances and occupies more land, some families find that their houses have cracks and are now on the edge of a precipice. There are armed security guards everywhere.' She said people faced chronic skin infections, hair loss and feared for the safety of their children living in houses that may collapse due to substantial cracks. 'The authorities don't want to know, we don't count.'

- Lina Solana, from Ecuador, has several charges against her for protesting against Canadian mining company Corriente Resources. 'The company's activities damage the Amazonian ecosystem.' She said the exploration not only caused environmental damage and problems with the water, but also social problems such as corruption and the criminalisation of protesters. 'There is a lot of verbal aggression from the police towards females protesting against the mines. They call us sluts and smelly Indians.'

None of the companies mentioned here were prepared to comment. The women have been supported by the Latin American Mining Monitoring Programme (LAMMP). This is a London-based charity that supports Latin American women and their communities in their campaign for human rights and responsible business development.

Source: adapted from www.guardian.co.uk

(a) How might the EU government intervene in this case? **(2 marks)**

(b) State two other ways in which a government can influence business decision making. **(2 marks)**

(c) Using this case as an example, explain what is meant by a pressure group. **(2 marks)**

(d) Outline the impact that mining companies appear to be having in South America on: (i) the environment; (ii) people; (iii) society. **(9 marks)**

(e) Describe the possible impact on South American economies that the mining companies mentioned in the case might have. **(5 marks)**

Chapter 58

The workforce and the working environment

Getting started...

One important aspect of government control over businesses concerns the working environment. In some jobs the working environment can be dangerous and workers need protection from employers who do not provide sufficient safeguards against accidents. Workers also need protection from exploitation, discrimination and unfair dismissal. Look at the information below.

Fatal injuries at work

Unfortunately, every year, workers are fatally injured at work. For example, in the UK in 2008–2009:

- In *agriculture* there were 26 fatal injuries, a rate of 5.7 deaths per 100,000 workers.

- In *construction* there were 53 fatal injuries, with a rate of 2.4 deaths per 100,000 workers. There is an overall downward trend in the rate of fatal injury to workers in this sector.

- In *manufacturing* there were 32 deaths and the rate of fatal injury was 1.1 per 100,000 workers.

- In the *services* sector there were 63 fatalities and the fatality rate was 0.3 per 100,000 workers.

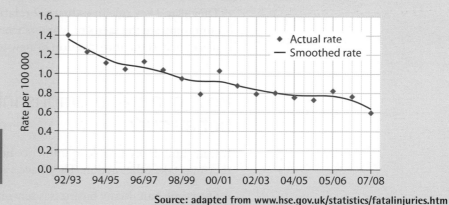

Figure 58.1 ▶
Rates of fatal injuries to workers

Source: adapted from www.hse.gov.uk/statistics/fatalinjuries.htm

(a) What evidence is there here to suggest that workers need protection at work?

(b) (i) Which business sector has the most fatalities?
    (ii) Give one possible reason for your answer in (i).

(c) What might account for the trend shown by the graph in Figure 58.1?

Trade unions

Employees need to have their voice heard at work – they need representation. This is because individual workers find it difficult to stand up for themselves – when trying to exert their rights against a large multinational, for example. They need a more powerful authority to represent them. **Trade unions** are able to provide this authority. Trade unions are organisations of workers who join together to further their own interests in the workplace.

Benefits of trade unions for their members

If workers join a trade union they will have to pay an annual membership fee. In return they get a number of benefits:

• Trade unions represent workers by negotiating with employers on their behalf. They employ skilled negotiators to get the best possible deal for workers. This is called collective bargaining. They press for higher pay, better working conditions, improved health and safety, and fight against redundancies.

• They have a legal network that will represent individual members in cases such as discrimination and unfair dismissal. The cost to workers of legal representation would be huge without the support of trade unions.

• They act as pressure groups to influence business decision making in general.

• They provide other benefits such as access to cheap insurance, discounts on mortgages and travel, social facilities and support when times are hard.

• They play a key role in **industrial relations** at work. For example, they communicate the views of workers when big changes are about to take place such as the introduction of new technology.

How can trade unions influence business behaviour?

If trade unions are unable to influence businesses through negotiation, they may take other action. They have a number of options:

• **Overtime ban**: Many businesses rely on workers volunteering to work overtime so that orders can be met. If workers stop overtime working, businesses might struggle to meet important orders.

• **Work to rule**: This is where workers carry out their duties strictly in accordance with their contract. They follow safety or other regulations to the letter in order to cause a slowdown. Workers cease to cooperate and stop taking short-cuts in their work.

• **Go slow**: This is where employees deliberately try to slow down production but without breaking the terms of their contract.

- **Sit-ins and work-ins:** This is where workers occupy the premises. Work-ins and sit-ins usually occur when a business is threatened with closure. With a work-in employees carry on with production in an effort to show that the business is still viable. In a sit-in there is no production. Workers occupy the workplace to protest and to prevent machinery and other resources from being removed.

- **Strike action:** The most powerful method of industrial action is for workers to withdraw their labour. This is called a strike and prevents output from being produced. This is usually destructive for both employers and employees because the future success of the business is put at risk. Figure 58.2 shows the principal causes of strikes in 2006.

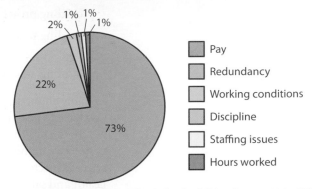

Source: Office for National Statistics, Social Trends 38: 2008 edition

▲ **Figure 58.2**
Working days lost: by principal cause of dispute, 2006

 QUESTION 1

In 2009 over 200 union members of the Ceylon Electricity Board (CEB), Sri Lanaka, launched a protest in front of the CEB head office in Colombo. During the protest the Secretary of the Joint Union Forum for CEB, Ranjan Jayalal, told the media they were only demanding the compulsory salary increase that they should receive every three years. According to the CEB unions, the government had failed to provide the pay rise. The unions threatened the government with a national strike joining with other major sectors if the government failed to meet their demand.

Source: adapted from www.colombopage.com

▲ **Figure 58.3** Protesters in Colombo

(a) Why is the CEB union threatening a national strike?

(b) Outline two other methods of industrial action.

Health and safety at work

Figure 58.1 shows that work can be a dangerous environment. Because of the danger to employees, governments aim to protect workers by passing legislation that forces businesses to provide a safe and healthy workplace. This might involve:

- providing and maintaining adequate safety equipment and protective clothing such as fire extinguishers, protective overalls, hard hats, ear plugs and safety goggles;

- ensuring workers have enough space to do their jobs;

- guaranteeing a hygienic environment with adequate toilet and washing facilities;

- maintaining workplace temperatures and reasonable noise levels;

- providing protection from hazardous substances;
- providing protection from violence, bullying, threats and stress in the workplace;
- providing adequate breaks for rest.

In many countries legislation exists to protect people at work. Businesses also have to give training, information, instruction and supervision to ensure the health and safety of workers. Many businesses also follow codes of practice to meet health and safety standards at work. Finally, health and safety inspectors have the right to enter business premises to ensure that health and safety measures are adequate.

Employment protection

Governments often pass legislation to protect people at work. Without such protection some businesses would exploit their workers. For example, they might pay low wages, make employees work long hours, discriminate against certain groups and dismiss employees unfairly. In addition to providing a healthy and safe working environment businesses have other legal obligations outlined below.

Employment contract Workers are entitled to a *contract of employment*. This is a legally binding agreement between the employer and the employee. It is likely to contain details such as the start date, term of employment, job title and duties, place and hours of work, pay and holiday entitlement, pension and sickness absence, termination conditions, and details relating to disciplinary, dismissal and grievance procedures. A range of employment legislation gives workers other rights, some of which are outlined below:

- maternity and paternity leave when children are born;
- sickness pay during illness;
- a legal minimum wage;
- the right to join a trade union;
- a limit to the number of hours worked during a week;
- an explanation of the rules of conduct and what will happen if they are broken.

Discrimination Legislation exists in many countries to protect workers from *discrimination* over gender, race, disability, sexual orientation and age.

For example, laws might exist to ensure that recruitment is not biased in favour of a particular gender. Or that people doing the same sort of work are entitled to the same pay and conditions, regardless of their race, gender, age or sexual orientation.

Unfair dismissal Sometimes workers are dismissed unfairly. For example, if workers are dismissed for joining a trade union or because they try to exercise their legal rights, they may have grounds to claim *unfair dismissal*. If an **employment tribunal** finds that a worker has been unfairly dismissed, it has the power to reinstate that worker.

Key terms

Business ethics – ideas, in business, about what is morally right or wrong.
Employment tribunal – a court which deals with cases involving disputes between employers and employees.
Industrial relations – the relationship between employers and employees (particularly when represented by trade unions).
Trade unions – organisations of workers which exist to promote the interests of their members.

Business ethics

Businesses often have to make ethical decisions. **Business ethics** is about morality – 'doing the right thing'. For example, should a business:

- Make more use of recycled materials even though profits will fall?
- Test its products on animals?
- Buy goods from suppliers that employ child labour?
- Use a bribe to secure an overseas contract in a country where bribery is a part of the culture?

Generally, if businesses adopt unethical practices, they will make more profit. However, more and more businesses want to be 'good corporate citizens'. Therefore, they are more likely to adopt an ethical stance. One way of doing this is to follow an ethical code of conduct. This lays down guidelines on how employees should respond in situations where ethical issues arise. The code helps businesses to meet ethical standards.

Chapter review – Kenyan flower pickers

Workers picking and packaging flowers in Kenya are no longer forced into overtime and casual contracts. This is a result of companies signing up to ethical codes of conduct. Pay slips are now available to staff, as are employment contracts, better medical facilities, improved housing and increased maternity leave. Better training on the use of pesticides and the stricter controls on the spraying of pesticides have also been introduced. More women have been promoted to supervisory roles and staff welfare committees have been established. Workers are also joining trade unions in increasing numbers. These changes were put into effect after an investigation by an ethical group showed workers' rights in the African flower industry were being violated.

Source: adapted from www.eti2.org.uk and allafrica.com

(a) What is a contract of employment? **(2 marks)**

(b) Some government legislation is designed to prevent discrimination at work. Explain two ways in which workers might be subject to such discrimination. **(4 marks)**

(c) Many Kenyan flower pickers have joined trade unions. Explain how they might benefit from membership. **(6 marks)**

(d) What is an ethical code of conduct? **(2 marks)**

(e) Why was an ethical code of conduct introduced for Kenyan flower pickers? **(2 marks)**

(f) How have the Kenyan flower pickers benefited from an ethical code of conduct? **(4 marks)**

Chapter 59

The consumer

Getting started...

One of the roles played by the government is to ensure that consumers are protected against businesses. For example, in many countries legislation exists to prevent the sale of substandard goods and the use of misleading information to sell products. The government will also ensure that competition exists in markets. Look at the example below.

Vehicle glass cartel

In 2008 the European Commission imposed a record fine of €1.4 billion on four car glass manufacturers for operating a cartel and sharing commercial secrets. France's Saint-Gobain was fined a €896 million. Fines were also imposed on Pilkington (€370 million), Japan's Asahi/AGC (€113.5 million) and Belgium's Soliver (€4.4 million). The four were found guilty of running a cartel between early 1998 and 2003. They discussed target prices, market-sharing and customer allocations during secret meetings in hotels and airports. The European Commission said these companies cheated the car industry and car buyers in a market worth €2 billion in the last year of the cartel. The commission urged victims to seek damages.

Source: adapted from *The Times* **13.11.08**

▲ **Figure 59.1** A car windscreen

(a) Using this case as an example, explain what is meant by a cartel?

(b) Who were the victims in this case?

(c) What is the role of the European Commission in this case?

The need for anti-competitive regulation

There is a need to monitor the activities of monopolies and markets that are dominated by a few large firms. Without government regulation some firms would exploit consumers by using **anti-competitive practices** or **restrictive trade practices** to reduce competition in the market. Such practices might include:

- **Increasing prices** to levels above what they would be in a competitive market. For example, some manufacturers supply goods to retailers and insist that they are resold at a fixed price.

- **Restricting consumer choice**. A manufacturer might refuse to supply a retailer if that retailer stocks rival products. This will reduce choice for the consumer.

- **Raising barriers to entry** by spending huge amounts of money on advertising, for example. A dominant firm might also lower its price for a temporary period. This would make it difficult for a new entrant to get established in the market. Once the new entrant disappears the price would go up again.

- **Market sharing** which might occur if there is collusion. This is what happened in the above example in the market for glass. If a market is shared out between the dominant firms, choice is restricted and the price rises.

How can a government promote competition?

One of the roles of the government in the economy is to promote competition and prevent anti-competitive practices. Some examples of the action a government might take are outlined below.

Encourage the growth of small firms If more small firms are encouraged to join markets, there will be more competition. Several measures can be used to help the growth of small firms.

Lower barriers to entry If barriers are lowered or removed, more firms will join a market. This will make it more competitive. For example, in some countries public transport was provided solely by the public sector. However, laws have been changed to allow private companies to provide transport services.

Introduce anti-competitive legislation Many countries have laws which help to promote competition. Such laws are often designed to protect consumers from exploitation by monopolies, mergers and restrictive practices. Some countries have special bodies or agencies that are responsible for overseeing all policy relating to competition and consumer protection. They may also carry out enquiries into mergers and anti-competitive practices.

 DID YOU KNOW?

Business start-up schemes have been used to provide funds for new businesses. Business advisory organisations such as Business Links provide information and advice on running a business and obtaining finance. Taxes are also lower for small firms.

Key terms

Anti-competitive practices or restrictive trade practices – an attempt by firms to prevent or restrict competition.

Consumer protection

Consumers want to buy good quality products at a fair price. They want information about products that is accurate and clear, and good customer service. They do not want to buy goods that may be dangerous, overpriced or sold to them on the grounds of false claims. Many businesses aim to match or exceed customer expectations. However, there are some that will try to exploit consumers. As a result, governments use legislation to provide protection. There has been a growth in consumer protection in recent years for a number of reasons.

- Many products have become more complex and sophisticated because of advances in technology. As a result, it is often difficult to evaluate their quality. This puts consumers at a disadvantage.

- There has been a huge increase in consumer incomes and the number of products marketed. This increase in the volume of trading suggests that the need for protection has also risen.

- An increasing number of consumers shop online, which is unregulated. This provides a lot of scope for consumer exploitation. For example, payments can be paid online to companies that then fail to deliver goods or simply 'disappear'.

- As a result of globalisation many goods now come from overseas. Protection may be necessary because imports may not match the quality standards of domestic goods. For example, certain toys have arrived in the UK from Asia with low safety standards.

- Increasingly competitive markets pressurise some businesses into taking advantage of consumers. They may reduce the quality of products to reduce costs, for example.

How does legislation protect the consumer?

Some countries have a lot of consumer legislation. It covers a variety of consumer issues and Figure 59.2 provides some examples.

Legislation is likely to prevent businesses from activities such as making false claims about the performance of their products, selling goods that are not fit for human consumption and selling goods that are not 'fit for purpose'. If businesses break consumer laws they may be fined and have to compensate consumers for any loss.

Figure 59.2 ▶
Consumer issues covered by legislation

QUESTION 1

JD Sports was fined £250 plus £240 court costs for misleading consumers on prices in its store in Bangor, Co. Down. The company pleaded guilty under the Consumer Protection From Unfair Trading Regulations Act. This states that it is a criminal offence to make misleading statements about the price of products. JD Sports claimed that customers were making a £40 saving on the tracksuits, displaying a sign saying that they had been reduced from £89.99 to £49.99. An investigation into the claims found that the suits had never been sold at the higher price. The retailer was trying to con customers into thinking they were getting a great deal.

JD Sports increased profits to £10.1 million, which was a significant rise of 11% on the £9.1 million it recorded for the same period last year. Revenue also rose 8.4% from a year ago to £324 million.

Source: adapted from www.insideireland.ie

(a)   What legislation has been used to prosecute JD Sports?

(b)   Use this case as an example to explain why consumer protection is needed.

(c)   Do you think the fine was severe enough? Explain your answer.

Chapter review – Consumer exploitation in UAE

In January 2010, all restaurants and cafes in UAE were ordered to stop adding any service charges to their bills. The Director General of the Ministry of Economy, Ahmed Bin Abul Aziz Al-Shehi, confirmed that it was illegal for non-tourist restaurants to add service charges. Restaurants and cafes operating inside hotels and those paying taxes to the local governments are the only exception. It was also said that inspection teams will be employed to ensure that the law was not broken.

The law prohibiting this practice is Consumer Protection Law Number 24/ 2006. The enforcement followed a flood of complaints about surcharges from consumers nation-wide. Consumers said that illegal service charges of 5 to 20% were imposed on bills by most restaurants and cafes in the country.

Source: adapted from www.uaeinteract.com

(a)   Explain how consumers are being exploited in this case. (2 marks)

(b)   Which businesses are allowed to make service charges? (2 marks)

(c)   (i)   Which law is being broken by many restaurants in this case? (2 marks)

  (ii)   How will the above law be enforced in UAE? (2 marks)

(d)   Why has there been a growth in consumer legislation in recent years? (6 marks)

(e)   In addition to legislation, outline two other measures a government can use to promote competition in a market. (6 marks)

Chapter 60

External costs and benefits

Getting started...

Business activity, such as building a new factory or transporting a tanker full of oil from Qatar to Japan, will affect those inside the business. However, sometimes business activity can also have an impact on the outside. There are 'spillover' effects that may be positive or negative. Look at the example below.

Empress Developments

In 2007 Empress Developments bought a plot of land in a run-down part of a Mumbai suburb. The plot was abandoned 18 years ago when a textile company ceased trading. It had become an eyesore and a danger to trespassers. Empress built a small retail centre, a restaurant and some accommodation for the elderly costing $32 million. During the construction period about 130 temporary jobs were created with a further 90 permanent jobs on completion. However, during the construction period local residents experienced some disruption. The demolition of the old site created a lot of noise and dust. There was also 12 months of congestion because of the temporary closure of an important road.

▲ **Figure 60.1** A new retail development

(a) Explain how people outside the business in the above example will be affected. (Consider both the positive and the negative effects.)

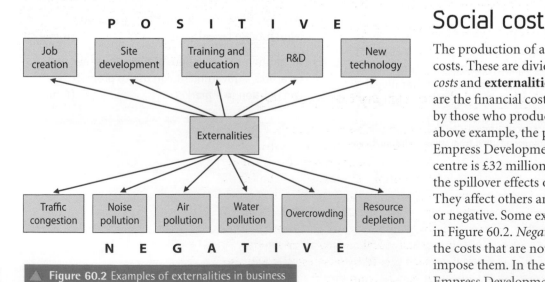

▲ **Figure 60.2** Examples of externalities in business

Social cost

The production of a good will have costs. These are divided into *private costs* and **externalities**. Private costs are the financial costs and are met by those who produce a good. In the above example, the private cost to Empress Developments of the retail centre is £32 million. Externalities are the spillover effects of production. They affect others and can be positive or negative. Some examples are shown in Figure 60.2. *Negative externalities* are the costs that are not met by those who impose them. In the above example, Empress Developments was responsible for some negative externalities. The demolition of the old site created a lot of noise and dust. There was also 12 months of congestion because of the closure of an important road. It was local residents that had to bear these costs. The costs to society as a whole of business activity, the **social costs**, are made up of private costs and external costs.

Social cost = Private cost + External cost (negative externalities)

Social benefit

The production of a good will also have benefits. These are divided into *private benefits* and *positive externalities*. Private benefits are enjoyed by those who produce a good. In the above example, the private benefits to Empress Developments are the financial returns it makes from the investment in the retail centre. This could be rent from those who lease the retail units, for example. Positive externalities are the benefits to anyone other than those responsible for business activity. Some general examples are shown in Figure 60.2. In the above case, examples of positive externalities include the removal of an eyesore and the creation of employment. The benefits to society as a whole of business activity, the **social benefits**, are made up of private benefits and external benefits.

Social benefit = Private benefit + External benefit (positive externalities)

 ## QUESTION 1

Factory farming involves raising a large number of farm animals in a confined space. The farm operates as a factory. It produces large quantities at the lowest cost by relying on economies of scale, modern machinery and biotechnology. However, this approach requires antibiotics and pesticides to control the spread of disease caused by crowded living conditions. Factory farming has resulted in farms that are easier to run with lower labour costs and more output. However, it has also resulted in:

- an increased number of antibiotic-resistant bacteria because of the overuse of antibiotics;
- air quality problems;
- the contamination of rivers, streams and coastal waters with animal waste;
- animal welfare problems.

(a) What examples of negative externalities are there in this case?

(b) What might be the private benefits of factory farming?

(c) What is meant by the social costs in this case?

Effect on stakeholders of externalities

All business decisions will have an impact on business stakeholders. The private costs and benefits will be felt by stakeholders inside the business. For example, a decision to launch a new product will incur private costs such as product development, production and promotion. These costs will be felt by the shareholders. Employees, managers, directors and suppliers will also be affected, though. The private benefits, profit for example, will go to the shareholders. In contrast, externalities, by their nature, will affect people outside the business. For example, it is usually local residents that have to suffer pollution and environmental damage caused by businesses. It will also be stakeholders outside the business that benefit from positive externalities.

Externalities – the spillover effects of consumption or production. They affect others and can be positive or negative.
Social benefit – the benefit of business activity to society as well as to the individual or firm.
Social cost – the cost of business activity to society as well as the individual or firm.

Government policies to deal with externalities

A government will want to discourage business activities that result in negative externalities and encourage those that result in positive externalities. How can this be done?

- **Taxation**: Taxes on pollution will raise business costs so there is a financial incentive to reduce pollution.

- **Subsidies**: The government can offer grants, tax allowances and other subsidies to firms as an incentive to reduce externalities. For example, a firm might receive a subsidy if it builds a plastics recycling plant.

- **Fines**: In some countries penalties are imposed on those who damage the environment.

- **Government regulation**: Pressure has grown on governments in recent years to pass more legislation to protect the environment. Much of the pressure has emerged as a result of the growing concerns about global warming. Legislation outlaws pollution and firms can be prosecuted.

- **Other measures**: A range of other measures have been used to try and reduce negative externalities. For example, targets have been set in an attempt to reduce global pollution. The Kyoto Protocol is one such agreement.

Government legislation designed to reduce environmental damage is discussed in more detail in Chapter 57.

Chapter review – Xang Xing

Xang Xing makes fibreglass-reinforced panels for the construction and transport industries. The company, based in Guangdong, China, recently opened a new plant. Initially, the new plant, which cost $80 million, was welcomed by local residents because 340 new jobs were created. There were also rumours that some local businesses would get supply contracts. However, after about six months it was discovered that the company had violated its air-pollution permit. It had discharged styrene into the atmosphere. Styrene can cause damage to the nervous-system if people are exposed to high concentrations. Several residents living close to the factory complained that they had been affected and threatened to sue Xang Xing. The company settled out of court, but complainants had to sign an agreement that cleared Xang Xing from blame. The company was fined and ordered to install an emission-reducing incinerator at a cost of $300,000.

After one year it was reported in the press that the new factory generated an operating profit of $12.1 million.

(a) Using examples from the case, explain the difference between private costs and social costs. **(4 marks)**

(b) Using examples from the case, explain the difference between private benefits and social benefits. **(4 marks)**

(c) State four ways in which the government might reduce negative externalities. **(4 marks)**

(d) State two stakeholders that might benefit from the decision to open the new plant. **(2 marks)**

(e) Do you think businesses care about externalities? Explain your answer. **(6 marks)**

Chapter 61

Exchange rates

Getting started...

Most countries in the world do not use the same currency. For example, China uses the yuan, Chile the peso, some European countries the euro and the UK the pound. When countries use different currencies, transactions between people and firms in different countries are affected. Look at the examples below.

Enfield Systems

Enfield Systems produces software for prison security systems. In 2009 the firm signed a contract with the German government to supply a system for a new high-security prison in Hamburg. Enfield Systems charged £24,000 for the contract. The cost in euros to the German government was €26,400. This was because £1 = €1.10 (24,000 × 1.10).

Sally Wong and Peter Robinson

Sally and Peter are going on a three week backpack tour of India before they start university. They planned to use credit cards to pay for their accommodation and other large expenses. However, they still needed some rupees for smaller payments. They had £1,000 for such expenses, which they exchanged for Rs72,880. At the travel agent's, where the exchange was made, £1 = Rs72.88.

(a) Which currencies are used in (i) Germany; (ii) India?

(b) Using an example from the case, explain why exchange rates are needed.

(c) What was the exchange rate in the case of Enfield Systems?

▲ **Figure 61.1** Euros

What is an exchange rate?

The examples above show that different countries use different currencies. India uses rupees, Germany uses the euro and Britain uses the pound. The examples also show the conversion rates of different currencies. In the first example £1 = €1.10. This is the **exchange rate**. It shows the price of pounds in terms of euros – £1 will cost Germans €1.10. Similarly, when Sally and Peter converted their £1,000 into rupees at the travel agent's, the exchange rate was £1 = Rs72.88. They got Rs72,880 for their £1,000. When businesses buy goods from other countries payments are often made in another currency. Some examples are given below.

Example 1 How much will it cost a French firm to buy goods from a British firm that cost £400,000 if £1 = €1.10? The cost to the French firm in euros is given by:

$$£400,000 \times 1.1 = €440,000$$

Example 2 How many US dollars will be needed by a British firm buying £55,000 of goods from an American firm if £1 = US$1.50? The cost to the British firm in US dollars is given by:

$$£55,000 \times \$1.50 = \$82,500$$

Example 3 How much will it cost a British firm in pounds to buy $300,000 of goods from a US firm if £1 = US$1.50? The cost in pounds is given by:

$$\$300,000 \div \$1.50 = £200,000$$

Example 4 How many pounds can a Japanese business person buy with ¥100,000 when visiting London if £1 = ¥150? The quantity of pounds that can be bought is given by:

$$¥100,000 \div ¥150 = £666.67$$

QUESTION 1

London-based Miskin plc manufactures machines and other equipment for production lines in the food processing industry. About 40% of its output is sold to American producers. However, Miskin buys materials and components from Germany and Spain. In May 2009, there were three important international transactions.

- A US firm bought machines from Miskin costing £3,600,000.

- Miskin bought components from a German firm for €2.5 million.

- Miskin bought materials from a Spanish firm for a sterling price of £200,000.

(a) Calculate the price in US dollars of the machines sold by Miskin to the US firm (assume £1 = $1.50).

(b) Calculate the amount paid in pounds by Miskin for the €2.5 million in components bought from Germany (assume £1 = €1.10).

(c) Calculate the amount in euros received by the Spanish supplier for the £200,000 of materials sold to Miskin (assume £1 = €1.10).

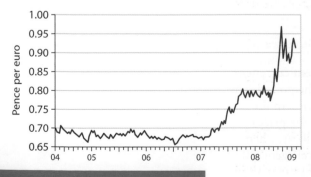

▲ **Figure 61.2**
Euro-pound exchange rate 2004–2009

Why do exchange rates change?

The exchange rate is the price of one currency in terms of another. Like all prices exchange rates can change. This is because prices are determined by market forces and at any time supply and demand conditions can change. For example, if the demand for UK exports rises, there will be an increase in the demand for pounds. This is because foreigners need pounds to pay for exports. The increase in demand for pounds will raise the exchange rate. Figures 61.2 and 61.3 show how some exchange rates have changed in the last few years.

When the exchange rate falls it is said that there has been a **devaluation** or *depreciation* in the exchange rate. When it rises, the exchange rate has *appreciated*.

Sixteen European countries use the euro including some of Britain's key trading partners such as France, Germany and Spain. Figure 61.2 shows the exchange rate between the euro and the pound between 2004 and 2009.

The US is one of Britain's main trading partners. In recent years the exchange rate has fluctuated between about £1 = $2 to £1 = $1. Figure 61.3 shows the exchange rate between the pound and the US dollar between 2006 and 2009.

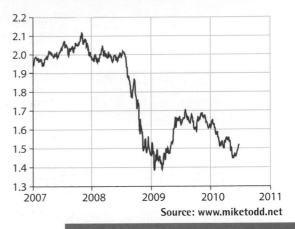

Source: www.miketodd.net

▲ **Figure 61.3**
Pound–US dollar exchange rate 2006–2009

The impact of a depreciation in the exchange rate on imports and exports

Changes in the exchange rate can have an impact on the demand for exports and imports. This is because when the exchange rate changes the prices of exports and imports also change. Look at what happens when the exchange rate falls from £1 = $1.50 to £1 = $1.20:

- **Impact on exports**: If a UK firm *sells* goods worth £2 million to a US customer, the dollar price at the original exchange rate is $3 million (£2m × $1.50). When the exchange falls the dollar price of the goods also falls to $2.4 million (£2m × $1.20). This means that demand for UK exports is likely to rise because they are now cheaper.

- **Impact on imports**: If another UK firm *buys* goods worth $600,000 from a US supplier, the price in pounds at the original exchange rate is £400,000 ($600,000 ÷ $1.50). When the exchange rate falls the sterling price to the importer rises to £500,000 ($600,000 ÷ $1.20). This means that demand for imports is likely to fall because they are dearer.

The impact of an appreciation in the exchange rate on imports and exports

A rise in the exchange rate will have the opposite affect on the demand for exports and imports. Look at what happens when the exchange rate rises from £1 = $1.50 to £1 = $2.

- **Impact on exports**: If a UK firm *sells* goods worth £2 million to a US customer, the dollar price at the original exchange rate is $3 million (£2m × $1.50). When the exchange rises the dollar price of the goods also rises to $4 million (£2m × $2). This means that demand for UK exports is likely to fall because they are now dearer.

- **Impact on imports**: If another UK firm *buys* goods worth $600,000 from a US supplier, the price in pounds at the original exchange rate is £400,000 ($600,000 ÷ $1.50). When the exchange rate rises the sterling price to the importer falls to £300,000 ($600,000 ÷ $2). This means that demand for imports is likely to rise because they are cheaper.

The effects of changes in the exchange rate on the demand for exports and imports are summarised in Figure 61.4.

Figure 61.4 ▶
A summary of the effects of changing exchange rates

Exchange rate	Price of Exports	Demand for Exports	Price of Imports	Demand for Imports
Falls	Falls	Rises	Rises	Falls
Rises	Rises	Falls	Falls	Rises

QUESTION 2

An airline carrier operating in the UK buys aviation fuel in dollars. In May 2009 the carrier paid $900,000 for a fuel order. The same carrier also sells seats to overseas travellers in Spain. In May 2009, the price of a return flight from Madrid to London was £220. Some information relating to exchange rates is given in Figure 61.5.

(a) (i)   Calculate the cost in pounds of the aviation fuel in 2009.
     (ii) Calculate the price in euros of the return flight in 2009.

(b) (i)   Recalculate the cost in pounds of the aviation fuel at the estimated 2010 exchange rate.
     (ii) Recalculate the price in euros of the return flight at the estimated 2010 exchange rate.

(c) How might the demand for aviation fuel and flights be affected by the changes in the exchange rates?

	2009	2010*
£1 =	$1.50	$1.75
£1 =	€1.10	€1.25

▲ **Figure 61.5**
Exchange rate information.
*Estimated rates

How are businesses affected by exchange rates?

The examples above show what happens to the prices of imports and exports when exchange rates appreciate and depreciate. Sometimes these changes will benefit a business, other times they will not. For example, if the value of the rupee falls, Indian exporters will benefit because the price of exports falls and demand should increase. However, Indian importers will lose out because their purchases will be more expensive.

Fluctuating exchange rates cause uncertainty. Businesses do not know what is going to happen to exchange rates in the future. This means that it is difficult to predict demand for exports and the cost of imports. This makes planning and budgeting more difficult.

Another problem is that it costs money to switch from one currency to another. There is a usually a commission charge of around 2%. This represents a cost to importers and therefore reduces profit.

Key terms

Devaluation – the depreciation or fall in the value of a currency.
Exchange rate – the price of one currency in terms of another.

Chapter review – The effects of changing exchange rates

Duberry's plc is a confectionery producer that supplies customers in Europe, the US and Japan. In 2009 the company was planning to open a new production line to make a range of chocolate biscuit bars. To do this Duberry's would have to buy €12m of machinery from a German supplier. However, the board of directors was not sure whether or not to wait a year before making the purchase because of possible movements in the exchange rate. Figure 61.6 shows some exchange rates for 2009 and predictions for 2010.

	2009	2010*
£1 =	€1.10	€1.00
£1 =	$1.65	$1.55
£1 =	¥150	¥180

▲ **Figure 61.6**
Exchange rate information affecting Duberry's plc. *Estimated rates

(a) Figure 61.6 shows that the predictions for the exchange rate in 2010 are different from the actual exchange rates in 2009. Why do exchange rates change? **(2 marks)**

(b) (i) In 2009 Duberry's sold £18,000 of goods to a Japanese customer. How much did the Japanese customer pay in yen? **(2 marks)**
   (ii) What happens to the price of these goods in 2010? **(2 marks)**
   (iii) Explain whether the change is likely to benefit Duberry's or not. **(2 marks)**

(c) Do you think that Duberry's should purchase the German machinery now or wait for another year? Show all your calculations. **(4 marks)**

(d) Explain whether Duberry's US customers will benefit or not from the predicted change in the exchange rate. **(2 marks)**

(e) Discuss the problems businesses like Duberry's are likely to have with fluctuating exchange rates. **(6 marks)**

▲ **Figure 61.7** A production line making biscuits

Chapter 62

The business cycle

Getting started...

Over a period of time most economies in the world grow. However, in many developed economies the pattern of economic growth is not smooth. It tends to fluctuate and sometimes the economy may even contract. This means that national income actually falls. Look at the example below.

Growth in Argentina

Argentina is the third largest economy in Latin America. It has plentiful natural resources, a well-educated population, an export-oriented agricultural sector and a diversified industrial base. However, as a result of domestic instability, Argentina fell from the world's 10th wealthiest nation in 1913 to the world's 47th wealthiest in 2008. For example, there was a serious financial crisis in 2002 that resulted in a very sharp fall in national income. Figure 62.1 shows Gross Domestic Product (GDP) for Argentina between 1970 and 2008.

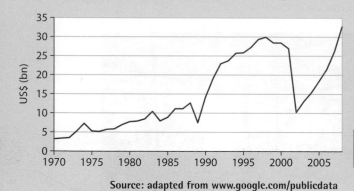

Figure 62.1
Argentina GDP 1970–2008 ($billion)

Source: adapted from www.google.com/publicdata

(a) In which years did national income fall in Argentina?

(b) How might an Argentine car manufacturer be affected by a sharp fall in national income?

(c) State one measure a government might take to help the economy recover after a sharp fall in national income.

The business cycle

Over a period of time GDP is expected to grow. However, the rate of growth is not likely to be smooth. There are likely to be some fluctuations. It is also possible for GDP to fall. These fluctuations are often referred to as the *economic, trade* or *business cycle*. Figure 62.2 shows these fluctuations and identifies four different phases.

Boom: The peak of the cycle is called a **boom**. During a boom GDP is growing fast because the economy is performing well. Existing firms will be expanding and new firms will be entering the market. Demand will be rising, jobs will be created, wages will be rising and the profits made by firms will be rising. However, prices may also be rising.

Downturn: A boom will be followed by a **downturn**. The economy is still growing but at a slower rate. Demand for goods and services will flatten out or begin to fall, unemployment will start to rise and wage increases will slow down. Many firms will stop expanding, profits may fall and some firms will leave the market. Prices will rise more slowly.

Recession or depression: At the bottom of the business cycle GDP may be flat. If GDP starts to fall, the bottom of the cycle may be referred to as a **slump** or **depression**. Such a period is often associated with hardship. Demand will start to fall for many goods and services – particularly non-essentials. Unemployment rises sharply, business confidence is very low, bankruptcies rise and prices become flat. The prices of some things may even fall. A less severe version of a depression is a **recession**.

Recovery: When GDP starts to rise again there is a **recovery** or an **upswing** in the economy. Businesses and consumers regain their confidence and economic activity is on the increase. Demand starts to rise, unemployment begins to fall and prices start to rise again.

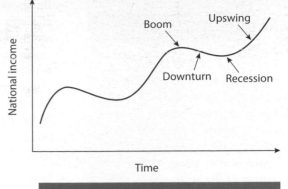

▲ **Figure 62.2**
The economic, trade or business cycle

The impact of the business cycle on business

The uneven pattern of growth, shown by the business cycle, can have an impact on businesses. However, the scale of the impact will depend on the financial position of the business and what it produces.

- **Output:** During a boom businesses increase output to meet rising demand. Some will increase capacity. Businesses providing non-essential products and luxury items will benefit more than those that produce necessities. In contrast, during a recession or a depression output will fall. Businesses respond by reducing output and cutting capacity. Businesses that trade in essential items, such as supermarkets, will avoid the worst of the downturn.

- **Profit:** During a boom business profits are likely to rise. This is because demand is rising and it is easier to raise prices. However, when national income starts to decline, it is harder to make a profit. Businesses may cut their costs to maintain profit levels. Many will have to tolerate lower profits and some will make losses.

 DID YOU KNOW?

During a boom businesses operating in the holiday, restaurant, air transport, jewellery and fashion industries are likely to benefit most.

Key terms

Boom – the peak of the economic cycle where GDP is growing at its fastest.

Business cycle – regular fluctuations in the level of output in the economy.

Depression or slump – the bottom of the economic cycle where GDP starts to fall with significant increases in unemployment.

Downturn – a period in the economic cycle where GDP grows, but more slowly.

Recession – a less severe form of depression.

Recovery or upswing – a period where economic growth begins to increase again after a recession.

- **Business confidence and investment**: During an economic recovery and into a boom business confidence is high. Business owners are optimistic about the future and are prepared to take more risks. For example, they are more inclined to launch new products, enter new markets and expand. In contrast, during a recession business confidence is low and business owners are pessimistic, cautious and anxious about the future. Consequently, they are not likely to take risks and are more inclined to contract their businesses. Investment is likely to fall. For example, instead of replacing outdated machinery they will make do with what they have.

- **Employment**: During a boom unemployment falls because businesses are taking on more workers to cope with rising demand. Sometimes firms might struggle to recruit the quantity and quality of staff that they need because of shortages. However, during a recession the opposite happens. Business lay off workers and unemployment rises.

- **Business start-ups and closures**: In a boom more people are prepared to set up a new business. This is because demand is rising and it is easier to make a profit. Business confidence will be high so new entrepreneurs will be more enthusiastic. However, during recession is not a good time to start a new business because business closures will be rising. Inefficient businesses, those with cash flow problems and those producing non-essential products are most at risk.

Chapter review – Air France–KLM

Air France–KLM, Europe's biggest airline, announced losses of €814 million for 2009. It also said that 2,700 jobs would have to be cut. The losses were the first incurred by the French–Dutch group after the 2003 merger of Air France and KLM. Some 2,700 jobs were slashed during 2008 and 2009, and further cuts were planned for 2010. To reduce costs the airline will also stop recruitment, ask staff to take holidays and make more use of part-time staff.

Air France–KLM employs around 104,000 people and has been hit hard by the economic crisis that has affected the global airline industry. The airline has suffered from a sharp drop in traffic that forced it to scale back services – by 4.5% for passengers and 11% for cargo. The worst global slump in decades has devastated the airline industry, with passenger numbers plunging more than 11% in March compared to a year earlier.

Source: adapted from www.france24.com

(a) What is meant by the business cycle? **(2 marks)**

(b) Use this case as an example to explain what is meant by a slump **(2marks)**

(c) Discuss how the current stage in the business cycle has affected Air France–KLM. **(8 marks)**

(d) How might Air France–KLM be affected if the economy starts to recover in 2010? **(8 marks)**

Index